Logical Thinking
An Introduction to Logic
Second Edition

JAMES STUART
DONALD SCHERER

Bowling Green State University

McGraw-Hill, Inc.
Primis Custom Publishing

New York St. Louis San Francisco Auckland Bogotá
Caracas Lisbon London Madrid Mexico Milan Montreal
New Delhi Paris San Juan Singapore Sydney Tokyo Toronto

McGraw·Hill

A Division of The McGraw·Hill Companies

Logical Thinking
An Introduction to Logic

McGraw-Hill's Primis Custom Publishing Series consists of products that are produced from camera-ready copy. Peer review, class testing, and accuracy are primarily the responsibility of the author(s).

1 2 3 4 5 6 7 8 9 0 BKM BKM 9 0 9 8 7

ISBN 0-07-289622-1

Editor: Jan Scipio
Printer/Binder: Bookmart Press

Acknowledgments

The authors wish to thank the many people who have assisted in the production of this book. A special thanks to Greg Hendee for his help in formatting and to Gene Torisky who read the entire manuscript in an earlier version and made many valuable suggestions for its improvement. Csaba Nyiri and Bill Kline each read the entire book in its first edition and caught many errors and made numerous suggestions for improving the second edition. Additionally, the following have read all or portions of the manuscript and made corrections and suggestions for changes: Kary Church, Mahesh Ananth, Natasha Williams, Drew Ackerman, Peter Found, Amanda Stuart, Kalevi Lehto, Alexi Marcoux, James Okapal, Steve Sheinberg, Matthew Stuart, Sean Whyte, Sam Zinaich, Sharon Stuart, Charles Hinckley, Christopher Pece, James Denvil and James Spence. Others who have helped in a variety of ways are Margy Deluca, Diane Petteys, Pat Bressler and Bob Werkmeister. Finally, special thanks to Jan Scipio, of McGraw-Hill, for her valuable assistance and advice.

J. S.
D. S.

Contents

CHAPTER ONE

LOGIC AND ARGUMENT

THE STUDY OF LOGIC

A book about logic is a book about reasoning. Reasoning, of course, is a familiar activity. For example, imagine a woman with the goal of getting to Cincinnati for a birthday celebration. Without private transportation, she rejects flying because it is too expensive for her. The only other available public transportation is by bus. The last bus to leave town and arrive in Cincinnati before the birthday celebration leaves at noon. So she infers that she must leave for the bus station by eleven.

The woman's thinking exhibits planning, an activity in which people typically reason. From the premise that Cincinnati is too far away to reach without a motored vehicle, and the premise that flying is too expensive, the woman reasons that she must take the bus because no other form of transportation is available to her. From the bus schedule, the set time for the birthday celebration, and her present location, she infers when she must leave in order to catch the bus. What has been described here is one person's *reasoning*.

Logic is a study of reasoning. However, logic is not just any study of reasoning. For in logic we do not study how people actually reason. We do not study when, where or why they reason. Rather, in logic we study the distinction between good and bad reasoning.

Logic, moreover, is a discipline. Logicians are accordingly not content merely to recognize individual examples of good or bad reasoning. As a discipline, **logic is a study of the principles or methods for distinguishing good from bad reasoning.**

Let us look back at a small portion of the reasoning of the woman who wanted to get to Cincinnati. She reasoned as follows:

I can get to Cincinnati only by plane or by bus.
The plane is too expensive.
So I can get to Cincinnati only by bus.

Logicians call such pieces of reasoning *arguments*. The argument just stated consists of three statements. While some arguments are long and some are short, all arguments consist of statements. Accordingly, let us wait to define what an argument is until after we have understood what *statements* are.

Exercises

Complete the following by filling in the blank.

1. Logic is a discipline that studies _____.

2. Rather than studying facts about people's reasoning, logicians study the difference between _____ and _____ reasoning.

3. To say that logic is a discipline implies that logicians study the _____ that distinguish good from bad reasoning.

4. Logicians call a piece of reasoning an _____.

STATEMENTS

All *statements* are sentences. But not all sentences are statements. Questions, for instance, are sentences, but they are not statements. For example, "What time is it?" is a question, not a statement. Imperatives also are sentences but they are not statements. "Don't you insult me!" is an imperative, not a statement. Likewise exclamations, such as, "Excuse me!," are not statements.

Unlike questions, imperatives and exclamations, **statements are sentences that are either true or false**. That is what sets statements apart from other sentences. "Many little children do not know what a question is," and "I did not intend to insult you" are examples of statements because each of these sentences is either true or false.

Any sentence that is true or false is a statement. The sentences we know to be true and those we know to be false are all statements. "At least 700,000 species of insects exist" is, for example, known to be true. "Unicorns exist" is known to be false. But there are also statements about which we are ignorant. "Over a million species of insects exist," for example, is a statement believed to be true by many biologists but not *known* to be true and not known to be false. Thus sentences that are either true or false, even if we do not know which, are statements.

Exercises

Which of the following are statements?

1. Most people have five toes on each foot.

2. Where did you find the hot peppers?

3. Please pass the peppers.

4. Both fundamentalist Christians and fundamentalist Shiite Muslims are literalists.

5. Religious beliefs are matters of opinion.

6. Do you think religious beliefs are never matters of history?

7. What a strange idea!

8. Stop or I'll shoot.

9. If you enter the contest, you will win.

10. What color is your book?

ARGUMENTS

With the understanding that statements are those sentences that are either true or false, we can build a correct understanding of the term "argument" as it is used in logic. To repeat the original point, arguments are composed entirely of statements.

A random collection of statements, however, does not necessarily make an argument. What, then, makes a group of statements into an argument? To answer this question, let us look at some statements that form an argument:

Grant Wood, a famous American painter, once used German glass as part of a memorial to the American soldiers who died in World War I. Members of the Daughters of the American Revolution, who learned what he did, thought he was shaming the memory of those soldiers. So if future artists who build war memorials want to avoid controversy, they will use American materials to construct their memorials.

In this argument we find three statements. After you have read the first two, you probably felt informed about some facts you did not previously know. There is no indication in those two statements, by themselves, that you are reading an argument. The third statement, however, not only makes a new assertion, it also shows that the three statements form an argument. The third statement is presented *as supported by* the preceding statements. In the light of the third statement, the first two statements are seen to be *reasons* asserted to provide *support* for the final statement. In other words, the word "so" conveys the idea that if the author's other statements are true, then their being true provides support for the truth of the statement following the word "so." That means that the above example is an argument.

Consider another example:

This course, according to the professor, is one that builds from session to session. That's why I should start reviewing every day, since I will otherwise tend to fall behind.

Let us focus on the statement that occurs early in the second sentence: "I should start reviewing every day." The way this passage is composed indicates that this statement is a *conclusion* in this passage. The composition of the passage indicates that the other statements are supposed to support it. They are presented as providing reasons why this statement is true. The fact that the other statements are presented as *reasons* meant to support the truth of the statement "That's why I should start reviewing daily" is crucial. It makes the passage an argument. In this example, however, only part of the support is in the statement preceding "That's why." Additional support is indicated in the final statement of the passage, following the word "since." From this example, then, you can see that when a set of statements form an argument, the statement that is presented as supported by other statements does not have to occur at the end of the passage. It may occur in the middle, as in this example, or it may occur first.

Arguments, therefore, are sets of statements. But in order for a set of statements to constitute an argument, at least one of the statements must be presented as providing support for another of them. In other words, if two or more statements are going to form an argument, then at least one of the statements must be used to support another statement.

Logicians have special terms for the parts of an argument. The statements that are presented as providing support are called *premises*. The statement that is presented as supported by the other statements is called a *conclusion*.

Here is another example of an argument:

> In the last fifteen years, ten of those years are the warmest in recorded history. This probably indicates that the earth is getting warmer.

The second statement of this argument begins "This probably indicates that." These words alert the reader that the last statement is the *conclusion*, the statement the speaker is aiming to support. This means that the first statement is being presented as a reason in support of the last statement. The first statement is, therefore, the *premise*. Notice that the reasoning structure of the passage is apparent independently of any evaluation of how good the argument is. How good this sample argument is, people dispute quite widely. At this point in the study of logic, however, no question of the evaluation of any argument is involved. Rather, you are learning to recognize structures that indicate that a passage contains a piece of reasoning, that is, an argument. When you see words like, "This probably indicates that. . ." you know what the author of those words is doing. The author is using these words to introduce a conclusion. That means that the preceding statement is a premise that is intended to provide support for the conclusion.

Suppose the author of the above passage said, "This probably indicates that the physical properties of the mercury in thermometers has recently changed." You might think that the statement is absurd. You might think that the first statement indicates nothing of the kind. But, even so, you would know from the words, "This probably indicates that . . .," that the author presented the second statement as a conclusion based on the premise of the first.

You may have thought about reasoning not in terms of "premises," "conclusions," and "arguments," but in terms of "inferences." It is certainly true that arguments are a result of a reasoning process. And, when one reasons, one draws an inference. Logicians, however, do not often talk about inferences. Logicians are less interested in the mental process of drawing inferences because they are more interested in identifying premises and conclusions and learning how to evaluate the support a given set of premises provides for a particular conclusion. Another reason logicians shun the word "inference" is because the term is ambiguous. By "inference" we may mean a process by which one statement is inferred, or derived, from one or more other statements. But "inference" does not need to refer to a process.

Consider the following passage:

> His inference, from the roar of the crowd, was that the new musical would be a box office success.

Here the word "inference" refers to what is being inferred: that the musical would be a success. Instead of referring to the process of inferring, the word refers to the product, the statement (conclusion) that is inferred.

Nothing is lost, however, in ignoring the term "inference." The logician attempts to discover the principles of good reasoning. To that end, it is sufficient to use the language of "argument," "premise" and "conclusion."

Exercises

Which of the following passages contain arguments? For those that do, which statements are premises and which are conclusions?

1. In contrast to the great work of Handel in the early 18th Century and Haydn later in the 18th Century, no great oratorio has been written in English since Mendelssohn completed his *Elijah* just before his death in 1847. So it seems safe to hold that the tradition of great English oratorio writing is dead.

2. Andrew Lloyd Webber could write a great oratorio if he tried.

3. Do you seriously believe Webber is a composer comparable to Haydn or Mendelssohn?

4. It is likely that new markets will soon develop in Eastern Europe and in South America. After all, the recently installed governments in those areas are receptive to the growth of private enterprises. And many clever and industrious people are ready to respond to their governments' willingness.

5. Compared to the many markets that are opening, available capital is scarce. So the demand for capital will probably increase the price people are willing to pay for it.

6. You should really go to sleep. For, if you don't then you'll be tired and cranky, and you don't want to be tired and cranky for the interview.

7. I wish I knew what time it was. If I knew, I would tell you.

8. The President of the United States in 1993 was Bill Clinton. Winston Churchill was Prime Minister of England during the Second World War. George Foreman is a boxer.

9. All scholarly books are dull. Kant's *Critique of Pure Reason* is not a scholarly book. Hence, it is not dull.

10. Historical accounts are intended to be objective accounts of past events. For a variety of reasons this intent is not always realized.

CHAPTER TWO

PREMISES AND CONCLUSIONS

Logic, we said in Chapter One, is the study of the principles for evaluating arguments. Eventually, then, our focus will be on the differences between good and bad arguments. The first part of our study, however, does not address the difference between good and bad arguments. The reason for this is that we must clarify what arguments are before we begin evaluating them. Thus, we shall ask, "How does one tell whether some set of statements amounts to an argument?" In Chapter One, we noted that arguments are composed of statements that function as premises and conclusions. In this chapter, we will elaborate our understanding of premises and conclusions, and in the process you will learn to distinguish arguments from other similar linguistic units.

PREMISES AND CONCLUSIONS

All premises and all conclusions are statements. Remember that a statement is a sentence that is either true or false. What makes a statement a premise or a conclusion is the role it plays in a given passage. Since a conclusion is a statement, it asserts that something is true. When a statement functions as a conclusion, it is presented as supported by reasons provided in one or more other statements. Because a premise is also a statement, it asserts that something is true. The function of a premise is to give a reason in support of the truth of the conclusion.

The new idea in the preceding paragraph is that statements can function in different ways, as premises and as conclusions. When we say that a statement functions as a premise or as a conclusion, we mean more than that it asserts something to be true. The statement is also being used to play a role. We are all aware that people play roles, not only in plays, but also as students, employees, investors, citizens, family members and the like. We can understand such roles in terms of how persons relate to one another.

In logic, we are talking about a relationship when we refer to the roles of statements as *premises* and *conclusions*. Just as the words "mother" and "daughter" describe how one person is related to another, so the words "premise" and "conclusion" describe how one statement is related to another. When a statement is presented as a reason in support of another statement, the two statements have been related to each other. They are related in terms of how the *one is presented as the support of the other*. The statement presented as a reason is playing the role of a premise. The statement presented as being supported is playing the role of a conclusion. This is the relationship of premise to conclusion.

ARGUMENTS VERSUS NON-ARGUMENTS

It is easy to be confused about how to determine whether a statement, in a given passage, is a part of an argument. Now that you know that arguments are composed of premises and conclusions, you can understand how to proceed. Questioning whether a statement is part of an argument amounts to asking whether it plays the role of either a premise or a conclusion. You should begin by understanding that the responsibility for conveying the role of a statement in a passage rests with the author of the statement. The author needs to indicate how he or she intends the statement to be used. If a set of statements is to play the roles of premise and conclusion, the author needs to indicate this. Otherwise, the set of statements will not amount to an argument.

Authors usually provide this indication by using special words that reveal when a statement is playing a special role, either as a premise or a conclusion.

Consider the following passage:

> Since Doug knows you will be waiting by the telephone to get the news, he will call you as soon as he hears.

Within this sentence, we find two assertions: "Doug knows you will be waiting by the telephone to get the news," and "he will call you as soon as he hears." Besides the two assertions, we find the word "since." The word "since" is an argument indicator. More specifically, it is a word which makes clear that the statement following it is the author's reason in support of the statement that Doug will call you as soon as he hears. A word which indicates that a statement serves as a reason for the truth of another statement, we shall call a *premise indicator*. This means that in this example the first statement, "Doug knows you will be waiting by the telephone to get the news," is the premise. It follows, then, that the last statement, "he will call you as soon as he hears," is the conclusion.

Consider the following continuation of the above scenario: When Doug hears the news, he puts in a call. He gets no answer. He then reasons as follows:

> Ellen is so concerned to get the news that she would not leave the phone unless she had already heard. Yet she doesn't answer the phone. That must mean that I either dialed the wrong number or somebody else has already told her.

In this argument, we find three statements. The third statement begins with "That must mean that. . ." These words are a *conclusion indicator*. They indicate that the statement following them is presented as supported by the statements preceding it. Thus, "I either dialed the wrong number or someone else has already told her" is the conclusion of this argument.

In general, then, arguments are marked as pieces of reasoning by words and phrases that indicate that statements within a passage are either premises or a conclusion. These words and phrases are called *premise indicators* or *conclusion indicators*, because they are the devices the author of a passage usually employs to indicate that statements within the passage are playing the role of a premise or a conclusion.

Here are two lists, of common premise and conclusion indicators:

Premise Indicators	Conclusion Indicators
since	therefore
because	hence
for	so
given that	thus
inasmuch as	consequently
My reason for this is that. . .	This proves that. . .

Sometimes an argument will have only a premise indicator. The author expects the reader or hearer to understand where the conclusion is once a premise has been indicated. Similarly, an argument may contain only a conclusion indicator. Again the author expects the reader to understand where the premise or premises are once the conclusion has been indicated.

Occasionally, there are no premise indicators and no conclusion indicators present. In that case, ask yourself, is the author trying to convince me of something. If not, then there is no argument. If so, whatever the author is trying to convince you of is the conclusion. The reasons supplied in support of the conclusion are the premises.

Exercises

In each of the following passages, pick out the premise indicators and the premises, the conclusion indicators and the conclusions.

1. I am simply looking for certain words. So I shouldn't have much trouble picking out premises and the conclusion.

2. You also need to know which words indicate premises and which indicate conclusions. Hence your task is not quite so simple.

3. Since the words on the premise indicator list convey the idea of being a reason, it is not hard to figure out which words belong on which lists.

4. In fact, I must have been wrong to say that I was looking for certain words, because I am really checking whether the author is using a statement either as support or as supported.

5. Since you are checking an author's statements to see whether they are performing these functions, it is not surprising that sometimes words not on the list, like "My proof is that," also perform the functions.

6. The price of oil will increase. For, the supply of oil has decreased.

7. Given that the sidewalk is wet, it follows that it must have rained, since only rain would make the sidewalk wet.

8. All persons are rational and John is a person. Hence, John must be rational.

9. If an elephant is bigger than a horse and a whale is bigger than an elephant, it would have to be true that a whale is bigger than a horse.

10. Because every plant is a living thing and all living things require oxygen, it must be the case that all plants require oxygen.

STATEMENTS, PREMISES AND CONCLUSIONS

In a family context a particular woman may be a mother, in another she is a daughter. In a work context, she is not a mother or daughter, but perhaps a professor. Similarly, a given statement may be a premise in one passage, a conclusion in another and neither in a third.

Consider an example. If someone asks whether Grant Wood was a famous American artist, the reply, "Grant Wood is certainly famous," would be, by itself a statement. In that simple context *it is neither a premise nor a conclusion.*

If you found this assertion of Grant Wood's fame surprising and you questioned it, someone might say,

"Oh, yes, he is famous. After all, he painted, *American Gothic.*"

You should be able to see that this last example is an argument. The statement "Grant Wood is famous" is *supported by* "he painted *American Gothic.*" This is made clear by the words "After all," which function as a premise indicator. These words tell you to understand the second statement as support for the first statement. The words "After all" tell you to interpret the two statements in the following way:

Premise: Grant Wood painted *American Gothic.*

Conclusion: Grant Wood is a famous American artist.

Suppose you have become convinced that Grant Wood is a famous American artist. On the basis of that conviction you infer,

So if I take a Survey of American Art course, Grant Wood will be on the syllabus.

The statement you have inferred is "If I take a Survey of American Art course, Grant Wood will be on the syllabus." The word "so" is used to indicate the role of that statement. "So" indicates that the statement is presented as supported. That means that the statement is functioning as a *conclusion*. Accordingly, the statement that is taken as providing the support for this conclusion is, "Grant Wood is a famous American artist." Following the format above, then, our new argument is this:

Premise: Grant Wood is a famous American artist.

Conclusion: If I take a Survey of American Art course,
                  Grant Wood will be on the syllabus.

In summary, then, a statement becomes a premise or a conclusion by the *role* it plays in a given passage. The same statement can function both as a premise in one argument and a conclusion in another. The use of premise and conclusion indicator words are the typical means by which authors indicate the functions or roles they wish their statements to serve.

Sometimes authors do not rely on indicator words to indicate a statement as a premise or a conclusion. Imagine the following conversation:

Student A: Professor Lewis will give a quiz on Friday.

Student B: What makes you say that?

Student A: Every week Professor Lewis has either a scheduled exam or a quiz on Friday. This week, as you know, no exam is scheduled.

In this conversation, Student A uses no words to indicate that her second and third statements are premises. Yet clearly the second and third statements are presented as providing support for the first. What makes this clear? In short, it is the *context* that makes it clear.

More precisely, Student B's question is a request for Student A to support her first statement. The fact that support has been requested provides the context within which to presume that Student A's second statement is A's attempt to respond to B's request. In other words, A's second statement is, in the context of B's request, a premise.

Statements, however, are frequently neither a premise nor a conclusion. If a statement is a premise or a conclusion, something must indicate that the statement is functioning in this special way. Indicator words, and the context in which the statements occur, are the only things that can show that a statement is functioning as either a premise or a conclusion.

At this point, a significant conclusion is in order. You have learned that only indicator words and context can reveal that statements are playing the roles of premises or conclusions. You know that every argument must contain at least one premise and one conclusion. Therefore, you can correctly infer that when neither premises nor conclusions are indicated, no argument is present. In other words, when neither indicator words nor context shows that statements are being used as premises or conclusions, the statements do not form an argument. In still other words, an argument exists only if, either through indicator words or context, it is revealed that statements are playing the roles of premise or conclusion.

Exercises

Identify those passages below that contain arguments. Use indicator words to distinguish premises of arguments from their conclusions.

1. When Mark and Bill first met, they were attending the same nursery school. Today they are still friends, after high school, college and years of work.

2. Mark and Bill have remained good friends, often socializing and working together, over many years. So it's very likely that they know each other's likes and dislikes pretty well.

3. "Logic helps students develop reasoning skills, just as the professor says." "How can you be so sure?" "When my sister took the LSAT, she said her logic course is what really saved her on the reasoning skills part of the test."

4. Many students take logic. Only a minority of them take the LSAT. The others, then, would probably lack such a direct confirmation of whether taking logic improves reasoning skills.

5. In a logic course some students learn well from a video presentation. For others reading a text is more helpful, although the video can

provide reinforcement. Still others benefit most from doing exercises on computers that provide immediate feedback.

6. I own all the photocopiers in this building. Since this photocopier is in this building, I own this photocopier.

7. All crows are black, this bird is white, consequently, it is not a crow.

8. Fire requires a lot of oxygen to burn. My house burned down. Hence, there was a lot of oxygen around my house at the time.

9. I knew that he was guilty. He was at the scene of the crime, he had a gun, and anyone who was both at the scene and had a gun must be the one who was guilty.

10. My life will be complete only if the Yankees win the World Series. Since they are not doing well this year, I should seek fulfillment elsewhere.

ARGUMENTS DISTINGUISHED FROM GOOD ARGUMENTS

One reason people sometimes have difficulty picking out premises and conclusions is that they try to decide *how strongly* a given statement supports another, rather than trying to decide whether it is *presented as* providing support for the other.

Consider the argument we discussed earlier:

> Oh, yes, Grant Wood is famous. After all, he painted *American Gothic*.

Some people, including some who are reading this book, will know that *American Gothic* is a very famous painting. It is the painting of a farmer, pitchfork in hand, standing in front of a house, beside a somewhat younger woman. A whole book could be written just about the parodies that have been done of that famous painting. Many people do not know the name Grant Wood, but they know his painting. Accordingly, the statement, "He painted, *American Gothic*" would do a lot to persuade them of Wood's fame.

Other people, however, may be totally unfamiliar with *American Gothic*. Some will never have seen the painting at all. Telling them that Grant Wood painted *American Gothic* will probably not persuade them that Wood is famous at all.

The fact that some people are familiar with *American Gothic*, and some are not, leads some people into confusion about whether "Grant Wood painted *American Gothic*" should be classified as a premise. This is indeed a confusion. Whether "He painted *American Gothic*" is a premise, has nothing to do with whether you are familiar with the painting. What makes the statement a premise is *how the statement is presented*. The words, "After all," present the statement as support for the statement that Grant Wood is famous.

Maybe you know that *American Gothic* is famous. Maybe you never heard of *American Gothic*. In either case, you know that you are looking at an argument. You know it because you know that "After all" is a premise indicator. Having one statement being used as a premise, of course, means that another statement is being used as a conclusion. That means that the example under discussion is an argument.

It is true that if *American Gothic* were not a famous painting, then Wood's having painted it would not *strongly support* his being a famous artist. But even if the painting were not famous, Wood's having painted it is *presented as* the author's support for the statement that Wood is famous. In that case the above example would still be an argument, even though the argument would have a false premise. What we are attempting to do now is to distinguish arguments from non-arguments. Once we have learned to do that, we can learn to distinguish good arguments from bad arguments.

In other words, one can make the task of picking out premises and conclusion more difficult than it is. You can do this by ignoring the simpler question, "How is this statement presented?" and concentrating on the harder question, "How well does the statement provide the support it is presented as providing?"

Let us not get ahead of ourselves, however. We are not discussing how strongly the premise supports the conclusion. The important point is that in the passage, "He (Grant Wood) is famous," is a statement which *functions as* a conclusion. What shows us the function of the statement is the words, "After all." They tell us that the statement following them is presented as a reason, and that the statement preceding them is presented as being supported by that reason.

CONTRASTING CONDITIONAL STATEMENTS WITH ARGUMENTS

Conditional statements and explanations both look enough like arguments that special care should be taken to understand that they are not. Let us begin by contrasting a conditional statement with an argument:

> **Conditional Statement:**
> If most Bowling Green students live over fifty miles from Bowling Green, then the University surely has many residence halls.

> **Argument:**
> Inasmuch as most Bowling Green students live over fifty miles from Bowling Green, the University surely has many residence halls.

Clearly the whole difference between the two passages is that the conditional (or hypothetical) statement begins with the word *"If"* while the argument begins with the phrase, "Inasmuch as." You can see what a big difference that is by asking yourself how many statements are asserted under each heading. The argument contains two statements. The argument contains the assertion that most Bowling Green students live over fifty miles from Bowling Green. It also contains the assertion that the University surely has many residence halls. (Additionally, the premise indicator 'inasmuch as' conveys the idea that the first statement is presented as supporting the second.)

The conditional statement, in contrast, is a compound statement. It does *not* tell you where any Bowling Green students live. Neither does the conditional statement tell you that the University has any residence halls. Instead, it asserts only that *if* the statement "Most Bowling Green students live over fifty miles from Bowling Green" were true, *then* the statement "The University surely has many residence halls" would also be true. In other words, a conditional statement is a compound statement that asserts how the truth of one of its components is related to the truth of another of its components. It does not assert that either of its component statements is true.

But, while the conditional statement does not assert where any Bowling Green students live, the argument does. Unlike the word "if," the premise indicator tells you that the author is relying on the truth of the premise to provide support for the conclusion. The bottom line, then, is that a conditional statement is not an argument. It is simply a statement.

Of course, since the conditional statement is a statement, it can function in all the ways that other statements can. It could be used as a premise, and it could be used as a conclusion. If it were used as support for another statement, it would be a premise. If it were used as a statement one is attempting to support, it would be a conclusion. Reconsider the following argument:

> Grant Wood is a famous American artist. So if I take a Survey of American Art course, Grant Wood will be on the syllabus.

Here "Grant Wood is a famous American artist," is a premise. "If I take a Survey of American Art course, Grant Wood will be on the syllabus," is a conditional statement used as a conclusion. What tells us that the conditional statement is functioning as a conclusion is the conclusion indicator "so."

Two simple arguments can summarize the above points about conditional statements.

1. A conditional statement is a statement. No statement, by itself, is an argument. Therefore, a conditional statement, by itself, is not an argument.

2. Yet, a conditional statement is a statement. Any statement can be used either as a premise or a conclusion. Therefore, a conditional statement can be used as a premise or a conclusion of an argument.

Exercises

Which of the examples below are arguments? Which are only statements? Underline any conditional statements and indicate if they are used as premises or conclusions.

1. I will read the book. After all, it is recommended by my instructor.

2. If the book is recommended by my instructor, I will read it.

3. I was asked politely. Therefore, I ought to comply.

4. If I am asked politely, I will comply.

5. If anyone receives an invitation but cannot accept it, the courteous action is to express one's regrets. Since you have received an invitation you cannot accept, you ought to express your regrets.

6. I would go to the game, if I had a ticket.

7. Since all problems in Logic are lovely, and this page contains logic problems, this page contains lovely things.

8. You'll look beautiful if you use our make-up.

9. All real problems have solutions. Because I know I have a real problem, it must have a solution.

10. I will go to the game only if I have a ticket.

CONTRASTING EXPLANATIONS AND ARGUMENTS

To round out your understanding of arguments, you need to learn to distinguish between arguments and explanations. Although it is not always easy to make this distinction in practice, it is conceptually clear. Arguments are attempted *proofs*. In other words, arguments are attempts to demonstrate the truth of their conclusions. In this they differ from explanations.

Explanations accept something as a fact, and attempt to explain why it is so. In an explanation one is giving reasons to provide an account of *why* something is so. In an argument one provides reasons in order to *prove that* something is so.

When someone says, "The economy is in a recession because consumers are not buying goods and services as fast as they become available for purchase," we have an explanation. True, the word "because," which is sometimes a premise indicator, occurs in the statement. You need to see, however, that "because" serves a different function in this passage. The author of the statement is saying "What explains the recession in the economy is. . ." The author is not saying, "I can prove to you that there is a recession by pointing out that . . ."

Words that generally function as premise indicators or conclusion indicators, as you know, do not always serve those functions. In particular, a word that often serves as a premise indicator may sometimes serve to indicate an author's explanation of (what is presumed to be) a fact, rather than the author's proof of a given statement. But explanations are not arguments. One should be careful not to infer the existence of an argument from words which sometimes serve as premise or conclusion indicators. Instead, one should examine how those words are functioning in a given passage.

In summary, then, arguments consist of two or more statements in which at least one statement is presented as supporting the truth of another statement. Whether a statement is being used as support, or is being supported by others, is often made clear by indicator words. In cases where there are no indicator words, statements play the role of premises and conclusions only if the context does the job that indicator words would otherwise do.

CHAPTER THREE

ENTHYMEMES AND ARGUMENT DIAGRAMS

When philosophers state arguments, they often try to mention any assumptions they are making. Thus, their arguments are often fully stated, with all the premises they are relying on spelled out. Usually, however, most of us express our arguments only to the extent we feel we need to in order to communicate with others.

Suppose, for example, that a friend of yours drops an empty beverage can as the two of you are walking down the street. You say to your friend, "You should hang on to your beverage can. After all, you wouldn't want someone littering the front of your house."

This argument makes at least two assumptions. It assumes that your friend was about to drop the beverage can in front of someone's house. It also assumes that you should not do something to someone else that you would not want anybody doing to you.

In other words, a more complete statement of your argument would look like this:

You wouldn't want someone littering the front of your house.

You were about to drop a beverage can in front of someone's house. *(assumed)*

You should not do something to someone that you would not want anybody doing to you. *(assumed)*

Therefore, you should hang on to your beverage can.

This more complete statement of the argument illustrates the great extent to which our arguments in ordinary speech are elliptical. We don't waste our words saying what is obvious. This is partly because we don't want to bore our listeners stating assumptions that are common knowledge. We expect our listeners to be able to fill in those assumptions for themselves. As a matter of fact, sometimes in ordinary speech, we don't even make the effort to state the conclusion of an argument, when that conclusion is obvious.

Consider the following snippet of conversation:

Student A: "Do you think she's still interested in me?"

Student B: "You know that she made a point of talking to you yesterday."

Student B is asking Student A to acknowledge that the woman in question made a point of speaking to him yesterday. In the context of Student A's question, Student B clearly takes what happened yesterday as a solid basis for concluding that the woman is still interested in Student A. Thus, although the statement "She is still interested in you," does not occur, the context makes it clear that it is the *conclusion* of Student B's argument.

Throughout the first two chapters of this book, we have worked with examples of fully stated arguments. We have ignored the fact that arguments may be stated elliptically. The examples we are looking at now, however, show us that arguments are often expressed in an incomplete way.

In the light of these examples, we may introduce the definition of an *enthymeme*.

An enthymeme is an argument, some part of which is not stated explicitly.

In an enthymeme, either a premise or a conclusion will be left unexpressed, to be filled in as part of the author's intention. Sometimes, as we have seen, two or more premises may be unstated. Arguments are often stated very elliptically. Thus, we should not expect to find all arguments fully stated. But before we can fully understand an argument and evaluate it, we must be able to supply its missing premises or conclusion.

Exercises

Below are some enthymemes. State the missing premise or conclusion.

1. Mammals suckle their young. Whales are mammals. The conclusion is obvious.

2. Every time I go grocery shopping I forget something. So I wonder what I'll forget today.

3. Water is seldom scarce in a swamp. Bowling Green is in the Black Swamp. So how often do you think there's a water shortage in Bowling Green?

4. My books were very cheap this semester. Why, they cost me under $100 for five courses.

5. I'm going to do just fine on the final exam. After all, I've studied just as hard for it as I did for the earlier exams.

6. The gun is hot, so it was shot recently.

7. She must be smart. After all, she reads a lot.

8. He drives a brand-new Porsche! So, he must be wealthy.

9. This product has a lot of fiber in it. Therefore, it is clearly going to be good for you.

10. Whenever I go out on a date that involves dinner and a movie, I always run out of money. I guess that means that I am going to run out of money tonight.

ONLY ARGUMENTS CAN BE ENTHYMEMES

Once we understand that some arguments are enthymemes, there is a temptation to think that whatever we read is an argument. This is a mistake, and recalling what we have learned about arguments should prevent us from making this mistake. Statements become arguments by playing a certain role. Premise indicator words and conclusion indicator words are the usual means of making that role clear. Especially in oral language, however, context may also clarify the role that a statement plays.

The main point, however, is that something must present a passage as an argument, indicating that some statement is presented as supporting another, or being supported by another, statement. Once that has occurred, there is an argument. Unless that occurs, no argument exists.

Moreover, an enthymeme is defined as an argument. It is, by definition, an argument in which either a premise or a conclusion is not stated explicitly. Because an enthymeme is an argument, it follows that *whatever is not an argument cannot be an enthymeme*. Consider this analogy: If you know that a retriever is a breed of dog, then it would make no sense to say, "This is not a dog, but I wonder whether it is a retriever." Similarly, suppose you say, "This is not an argument. After all, there are no statements functioning here as either premises or conclusions." In that case, you should not add, "But even if it isn't an argument, I wonder whether it is an enthymeme." If the passage is not an argument, it is not an enthymeme.

ARGUMENT DIAGRAMS

The rest of this chapter is devoted to teaching a technique for picturing the relationship between premises and conclusions. We will be diagramming argument structures. Let us begin with a simple example.

> Carpenters and plumbers do equal work. So they should receive equal pay.

1. Our procedure begins by marking the statements in the passage. We will do this by putting brackets around them. Accordingly we have:

> [Carpenters and plumbers do equal work.] So [they should receive equal pay.]

2. We next number each statement in the order of its occurrence:

> ①
> [Carpenters and plumbers do equal work.]
> ②
> So [they should receive equal pay.]

3. We then put parentheses around any premise or conclusion markers:

①
[Carpenters and plumbers do equal work.]

②
(So) [they should receive equal pay.]

4. Our next step is to let the numbers stand for the statements.

① So ②

Our convention will be to place the conclusion below the premise(s) and to draw an arrow from the premise(s) to the conclusion. In our simple example, we get the following diagram:

This diagram tells us that our original argument has the following structure: The first statement, serving as the premise, is represented as implying the second statement which serves as the conclusion.

You have now learned the basics of argument diagramming. You know, however, that arguments can be more complex than the simple example above. We will now consider how to adapt argument diagramming techniques to more complex cases.

Independent Support

An important complication arises when an argument has more than one premise. In such cases, two possibilities need to be distinguished. The first is that each premise, by itself, provides some support for the conclusion. That is, each premise supports the conclusion *independently* of the other. For instance, look at the following example of an argument.

Pregnant women should avoid intoxication for two important reasons. First, the effects of intoxication on women are more long lasting than they are on men. And, second, repeated intoxication during pregnancy has been correlated with the effects of fetal alcohol syndrome.

Following the first steps of our procedure we obtain:

①

[Pregnant women should avoid intoxication] (for two reasons).

②

(First,) [the effects of intoxication on women are more long lasting than they are on men.] And (second,)

③

[intoxication during pregnancy has been correlated with the effects of fetal alcohol syndrome.]

In this passage, statements (2) and (3) are premises in support of the conclusion, statement (1). The new point is that each of the premises provides a reason by itself. The first reason relates to the dangers of intoxication for the woman. The second relates to the dangers of intoxication for the fetus. Each, by itself, would be a reason to avoid intoxication, *independent* of the other.

When premises supply their support for the conclusion *independently* of one another, we follow the convention of drawing an arrow directly from each premise to the conclusion it supports. Thus our diagram for the argument looks like this:

The separate arrows indicate that each premise supports the conclusion *all by itself.*

Cooperative Support

In contrast to premises that provide independent support, sometimes an argument's premises support a conclusion *only when taken together*. In that case, the fact that one premise provides support depends upon putting it together with another premise. For example, consider this argument:

Either the president or the president's secretary made the error. But the secretary was out of town when the error was made. So, the president made the error.

Again, following the first steps of our procedure, we obtain:

①
[Either the president or the president's secretary made the error.]
②
[the secretary was out of town when the error was made.]
③
(So,)   [the president made the error.]

In examining this argument, you should concentrate on (2). By itself, the fact that the secretary was out of town provides no support for the conclusion that the president made the error. To put the point differently, the only support the secretary's being out of town provides depends upon relating the secretary's being gone to (1). Together or cooperatively, as we shall say, (1) and (2) support (3), even though at least one of the premises by itself would not support the conclusion at all.

Because the support for (3), provided by (1) and (2) is *cooperative* in this example, we shall use a bracket which groups the premises together with one arrow pointing toward the conclusion. Thus we get the following:

More than one conclusion in a passage. Once you have learned how to distinguish independent and cooperative support and how to diagram each, you are ready to turn your attention to conclusions. Sometimes, in a given passage, an author will draw more than one conclusion. As logicians understand conclusions, each conclusion indicates a separate argument. For example:

Since the Shenandoah Valley already suffers heavy air pollution, the beauty of Shenandoah National Park is compromised and further upwind power plants should be subject to very stringent air pollution standards.

The initial analysis of this passage gives us:

①

(Since) [the Shenandoah Valley already suffers heavy air pollution,]

②

[the beauty of Shenandoah National Park is compromised]

③

and [further upwind power plants should be subject to very stringent air pollution standards.]

The premise indicator "since" tells us that in this passage, (1) is presented as supporting two conclusions, (2) and (3). Thus, in order to diagram the two arguments in this passage, we put (1) above (2) and (3), place (2) and (3) beside each other, and use two arrows from (1) pointing towards (2) and (3). Here is the diagram:

This diagram says that both conclusions (2) and (3) are supported by premise (1). Since the passage has two conclusions, it follows that our diagram actually represents two distinct arguments that share a common premise.

One statement as both conclusion and premise. In Chapter Two, you learned that the same statement can be a premise in one argument and a conclusion in another. We can see that relationship in the following argument:

Since it is Saturday, I'm going to buy some groceries. So, I'll pick up the cleaning while I am out.

The initial analysis of this passage yields the following diagram.

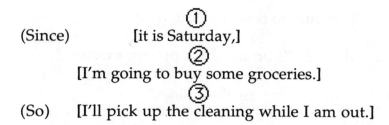

(Since)   [it is Saturday,]

[I'm going to buy some groceries.]

(So)   [I'll pick up the cleaning while I am out.]

Notice that the premise marker "since" presents (1) as a premise supporting (2) as a conclusion. At the same time, though, the conclusion marker "so" presents (3) as a conclusion drawn from (2). Using the arrow to represent the premise-conclusion relationship, we may diagram the arguments in this passage as follows:

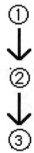

Chain Arguments. You should think of an example like the preceding as two arguments in one passage, each argument being defined by its own conclusion. In that light, the preceding example is the simplest form of a chain argument. The middle statement, which is a conclusion in the first argument and a premise in the second, links the two arguments together into the chain.

A somewhat more complex chain of arguments occurs in the following example:

Given that I have studied very carefully, I'm sure I'll pass the exam. And since I have C's on the three previous exams, I'm sure to pass the course.

Here is the initial analysis of this argument:

①

(Given that)   [I have studied very carefully,]

②

[I'm sure to pass the exam.]

③

And (since)   [I have C's on the three previous exams,]

④

[I'm sure to pass the course.]

(2) is a conclusion supported by (1). (2), however, is also a premise which cooperates with (3) in support of a second conclusion (4). Thus, we may diagram this example of a chain argument as follows:

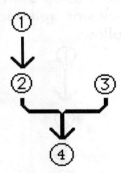

Enthymemes. If you examine the previous example carefully, you will notice that the second argument is an enthymeme. Besides the stated premises "I'll pass the exam," and "I have C's on the three previous exams," the argument rests on an unstated assumption that the grade will be based largely on the exam results. Thus, we should think of that assumption as an additional premise in the argument.

To complete our study of diagramming, we should learn how to diagram enthymemes. Here we simply need one additional convention. We will use these brackets { } around numbers of statements that are not stated, but are only implicit in the argument structure. If we assign the number 5 to the implicit premise that the grade will be based largely on the exam results, how will our diagram look? Since that implicit premise is part of the cooperative support for the second conclusion, the resulting diagram will look like this:

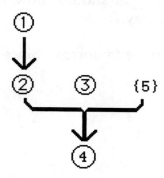

Exercises

Diagram the following arguments:

1. Baton Rouge is the capital of Louisiana. So New Orleans is not.

2. South Dakota is north of Nebraska. Kansas is south of Nebraska. So Kansas is south of South Dakota.

3. You should go to the fair because it is entertaining and because you get a chance to socialize with a lot of friends.

4. Since the Americans had several injuries, the Canadians were able to win. The Canadian public thus became more enthusiastic about the sport. Therefore, Canadian broadcasters bought the television rights.

5. You wouldn't want someone littering the front of your house. Therefore, you should hang on to your beverage can.

6. You really ought to buy this car today. The price will never be lower and neither will the interest rate on car loans.

7. Since all teachers are college graduates and John is a teacher, it follows that John is a college graduate.

8.   You really ought to exercise, because exercise is good for you.

9.   Since today is Saturday, you should mow the lawn today. Saturday, after all is your only free day.

10. Either you will win today or tomorrow. Since you didn't win today, you will win tomorrow.

CHAPTER FOUR

DEDUCTIVE ARGUMENTS

The principal aim of logic is the *evaluation* of arguments. When somebody evaluates an argument, they assess how good the argument is. In evaluating an argument, the focus is on the *relationship* between the premises and the conclusion. As you have already learned, the premises of an argument are presented as providing evidence for their conclusion. A *good* argument is one in which the premises *actually do provide* the support they are presented as providing.

Statements, as we have seen, are either true or false. Thus, they are evaluated in terms of their truth or falsity. Arguments, however, are *not* true or false. With an argument, we are concerned with whether its premises provide good reasons for believing that the conclusion is true. Thus, we are concerned with whether the argument is *logically correct*. Logical correctness is an important element of what makes an argument good. An argument is logically correct if its premises provide adequate support for its conclusion. So while statements are *true* or *false*, arguments are either *logically correct* or *logically incorrect*.

DEDUCTIVE ARGUMENTS

An argument is a set of statements in which some statements are presented as entailing or supporting another. As you have learned, a set of statements is an argument because some of the statements are *presented as* implying or supporting another. This is what distinguishes a mere set of statements from an argument.

This emphasis on how the argument is presented is carried through in the definitions of deductive and inductive arguments. *What makes arguments deductive or inductive is the way they are presented.* The contrast between a deductive or inductive argument rests on the different connection claimed between the premises and the conclusion. Inductive arguments will be discussed in Chapter Five. We now turn our attention to deductive arguments.

In a deductive argument, the presented relationship is *entailment* or *implication*. In a deductive argument it is presented that if its premises are true, then its conclusion *must* be true as well. That is, deductive arguments involve the implicit claim that its conclusion follows from its premises with necessity. Here is our definition of a deductive argument.

Deductive argument = an argument in which it is presented that if all its premises were true, then it conclusion would have to be true.

Here are some examples of deductive arguments. Note that in each case the conclusion is either implicitly or explicitly presented as a necessary consequence of the premises taken together. As you examine these examples, do not be distracted by the subject matter or the truth-value of any of the statements. Look instead at how the connection between the premises and the conclusion is presented.

> All my children went to the fair. Everyone who went to the fair was surprised at the crowd size. Everyone who was surprised at the crowd size left quickly to return home. So my kids must have left quickly to return home.

> John will attend the rehearsal if his parents are not going to be out of town that night. Since his parents are not going to be out of town that night, John definitely will attend the rehearsal.

> The fact that everybody believes in something follows necessarily from the fact that there is something that everyone believes in.

> Teresa enjoys barbecues. This is entailed by two facts: she enjoys whatever her family enjoys, and her family enjoys barbecues.

> If it rains, the game will be called. Look, it's raining now. Therefore, the game will be called.

> All persons are mortal. John is a person. So, John is mortal.

> I must get at least a C on the final or I will fail. I received a D on the final. Hence, I failed.

Notice that in the above examples the arguments present their conclusions as being *entailed* by their premises. That is, the arguments appear to claim that if their premises are true, their conclusions must also be true. *It is the way that the connection between the premises and conclusion is presented that makes the argument deductive.* In other words, it doesn't have to be the case that the premises of the argument actually do entail the conclusion for the argument to be deductive. Neither must it be the case that the premises are true. The argument is deductive when it is *presented* in such a way that it claims that *if* the premises are true, then the conclusion *must* be true. This is what makes the argument deductive.

So, for an argument to be deductive, it need not have true premises. Moreover, it need not be true that its premises do, in fact, imply or entail its conclusion. It only needs to be true that the argument *claims* that this is so. Again, it is the making this *claim* that causes the argument to be deductive.

DEDUCTIVE INDICATORS

How do we know that an argument is making this deductive claim? The way to recognize or identify deductive arguments is to ask: Is this conclusion being presented as a necessary consequence of its premises? If yes, the argument is deductive. Do not ask whether the conclusion actually is a necessary consequence: that question is concerned with logical correctness, which is a later issue. For now we are only concerned with how things are *presented* as being, not how they actually are. As an aid in answering the question "Is this conclusion presented as a necessary consequence of these premises?" you should (1) look for *indicator* words that present the conclusion as a necessary consequence of its premises and (2) look at the *intention* of the author as either directly stated or as made known through clues in the context of the argument's presentation. Indicator words that *tip-off* an argument as deductive include the following:

> It must be true that. . .
> It cannot fail to be that. . .
> It is necessary that. . .
> The premises imply that. . .
> We cannot escape concluding that. . .
> The premises entail that. . .
> It follows necessarily that. . .
> It is a necessary consequence that. . .

These words preceding an argument's conclusion indicate that the argument is deductive. Sometimes, however, no tip-off words may be given. When that happens, if the conclusion is presented as following from the premises without qualifications such as "probably" or "likely," then the argument should be regarded as deductive.

Exercises

Pick out the deductive indicator words in the following arguments.

1. Chess is a game of skill, and in any game of skill players maintain their abilities only through continued practice. Since Bobby Fischer has not been practicing in recent years, it follows that he can't be as good as he once was.

2. All bears love honey. Since all animals that love honey live in forests, bears must live in forests.

3. My conclusion follows necessarily because I have ruled out all the other options.

4. If Brenda is a senior, she's bound to graduate in June, since all seniors will graduate then.

5. He has to be the red-head. I know everybody else by name.

6. It was either raining or snowing. It was not raining. We cannot escape the conclusion, then, that it was snowing.

7. Working with computers requires both education and skill. Since Sally works with computers, it has to be the case that she has both education and skill.

8. All who failed to attend the last meeting will be fired. Consequently, you will be fired, because you failed to attend the last meeting.

9. It is undeniably true that I ran in the marathon. After all, I promised to do so, and I always do what I promise to do.

10. It's clear that I was snoring. Whenever I sleep, I snore, and I was sleeping.

ARGUMENT VERSUS LOGICALLY CORRECT ARGUMENT

We have defined an argument as a set of statements one of which is presented as supported or entailed by the others. In this chapter we have stressed that this definition is descriptive. It describes the roles that different statements are playing. You have learned that indicator words and context in which statements occur are the means by which you can figure out whether a statement is functioning as either a premise or a conclusion.

Earlier in this chapter we indicated that the phrase "logically correct argument" is used to *evaluate* arguments, rather than to describe them. The central concern of the logician is to devise a method of evaluating whether an argument does what it claims to do. Do its premises actually support or entail its conclusion? **We shall define a logically correct argument as an argument in which the premises actually support or entail the conclusion.**

In order to understand the significance of the preceding two paragraphs, you need to notice the difference as well as the similarities between the definitions of "argument" and "logically correct argument." Both talk about premises and a conclusion. Both mention support or entailment. But in contrast, what they say about support or entailment differs decisively. In order to see this, consider the following two definitions:

> An <u>argument</u> is a set of statements in which the conclusion is *presented as* strongly supported or entailed by the premises.

> A <u>logically correct</u> argument is a set of statements one of which (the conclusion) *is* strongly supported or entailed by the others (the premises).

Notice that the only difference in these two definitions is that the definition of an argument contains the words *"is presented as."* Thus an argument is a set of statements in which the conclusion is presented as strongly supported or entailed by the premises. However, when we say that an argument is logically correct we are further saying that the premises do *in fact* strongly support or entail their conclusion. The strong support or entailment is not merely presented as existing. The strong support or entailment actually *exists* in a logically correct argument.

LOGICALLY CORRECT DEDUCTIVE ARGUMENT

We have seen that deductive arguments *claim* that their premises entail or imply their conclusions. Put differently, they claim that if their premises are true, then their conclusions *must* be true as well. Now whether a deductive argument is logically correct is simply the question of whether it lives up to this claim. If a deductive argument does imply or entail its conclusion, then it is logically correct. If it fails to do so, then it is logically incorrect.

VALID ARGUMENTS

Logicians reserve the word *valid* for a logically correct deductive argument. **A valid argument is one in which its premises *entail* or *imply* its conclusion.** Or, what amounts to the same thing, **a valid argument is one in which if its premises are true, then its conclusion *must* be true.**

The concept of validity is the most important concept used for evaluating deductive arguments. Several facts about validity need to be clear to students. When we say that an argument is valid, we are *not* saying (1) it has true premises. We are *not* saying (2) it has a true conclusion. Consider the following argument:

> It snows only if the temperature gets below 20 degrees.
> The temperature never gets below 20 degrees on Tuesdays.
> Therefore, it never snows on Tuesday.

The premises and the conclusion of this argument are obviously all false. But is the argument valid? To decide this, it is irrelevant that the premises and conclusion are actually false. The question of validity is the question "Would the conclusion *have* to be true *if* all the premises were true?" In other words, suppose that "It snows only if the temperature gets below 20 degrees" and "The temperature never gets below 20 degrees on Tuesday" were both true. In that case would the conclusion "It never snows on Tuesday" have to be true as well? The answer is yes. *If* the premises were true, then the conclusion would have to be true too.

Therefore, this is a *valid argument*.

The notion of validity, then, has nothing to do with whether the statements in the argument are in fact true. Rather, validity has to do with the *logical connection* between the premises and the conclusion. If that connection is such that if the premises were true, then the conclusion would have to be true, then the argument is valid. If the connection between the premises and the conclusion is *not* such that if all the premises were true then the conclusion would have to be true, then we call the argument *invalid*.

As we have just seen, some valid arguments have false premises. In that case, they may have false conclusions as well. Even though they are valid arguments, as proofs of their conclusions, these arguments are failures. In the other words, they are not "good" arguments. Clearly, any argument that has both validity and true premises going for it meets a higher standard of evaluation than one which is valid but suffers from at least one false premise. Consider the following argument:

> Detroit is in Ohio, and Ohio is in the United States. So Detroit is in the United States.

Clearly, this argument, although valid, leaves something to be desired. Obviously, what is wrong with the argument is that it has a false premise. In contrast, compare the above argument with this argument:

> Detroit is in Michigan, and Michigan is in the United
> States. So Detroit is in the United States.

The second argument is not only valid, but it has true premises as well. Deductive arguments that are *both* valid and have all true premises are worthy of a special name because of their importance. These arguments are called *sound*. **A sound deductive argument is one that is both valid and has all true premises.**

A deductive argument, therefore, can fail to be sound for either of two reasons. It will fail to be sound if it is invalid. Secondly, deductive argument will not be sound if it has even one false premise. A deductive argument that fails either of these tests will not be sound. Such arguments are called *unsound*.

The central terms for evaluating deductive arguments focus on the connection of the premises to the conclusion. The job of the premises is to provide reasons in support of the conclusion. Accordingly, the central evaluative question in logic is this: If we accept somebody's reasons (premises) as true, how good are those reasons at showing that the conclusion is itself true?

Notice that, even though this question asks us to assume that the premises are true and even though it mentions that the conclusion is true, the question is not focused on truth. It does not say that the premises are true. It does not say that the conclusion is true. It asks whether the premises, *if* true, *would guarantee the truth* of the conclusion. This, of course, is the question of *validity*.

Exercises

Which of the following statements are true?

1. All valid arguments have true premises.

2. All sound deductive arguments have true conclusions.

3. All valid arguments are sound.

4. All deductive arguments claim that they are valid.

5. All valid arguments have true conclusions.

6. All logically correct deductive arguments are valid.

7. All sound arguments are logically correct.

8. All logically correct arguments are sound.

9. All sound arguments have true premises.

10. All deductive arguments are valid.

CHAPTER FIVE

INDUCTIVE ARGUMENTS

An argument, you will remember, is a set of statements in which some of the statements are presented as entailing or supporting another statement. As you have seen, this emphasis on how the argument is presented is carried through in the definition of deductive arguments. The definition of an inductive argument is similar in this regard. What makes an argument either deductive or inductive is the way it is presented.

The contrast between deductive and inductive arguments is the different connection *claimed* between the premises and the conclusion. As we have seen, in a deductive argument the connection claimed between the premises and the conclusion is one of entailment. That is, a deductive argument claims that if its premises are true, then its conclusion must be true also. In an inductive argument, the premises are presented as *strongly supporting* or *warranting* their conclusion. In other words, an inductive argument makes the claim that if its premises are all true, then its conclusion is *very likely* true as well. An equivalent way of speaking is given in the definition of an inductive argument.

> **Inductive argument** = an argument in which it is presented that if all its premises were true, then its conclusion would *very probably* be true.

The conclusions of inductive arguments are *presented as* being very probably true but still possibly false.

INDUCTIVE INDICATORS

The way to recognize inductive arguments is to ask: Is this conclusion being presented as *probably*, but not necessarily, true? If yes, the argument is inductive. Do not ask whether the premises actually do strongly support or strongly warrant the conclusion. That would be to ask if the argument is logically correct. Whether an argument is inductive is a matter of how the argument is presented, not a matter of logical correctness. In this section our concern is with describing a kind of argument, not with how to evaluate its logical correctness.

As an aid in answering the question "Is this conclusion being presented as probably but not as necessarily true?," we suggest: (1) looking for inductive *indicator* words leading into the conclusion or (2) relying on contextual clues in the way the argument is presented. Common *indicator* words for inductive arguments are:

> So *probably*. . .
> It *seems* that. . .
> It is *likely* that. . .
> It's a *good bet* that. . .
> We can *probably* conclude that. . .
> The facts *strongly suggest* that. . .
> The facts *strongly warrant* believing that. . .
> The evidence *strongly indicates* that. . .
> The facts *strongly support* concluding that. . .
> It seems *beyond reasonable doubt* that. . .
> It is *not improbable* that. . .

WHEN INDICATOR WORDS ARE MISSING

Indicator words and context usually allow you to decide if an argument is either deductive or inductive. Sometimes, however, an argument contains no words which indicate that it is either deductive or inductive. The context may not make it clear either. In that case you lack obvious evidence for making a decision. The *rule* you should follow in such cases is as follows: "Presume that the argument is deductive unless the conclusion is presented hesitantly, tentatively, cautiously, or as something less than a flat bold assertion."

Contrast the three following arguments:

> In the course of the day, the temperature will likely climb at least twenty degrees because the sun is going to shine all day.

> In the course of the day, the temperature is bound to climb at least twenty degrees because the sun is going to shine all day.

> In the course of the day, the temperature will climb at least twenty degrees because the sun is going to shine all day.

In each case, *because* marks the premise. In each case the predicted temperature rise is the conclusion. The only difference between the three arguments is in how the conclusion is presented. The conclusion of the first argument contains the word *"likely,"* which marks the argument as *inductive.* The conclusion of the second argument contains the phrase *"is bound to,"* which marks the argument as *deductive.*

The conclusion of the third argument has no marker. We know nothing about the context to indicate probability or necessity. The rule given above tells us to regard the third argument as deductive, since its conclusion is presented without hesitancy, tentativeness or other clear inductive markings.

DIFFERENCE BETWEEN INDUCTIVE AND DEDUCTIVE ARGUMENTS

In classifying arguments as either deductive or inductive we are talking about how the premises, taken as a group, are *presented* as relating to the conclusion. In the deductive relationship the premises are presented as *entailing* or *implying* the conclusion. In the inductive relationship the premises are presented as *strongly warranting* or *strongly supporting* (but not entailing) the conclusion.

When an argument is deductive, it *claims* that its premises entail or imply its conclusion. The suggestion of a deductive argument is that if the premises are all true, then the conclusion *must* be true. If, on the other hand, we are dealing with an inductive argument, then the premises taken together are *presented as* making the conclusion probably true. The conclusion is presented as being probably, but not necessarily, true. Unlike deductive arguments, the suggestion of an inductive argument is that if the premises are all true, then the conclusion will *probably* also be true. Look for the presentation of this relationship in these examples of inductive arguments:

> My children went to the fair. Most of the folks who went to the fair had a good time. So my children probably had a good time.

> Everybody pays taxes, but only lucky people win at poker. I'm usually not too lucky, so I'll probably do more tax paying than poker winning.

Teresa, it seems, enjoys barbecues. I say that because she usually enjoys whatever her family enjoys and her family enjoys barbecues.

John will attend the rehearsal if his folks are not going out of town that night. His folks are probably not going out of town that night. So it's a fair bet that he will attend the rehearsal.

You might find it helpful to compare these examples with the examples of deductive arguments given in Chapter Four. Notice the continual contrasts in the indicator words. An inductive argument is not presented as necessitating its conclusion; it merely claims to strongly support it. The presentation of an argument as inductive leaves it possible (though not likely) for all the premises of a good inductive argument to be true and yet for the conclusion to be false.

Exercises

Part I: Here are some tip-off words. Distinguish those which indicate *deductive* arguments from those that indicate *inductive* arguments.

1. So it is very likely that. . .

2. We must thus accept that. . .

3. Therefore. . .

4. Therefore probably. . .

5. The evidence strongly indicates that. . .

6. It is inevitable that. . .

7. The premises entail that. . .

8. It follows that. . .

9. Hence. . .

10. Thus it seems that...

Part II: Distinguish deductive arguments from inductive arguments in the examples below.

1. Bethany is athletic. Athletic people tend to be slim. So Bethany is probably a slim person.

2. If capital punishment deterred crime, it would be justified. But capital punishment does not deter crime. Therefore, we must acknowledge that capital punishment is not justified.

3. So far all intelligent students have done A work in logic. Thus, it seems that all intelligent students in the class will get an A.

4. If Karl Marx had been J. D. Rockefeller, then he would have been a capitalist. But Karl Marx was not a capitalist. Therefore Karl Marx was not J. D. Rockefeller.

5. I bought a pair of socks of this brand and style before, and they lasted a long time. If I buy another pair, they will last a long time, I expect.

6. Two-thirds of the last 100 tosses of this coin came up heads. So two-thirds of the next 50 tosses will come up heads.

7. Four out of five dentists recommend our chewing *Sticky Sweet* gum. It is likely that your dentist does too.

8. Only when the cows come home can we rest. The cows have come home. Therefore, we can rest.

9. Most women are overworked and underpaid. Since Mary is a woman, chances are she is both overworked and underpaid.

10. Most trees are tall and graceful. Sarah just planted a tree. Chances are it is tall and graceful too.

INDUCTIVE ARGUMENT VERSUS JUSTIFIED ARGUMENT

So far in this chapter we have discussed inductive arguments, that is, arguments whose conclusions are *presented as* probably true if their premises are true. Like the category of deductive arguments, inductive arguments are classified by how they are presented.

You will remember, however, our discussion of the concept of validity in Chapter Four. It is a concept for evaluating *deductive* arguments. An argument is valid when the presented deductive relationship between premises and conclusion actually holds. That is, an argument is valid if its conclusion must be true whenever all its premises are true. "Valid," as we have seen, is our special term for logically correct *deductive* arguments.

Inductive arguments can also be evaluated in terms of logically correctness. Since it is presented in any inductive argument that if its premises are all true, its conclusion is *probably* true, we can raise the evaluative question, "Is it indeed probable that the conclusion is true, given the truth of the premises?" This, as we have seen, is the question of logical correctness. Accordingly, we shall introduce the term "justified" as our special evaluative term for inductive arguments. If an argument is *justified,* then if all its premises are true, its conclusion is probably true. "Justified," then, is our special term for logically correct *inductive* arguments.

VALIDITY AND JUSTIFICATION

The general evaluation of an argument as logically correct, can be broken down into two specific evaluations. Each evaluation corresponds to the type of argument we are dealing with.

A deductive argument is *logically correct* if its premises entail or imply its conclusion. In other words, a deductive argument is logically correct if whenever all of its premises are true, its conclusion *must* be true. Our special term for a logically correct deductive argument is *valid.*

An inductive argument is *logically correct* if its premises *strongly support* or *warrant* its conclusion. In other words, an inductive argument is logically correct if whenever all of its premises are true, its conclusion is *probably true.* Our special term for a logically correct inductive argument is, *justified.*

Validity and justification, then, are both evaluative concepts. Both apply to arguments. Both are species of the general concept of logical correctness. The difference is that *validity* refers to the concept of entailment and therefore applies *only* to deductive arguments. A deductive argument is valid if whenever all of its premises are true, its conclusion must also be true.

Justification refers to the concept of strong support and therefore applies *only* to inductive arguments. An inductive argument is justified if whenever all of its premises are true, its conclusion is probably true. That is, its premises strongly support its conclusion. Hence logical correctness is a general term applied to both deductive and inductive arguments. In both cases it refers to the connection existing between the premises and the conclusion of an argument. However, as we have seen, logical correctness means something quite different when applied to deductive and inductive arguments. As a result of this difference, a logically correct deductive argument is called "valid," while a logically correct inductive argument is called "justified."

Thus we can say the following:

> **Logically correct argument** = an argument that is either valid or justified.

SOUNDNESS

In Chapter Four we introduced the evaluation of arguments as sound. We may use the following definition:

> **Sound Argument** = a logically correct argument having all true premises.

While our specific concern in Chapter Four was with deductive arguments, we did not confine our definition of soundness to deductive arguments. Instead we used a general definition phrased in terms of logical correctness. The result is that you can apply the concept of soundness to inductive arguments as well. As we have seen, an inductive argument is logically correct if whenever all of it premises are true, its conclusion is probably true. Such an argument is called "justified." Thus, if all of the premises of an inductive argument are true and the argument is justified, then it is *sound*.

Just as with deductive arguments, an inductive argument can fail to be sound for either of *two* reasons. First, if an inductive argument has even one false premise, it is unsound. Second, if an inductive argument is not logically correct, it is unsound. For an inductive argument to be sound it must be both logically correct, or justified, and have all true premises. If it fails to meet either condition, it will be unsound.

SOUNDNESS IN VALID AND IN JUSTIFIED ARGUMENTS

There is one significant contrast between a sound deductive argument and a sound inductive argument. Both are sound because they are logically correct and they have true premises. But the implications are different in the two cases. When a deductive argument is logically correct (valid) and has all true premises then its conclusion *must* be true.

In other words, a *sound* deductive argument *must* have a true conclusion. However, when an inductive argument is logically correct (justified) and has all true premises, its conclusion does not have to be true. Rather, in the case of a sound inductive argument, its conclusion will very probably be true. In other words a sound inductive argument will *probably* have a true conclusion, but its conclusion does not have to be true. Sound deductive arguments, in contrast, must have true conclusions.

Exercises

Which of the following are true?

1. All sound inductive arguments are justified.

2. If an argument is justified, it must have all true premises.

3. Every sound argument is either valid or justified.

4. If a deductive argument has true premises and a false conclusion, then it *must* be invalid.

5. All logically correct arguments have premises that either entail or imply their conclusions.

6. All deductive arguments have premises that imply their conclusions.

7. All deductive arguments are presented as having premises that imply their conclusions.

8. All inductive arguments have premises that, if true, would strongly support their conclusions.

9. It is possible for a justified argument to have a false conclusion.

10. It is possible for a valid argument to have a false conclusion.

CHAPTER SIX

CATEGORICAL STATEMENTS

We now turn our attention to categorical logic. Categorical logic, also called Aristotelian or syllogistic logic, is a deductive form of logic. It will be recalled that a deductive argument is one that *claims* that if its premises are true, then its conclusion *must* be true as well. Categorical logic is used to distinguish between some types of valid and invalid deductive arguments. An argument is valid, it will be recalled, if its conclusion must be true whenever its premises are all true. Otherwise, it is invalid.

Categorical logic employs what are known as categorical statements. These are statements that refer to *classes* or *categories* of things. In this section we will concentrate on learning the basic parts or elements of categorical statements. Overall, this chapter has two sections. The first focuses on the special *terms* that are used to identify the *concepts* of categorical logic. And, once we have learned to identify these concepts, the focus will be on how they are used.

WHAT ARE CATEGORICAL STATEMENTS?

Categorical statements are statements about *two* classes of things or objects. A *class* is a set or collection of objects of a particular sort. For example, imagine the class of all desks. The class of desks includes everything that is called a desk. A smaller class would be the class of all desks in some classroom. Categorical statements may also include statements about classes that do not have any members, since it is possible for you to be in a room in which there are no desks. The class of desks in that room would be an empty or null class.

What makes an object a member of a particular class? Class membership is determined by the object's having the particular characteristics or properties required by members of the class. For example, to be a Minnesota lake, something must be a still body of water and be within the state of Minnesota.

Corresponding to the concept of a class or set of objects, there is also the notion of a *class term*. A class term is a word that stands for a collection or set of objects. Examples of class terms are "professors" and "lakes." A class term can also be more than one word, like "twentieth century brick buildings" or "professors of philosophy." The difference between a class of objects and a class term is that a class term is a *word* or *phrase* used to talk about the members of a class, while a class is a collection or set of objects. A categorical statement then, will employ two class terms that make an assertion about exactly two classes. "All elephants are mammals" is an example of a categorical statement. As we shall see, it asserts something about both the class of "elephants" and the class of "mammals."

THE RELATIONS BETWEEN CLASSES

Because categorical statements make assertions they, like all statements, are either *true* or *false*. All categorical statements make assertions about two classes. For example, "All soldiers are brave persons." In this case the two classes are "soldiers" and "brave persons." The first class term in a categorical statement is called the *subject term* and the second term is known as the *predicate term*. A categorical statement will assert that the subject class is either *included* in or *excluded* from the predicate class. "All soldiers are brave persons," for example, asserts that the entire class of "soldiers" is included in the class of "brave persons."

Now consider, for example, the categorical statement "No humans are mortals." Here the assertion is that the class of things that are "humans" is entirely *excluded* from the class of things that are "mortals." As we will see later, other categorical statements make assertions about *part* of the subject class being either included or excluded from the predicate class.

Exercises

Complete the following statements.

1. A class is a _____ or _____ of objects.

2. A categorical statement is a statement which makes a claim about _____ classes of things or objects.

3. A class term is a word which is used to talk about the _____ of a class.

4. A categorical statement asserts that one of the classes to which it refers is either _____ in or _____ from the other class.

5. In the statement "All custard pies are dessert treats," _____ is the subject term and _____ is the predicate term.

QUALITY AND QUANTITY

Whether or not a categorical statement is an inclusion or an exclusion statement depends upon its *quality*. The quality of a statement is either *affirmative* or *negative*. **Statements that are *affirmative* in quality are *inclusion* statements**. An affirmative statement such as "All soldiers are brave people" asserts that all of the members of the class of soldiers are *included* in the class of brave people. **Statements that are *negative* in quality are *exclusion* statements**. The negative statement "Some soldiers are not brave people" asserts that some of the members of the class of soldiers are *excluded* from the class of brave people. All categorical statements that are inclusions have an affirmative quality, and all categorical statements that are exclusions have a negative quality.

In addition to its quality, categorical statements also have the characteristic of *quantity*. The quantity of a categorical statement is determined by whether the statement makes an assertion about the *entire* subject class or only about *part* of the subject class. If the statement makes an assertion about the entire subject class, it is called a *universal* statement. The statement "All soldiers are brave persons" is an example of a universal statement. The word "all" makes it clear that the *entire* subject class is being referred to. Since, as indicated above "All soldiers are brave persons" is also an affirmative statement, it is known as a *universal affirmative* statement.

"No soldiers are brave people" illustrates the other sort of universal statement. The word "*no*" indicates the *universal* quantity of the statement, since it makes reference to the entire subject class. The quality of this statement is *negative*, since it asserts that the entire class of soldiers is *excluded* from the class of brave people. In other words, it says that none of the members of the class of soldiers is a brave person. "No soldiers are brave people," therefore, is a *universal negative* categorical statement.

Categorical statements that refer only to *part* of the subject class are called *particular* statements. An example of a particular statement would be, "Some soldiers are brave people." The word "some" determines its quantity. That is, it refers to only *part* of the class of soldiers. Since it asserts that there are some members of the class of soldiers that are *included* in the class of brave people, its quality is affirmative. "Some soldiers are brave people," then, is called a *particular affirmative* statement.

There are also particular statements that *exclude* members of one class from another class. "Some soldiers are not brave people" is an example of such a statement. Again, the word "some" determines its quantity, since it only refers to *part* of the class of soldiers. It is, therefore, a particular statement. Because the statement asserts that part of the class of soldiers, the subject class, is *excluded* from the class of brave people, then its quality is negative. "Some soldiers are not brave people," therefore, is called a *particular negative* statement.

It should be pointed out that the word "some" appearing in statements having a particular quantity is vague. When we say, for example, that "Some cars are blue things," how many cars are we referring to? The point is that particular statements, because of the vagueness of the word "some," do not tell us exactly how many individuals are referred to in the statement. In order to ensure that we are using the word "some" the same way every time we use it in categorical logic, we need to define or stipulate its meaning. So, for the purposes of categorical logic, the word **"some" will be defined to mean *at least one*.** For example, if *some* television manufacturers are also VCR manufacturers, we will interpret this to mean that *there is at least one* television manufacturer who is also a VCR manufacturer.

Exercises

Part I: Complete the following statements.

1. The quality of a statement is either _____ or _____.

2. The quantity of a statement is either _____ or _____.

3. The word "some" means _____ _____ _____.

4. If a categorical statement is negative in quality, it is called an _____ statement.

5. If a categorical statement is affirmative in quality, it is called an _____ statement.

6. If a categorical statement refers to all of its subject class, it is called a _____ statement.

7. If a categorical statement refers only to part of its subject class, it is called a _____ statement.

8. Every categorical statement has both a _____ and a _____.

9. Every categorical statement can be analyzed with respect to both its _____ and _____.

10. The words "all" and "no" tell us that a statement is _____ with respect to its _____.

Part II: For each of the following statements below, determine whether it is a universal affirmative (UA), an universal negative (UN), a particular affirmative (PA), or a particular negative statement (PN).

_____ 1.   All computers are useful tools.

_____ 2.   Some books are boring things.

_____ 3.   Some people are not nice individuals.

_____ 4.   No bugs are cute things.

_____ 5.   Some dogs are brown animals.

_____ 6.   Some students are not scholars.

_____ 7.   No dogs are felines.

_____ 8.   Some really rich people are owners of blue-chip stock.

_____ 9.   No athletic events are things covered by enough insurance.

_____ 10. All doctors are persons opposed to socialized medicine.

THE A, E, I, AND O STATEMENTS

As we have observed, there are exactly four types of categorical statements. They are:

1. **Universal affirmative:** "All soldiers are brave persons."
2. **Universal negative:** "No soldiers are brave persons."
3. **Particular affirmative:** "Some soldiers are brave persons."
4. **Particular negative:** "Some soldiers are not brave persons."

Traditionally, the four different categorical statements are identified or designated by a letter of the alphabet. The letters that correspond to the statements are **A, E, I,** and **O,** respectively. That is, an universal affirmative statement such as, "All bears are animals" is an **A** statement, and an universal negative statement such as "No millionaires are paupers" is an **E** statement. Thus, **A** and **E** are letters that identify the two *universal* statements.

The *particular* statements correspond to the letters **I** and **O**. For example, a particular affirmative statement like "Some dogs are Terriers" is an **I** statement, and a particular negative statement such as "Some cats are not friendly animals" is an **O** statement. Following custom, we will identify the four categorical statements by these four letters:

A: "All bears are animals."   (universal affirmative)
E: "No bears are animals."   (universal negative)
I: "Some bears are animals."   (particular affirmative)
O: "Some bears are not animals."   (particular negative)

The four types of categorical statements can also be represented in a more general way. In order to clarify this more general notation, take an example of a categorical statement such as "All birds are warm blooded animals." Now, replace the *subject term* "birds" with the letter S, and replace the *predicate term* "warm blooded" animals" with the letter P. The result will be the general statement form:

All S is P

The general statement form "All S is P" will be used to represent any **A** form statement whatever.

Now, if we consider the statement "Some women are not Hispanics," we can replace the *subject term* "women" with the letter *S*, and the *predicate term* "Hispanics" with the letter *P*. The result will be the general statement form:

Some S is not P

The general statement form "Some S is not P" will be used to represent any **O** form statement whatever.

Obviously, we can do the same for **E** and **I** form statements with the resulting general forms for **E** and **I** respectively being:

E: No S is P   **I:** Some S is P

The technique of using the letters *S* and *P* to represent the subject and predicate classes of categorical statements allows us to grasp the statement's *form* . The *form* of a statement is the general structure that statements of the same sort have in common. Consider, for example, the two categorical statements: "All bats are blind animals," and "All tables are material things." These statements have different meanings, expressed by different words, but they share a common *form* expressed as "All S is P."

Because we are using the letter *S* to stand for the subject term of *any* categorical statement and the letter *P* to stand for the predicate term of *any* categorical statement, we can represent the form of *any* categorical statement in one of the following four ways:

A: All S is P
E: No S is P
I: Some S is P
O: Some S is not P

In the next two chapters you will learn precisely what the four different categorical statement forms express and the logical relations that hold between them.

Exercises

Part I: Complete the following statements.

1. A categorical statement contains two terms, a _____ term and a _____ term.

2. The letter _____ is used to represent the subject term, and the letter _____ is used to represent the predicate term.

3. The general structure of a statement is known as its _____.

4. The letters _____ and _____ are used to represent universal statements.

5. The letters _____ and _____ are used to represent particular statements.

Part II: Translate the following categorical statements into their form. Label each statement as either **A, E, I,** or **O**.

1. All cars are motorized vehicles.

2. All chickens are fowls.

3. Some flowers are not beautiful things.

4. No persons are slaves.

5. Some cities are havens for criminals.

6. No rules are restrictions that are justified.

7. Some supporters of arms control are persons disappointed with history.

8. All supporters of Richard Nixon are Republicans.

9. Some havens for criminals are not police stations.

10. All guitarists are musicians.

SUMMARY

Categorical statements, as we have seen, are concerned with *classes* of objects, and how those classes of objects relate to one another.

Class terms are the *words* or *phrases* that are used to talk about a class or set of objects. Each categorical statement contains a subject term and a predicate term. These terms are customarily represented by the letters S and P.

Two concepts used to characterize categorical statements are *quality* and *quantity*. The *quality* of a categorical statement is either *affirmative* or *negative*. A categorical statement is affirmative when it asserts the *inclusion* of part or all of its subject class within its predicate class. A statement is *negative* when it asserts the *exclusion* of part or all of its subject class from its predicate class.

The *quantity* of a categorical statement is either *universal* or *particular*. A categorical statement is *universal* when it makes an assertion about *all* of the members of the subject class. A categorical statement is *particular* when it makes an assertion about *some* of the members of the subject class. For clarity, the word "some" is defined as meaning "at least one."

Combining the notions of quality and quantity gives rise to four different kinds of categorical statements, known as the **A, E, I,** and **O** forms. They may be represented in their general form or structure as:

A: All S is P
E: No S is P
I: Some S is P
O: Some S is not P

CHAPTER SEVEN

CATEGORICAL LOGIC

In the last chapter categorical statements were introduced as statements that relate two classes or sets of objects to each other. This chapter introduces *Venn Diagrams*, the standard method used to diagram categorical statements. We will also describe a method of symbolizing categorical statements that will facilitate the diagramming process. Finally, the notion of *existential import* will be explained with its implications for the interpretation of categorical statements.

VENN DIAGRAMS

In 1880 the logician, John Venn, developed what are called *Venn Diagrams*. Venn Diagrams graphically illustrate the relationships between the two classes referred to by categorical statements. Each class is represented by a circle. The circles overlap to represent assertions of class inclusion or exclusion made by categorical statements.

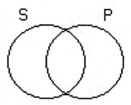

The circle on the left is labeled "S," representing the subject class of a categorical statement, and the circle on the right is labeled "P," representing the predicate class. Notice that the overlapping circles result in three distinct regions. For convenience in referring to them, we may label the three regions moving from left to right, regions 1, 2 and 3.

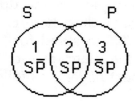

Region 1 represents things that are in the "S" class, but are outside the "P" class. Region 2 stands for things included in both the "S" and "P" classes, and region 3 stands for things that are within the "P" class, but are outside of the "S" class.

Since region 1 represents things that are in "S" but are not in "P," region 1 can be labeled "S$\overline{P}$" (using the bar above a letter to stand for "non"). "S$\overline{P}$" is read "S, non-P." Region 3, which represents those individuals which are not members of the subject class but are members of the predicate class, is written "$\overline{S}$P." It is read "non-S, P." Finally, region 2, representing those individuals that are members of both the subject and predicate class, is written "SP." It is read "SP."

DIAGRAMMING I AND O STATEMENTS

We are now ready to learn how to diagram categorical statements. Consider, for example, the **I** statement: "Some dogs are Terriers." The form of this statement is represented as "Some S is P." You should remember that an **I** form statement asserts that *there is at least one* S included in the class of P." If we use an "x" to denote *"there is at least one,"* we can diagram the **I** form statement, "Some dogs are Terriers," as follows:

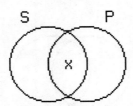

Notice that we have placed an "x" in the "SP" region, or region 2, indicating that "there is at least one dog that is also a Terrier." If we focus only on the *form* of the statement, "Some S is P," we have captured in our diagram the claim that "there is at least one S that is a P." The diagram illustrates how we diagram *any* **I** form statement, that is, any statement of the form "Some S is P."

An **O** statement, for example, "Some dogs are not Terriers," has the form "Some S is not P." It says that there is *"at least one S that is excluded* from the class of P." Using "x" to stand for *"there is at least one,"* we place an "x" in region 1. Thus, the diagram for "Some dogs are not Terriers," appearing at the top of the next page, is as follows:

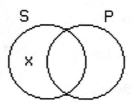

Placing an "x" in region 1, the "S$\overline{P}$" region, tells us that there is an S that is not a P. Again, *any* **O** form statement, that is, any statement of the form "Some S is not P," will be diagrammed in exactly the same way.

Exercises

Part I: Complete the blanks in the following sentences.

1. The diagrams that we are using to represent categorical statements are called: _____ _____.

2. The two circles in a Venn Diagram that represent the classes referred to in a categorical statement are labeled _____ and _____.

3. The three regions of a Venn Diagram are labeled: _____ _____ and _____.

4. When diagramming an **I** statement an ____ is placed in the ____ region to show that there is at least one thing that is both an ____ and a ____.

5. When diagramming an **O** statement an ____ is placed in the ____ area to show that there is at least one thing that is an ____ and not a _____.

Part II: Diagram the following examples using Venn Diagrams:

1. Some students are not persons who have part-time jobs.

2. Some drinks are red beverages.

3.   Some students are athletes.

4.   Some students are not athletes

5.   Some women are not students.

EXISTENTIAL IMPORT

The **I** form statement, "Some of my pets are cats," asserts that "There is at least one of my pets that is a cat." As we have seen, the Venn Diagram for an **I** statement looks like this:

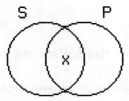

You should recall that the "x" in the SP region means that *"there is at least one* S that is also P."

Similarly, an **O** statement such as "Some of my pets are not cats" says that *"there is at least one* of my pets that is not a cat." The Venn diagram for an **O** statement looks like this:

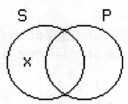

The "x" in region 1 says that *"there is at least one* S that is not a P."

Now we want to introduce a technical term. When a statement asserts or implies that its subject class has at least one member, we will say that the statement has *existential import*. It should be obvious that **I** and **O** statements have existential import. When I assert that "Some students are intelligent," I am saying that *"there is at least one* student who is intelligent." Or if I assert that "Some books are not worth reading," I am claiming that *"there is at least one* book that is not worth reading." In both cases it is clear that I am asserting the *existence* of the entities that I am talking about. Therefore, both **I** and **O** statements have *existential import*.

However, **A** and **E** statements do not necessarily assert that the classes they refer to have members. This can be clearly seen by looking at an example. Suppose your logic professor announces before an exam that "All cheaters in this class will be students who flunk." This, of course, is an example of an **A** form statement. Notice that by making this statement the professor is not asserting that there are or will be cheaters in the class. In fact it is likely that the professor is making this statement in an attempt to ensure that there will be no cheaters in the class.

But if "All cheaters in this class will be students who flunk" doesn't assert or imply the existence of cheaters in the class, then it doesn't have existential import. How, then, should we interpret the statement? It appears to be saying that *"If* there are any cheaters in the class, they will flunk." This interpretation of the **A** statement makes it clear that the *existence* of the subject class, (cheaters, in this case) is not always being asserted or implied by an **A** form statement.

Thus, it is clear that, unlike **I** and **O** statements, **A** statements do not always have existential import. The same is true for the **E** form statement. Consider, for example, the statement "No cheaters are persons who will win." It neither asserts nor implies that there are cheaters. It can be interpreted, instead, to say that *"If* there are any cheaters, they will not win." So, like **A** statements, **E** statements do not always assert or imply the *existence* of the classes they refer to. Therefore, they do not always have existential import.

DIAGRAMMING A AND E STATEMENTS

The English logician and mathematician, George Boole, first noticed that **A** and **E** statements need not be interpreted as having existential import. This interpretation of the universal statements, **A** and **E**, as lacking existential import, is accordingly known as the *Boolean interpretation* of categorical statements.

The fact that on the Boolean interpretation, **A** and **E** statements do not assert or imply the existence of the objects they refer to is reflected in the way they are diagrammed. Let's begin with an **E** statement that clearly lacks existential import. Consider the following **E** statement:

No space aliens are football players.

Obviously, the *existence* of space aliens is not being asserted by this statement. That is, it is neither being asserted nor being assumed that there are aliens from outer space. Even if the statement is true, it is not necessary that space aliens exist. The statement asserts only that "If there are any space aliens, they are not football players."

The Boolean interpretation of the **E** statement is reflected in the way we diagram it. Notice that the statement, "No space aliens are football players" asserts that the entire class of space aliens is excluded from the class of football players. Since, space aliens is the "S" class and football players the "P" class, the statement says that the class of things that are both space aliens and football players is empty. Now to indicate, on a Venn Diagram, that an area is empty we will shade it. So we diagram, "No space aliens are football players" by shading the "SP" region to indicate that it is empty. Here is the diagram:

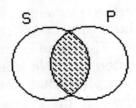

Notice that there is nothing in the diagram to indicate the existence of an "S" that is not a member of the "P" class. (Region 1 is unmarked.) Rather, what is asserted on the Boolean interpretation of *any* E statement is "*If* there is an S, then it is not a member of the P class." We capture what statements of the form "No S is P" assert by shading the SP region to show that it is empty. This, of course, is how we diagram *any* E form statement on the Boolean interpretation.

THE A STATEMENT

We are now ready to learn how to diagram the **A** statement. Consider the following example:

All space aliens are spies.

Clearly, the existence of space aliens is not being asserted by this statement. Moreover, by talking about space aliens, there is no assumption that there are aliens from outer space. Even if the statement is true, it is not necessary that space aliens exist. The statement asserts only that "*If* there are any aliens from outer space, they are spies."

How do we represent what this statement is asserting in a Venn Diagram? Notice that it is saying that the entire class of space aliens is *included* in the class of spies. Thus, it is asserting that there are no space aliens outside the class of spies. Using "S" to stand for "space aliens" and "P" to stand for "spies," the statement is saying that "there is no 'S' outside of 'P.'" If we shade the "S$\overline{\text{P}}$" region we can show that there is no "S" outside of "P." That is, the **A** form statement is asserting there are no space aliens outside the class of spies, since it claims that "If there are any space aliens they are all included in the class of spies." Thus, the class of space aliens who are not spies is empty. Here is the diagram for this statement:

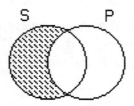

Notice that our diagram does not indicate that there are any space aliens that are spies; region 2 is unmarked. The diagram only says that there are no aliens outside the class of spies. This is what shading region 1 represents. The diagram reflects the Boolean interpretation of "*If* there are any space aliens, then they are spies." The above diagram indicates how to diagram any **A** form statement on the Boolean interpretation.

SYMBOLIZING A, E, I, AND O STATEMENTS

We have seen already that when we symbolize **A**, **E**, **I** and **O** statements, we capture their general form. For instance, an **A** statement such as "All dogs are animals" is symbolized as "All S is P."

An alternative method of symbolization can be used that more clearly reflects the Boolean interpretation of categorical statements. Once you learn it, it will also make diagramming categorical statements easier. As we have seen, "All S is P," on the Boolean interpretation says that "there are no S's outside the class of P." In other words, **A** form statements say that the class of "S$\overline{\text{P}}$" is empty. We can symbolize the **A** statement, then, as "S$\overline{\text{P}}$ = 0." This asserts that the "S$\overline{\text{P}}$" class is empty or null. Notice how this symbolization of the **A** form statement is captured in its Venn diagram:

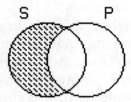

The "S$\overline{\text{P}}$" region is shaded to indicate that it is empty. This reflects the fact that, on the Boolean interpretation, the **A** statement does not assert the *existence* of the objects it talks about. Thus both the symbolization, "S$\overline{\text{P}}$ = 0," and the diagram only indicate that a certain region is empty. Neither says anything about a region having any members.

The **E** form statement, "No S is P," is symbolized, "SP = O." Symbolizing the **E** statement like this reflects the Boolean interpretation of the **E** statement as asserting only that the "SP" class is empty or null. Again this symbolization of the **E** statement is captured in its diagram:

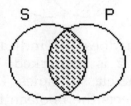

Both **I** and **O** statements, as we have seen, have existential import. That is, they assert that the classes they refer to have members. The **I** form statement, "Some S is P" says "there is at least one S that is also a P." We can symbolize this as "SP ≠ 0." The slash through the equal sign is used to deny that the class being referred to is empty. In other words, "SP ≠ O" asserts that "there exists at least one S that is included in the P class." This is reflected in the Venn diagram for the **I** form statement.

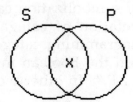

The **O** form statement, "Some S is not P," is symbolized "$S\overline{P} \neq 0$." It says that "there exists at least one S that lies outside the class of P." This is reflected in the Venn diagram for an **O** statement.

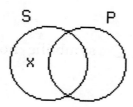

Exercises

Part I: Complete the following statements.

1. A statement having existential import asserts that there is _____ _____ _____ member of the subject class.

2. To show that a region of a Venn Diagram is empty, it is _____.

3. When diagramming an **A** statement using the Boolean interpretation the _____ region is shaded to illustrate that it is _____.

4. When diagramming an **E** statement employing the Boolean interpretation the _____ region is shaded to illustrate that it is _____.

Part II; Determine for each of the following whether it is an **A, E, I,** or **O** statement. Then, using our new symbolic notation, symbolize each statement.

1. No bears are vicious animals.

   type of statement _____ symbolic notation _____

2. Some turtles are not slow animals.

      type of statement _____   symbolic notation _____

3.   All snakes are animals.

      type of statement _____   symbolic notation _____

4.   Some birds are bipeds.

      type of statement _____   symbolic notation _____

5. All dogs are canines.

      type of statement _____   symbolic notation _____

6. Some wines are not red drinks.

      type of statement _____   symbolic notation _____

7. Some wines are white drinks.

      type of statement _____   symbolic notation _____

8. No Democrats are Republicans.

      type of statement _____   symbolic notation _____

9. Some baseball players are wealthy individuals.

      type of statement _____   symbolic notation _____

10. All paintings are works of art.

      type of statement _____   symbolic notation _____

Part III: Do a Venn Diagram for each of the statements in **Part II**.

VENN DIAGRAMS AND THE ARISTOTELIAN INTERPRETATION

As we have seen, the universal statements, **A** and **E**, do not always have existential import. That is, **A** and **E** statements do not always assert or imply the existence of the objects to which they refer. Often, however, when we make such statements we do intend to assert the existence of the objects to which we refer. For example, consider the following **A** form statement:

> All of my cats are animals that have fleas.

Now, this statement would ordinarily be understood to imply that the speaker does in fact have cats. It would be strange for one to make this statement without owning any cats. There are many other similar examples in which **A** and **E** statements are best understood as asserting or implying that the classes to which they refer have members.

Obviously, then, universal statements are sometimes used when it is reasonable to suppose that they are intended to assert or imply the existence of the things they talk about. In such cases, **A** and **E** statements should be regarded as having existential import. It seems that Aristotle, the inventor of categorical logic, understood both **A** and **E** statements in this way. When **A** and **E** statements are interpreted as having existential import, we will refer to this as the *Aristotelian interpretation.*

Thus, **A** and **E** statements can sometimes be interpreted as having existential import. However, you will recall that Venn Diagrams are designed to reflect the Boolean interpretation of **A** and **E** statements, where they are interpreted as not having existential import. As we have seen, such diagrams do not show that any class has a member. If we are to use Venn Diagrams to represent **A** and **E** statements in those cases where they are interpreted as having existential import, then we must modify them.

Consider the **A** statement mentioned above: "All of my cats are animals that have fleas." Remember, that **A** statements all have the form, "All S is P." In order to diagram an **A** statement on the Aristotelian interpretation, where we interpret the statement to either assert or imply the existence of the classes it talks about, we first diagram it exactly as we do on the Boolean interpretation:

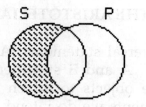

Then, since we are interpreting the statement to imply that the subject class has a member, we put an "x" in that region to reflect the Aristotelian interpretation. (The "x" you recall, means that "there is at least one.") In this case that means the statement is asserting or implying that there is at least one "S." Since the "SP̄" area is already declared empty, the "x" must be placed in the "SP" area. Our diagram, reflecting the Aristotelian interpretation of the **A** form statement is as follows:

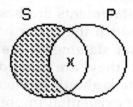

Our diagram now says two things. It says that the "SP̄" region is empty and it asserts that there exists at least one S that is also a P. The above diagram illustrates how we diagram *any* **A** form statement on the Aristotelian interpretation.

Next consider the **E** statement: "No cats are dogs." This statement has the form, "No S is P." First, as in the Boolean diagram of the **E** statement, the SP region is shaded. Then, in order to reflect the Aristotelian interpretation that the subject class referred to in the statement has at least one member, an "x" is placed in the "SP̄" region. This indicates that there is an "S" that is not a "P."

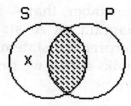

The diagram, again, says two things. It says that the "SP" region is empty and it asserts that "there exists at least one S that is not a P." The diagram illustrates how we diagram *any* **E** form statement using the Aristotelian interpretation.

Under the Aristotelian interpretation, then, the subject classes of the **A** and **E** statements are assumed to have at least one member. The information provided in the modified Venn Diagrams reflect this *existential assumption*.

The *existential assumption* applies only to **A** and **E** statements. Since, as we have seen, **I** and **O** statements already assert the existence of at least one member of the classes they talk about, the question of whether they have existential import does not arise for them. In short, **I** and **O** statements *always* have existential import. Thus the diagrams for them are not affected regardless of which viewpoint we employ. They will always be diagrammed as follows:

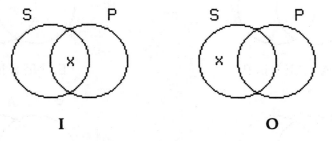

Exercises

Part I: Complete the following statements.

1. When an **A** or **E** statement is interpreted as asserting or implying that its subject class has at least one member, the statement has _____ _____.

2. When diagramming an **A** form statement on the Aristotelian interpretation, we first shade out the _____ region of the diagram.

3. Then, in order to reflect the Aristotelian interpretation of an **A** statement, an "x" is placed in the _____ area of the diagram.

4. When diagramming an **E** form statement on the Aristotelian interpretation, we first shade out the _____ region of the diagram.

5. Then, in order to reflect the Aristotelian interpretation of an **E** statement, an "x" is placed in the _____ area of the diagram.

Part II: Complete the first four Venn Diagrams by diagramming the categorical statement forms using the Boolean interpretation. Then, diagram the second four using the Aristotelian interpretation. Finally, compare the two sets of diagrams.

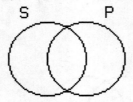

A: All S is P

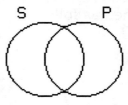

E: No S is P

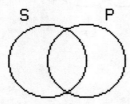

I: Some S is P

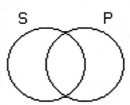

O: Some S is not P

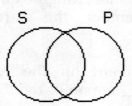

A: All S is P

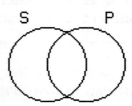

E: No S is P

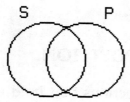

I: Some S is P

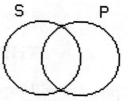

O: Some S is not P

CHAPTER EIGHT

THE SQUARE OF OPPOSITION

In this chapter we will explore the logical connections that hold among the four types of categorical statements. Assuming that we know the truth value of a given categorical statement, that is whether it is true or false, what can we infer about the truth or falsity of another categorical statement?

Suppose, for instance, that we know "No baseball players are poor people" is true. What could we then infer about the truth or falsity of the statement "Some baseball players are poor people?" Since the logical connections will differ depending on whether we use the Aristotelian or Boolean interpretations of categorical statements, we will examine the logical relationships from each perspective.

THE TRADITIONAL (ARISTOTELIAN) SQUARE OF OPPOSITION

Let's begin by using the Aristotelian interpretation of categorical statements. Consider the following two categorical statements:

    A: All lawyers are rich people.

    O: Some lawyers are not rich people.

If the **A** statement is assumed to be true, then what would be the truth-value of the **O** statement? If "All lawyers are rich" is true, it should be obvious that "Some lawyers are not rich," would have to be false. After all, if every lawyer is rich, then it would have to be false that there are lawyers who are not rich.

The procedure of reasoning from one form of categorical statement, say an **A** form statement, to a categorical statement of another form, say an **O** form statement, is known as *immediate inference*. Such reasoning is called *immediate*, since a conclusion is drawn from a single statement rather than from two or more statements. The most obvious instances of immediate inference can be represented on what is known as the *square of opposition*. As we shall see, there are several logical relations represented on the "square." Since at this point we are using the traditional or

Aristotelian interpretation of categorical statements, we will refer to it as the "traditional" or "Aristotelian" square of opposition.

The traditional or Aristotelian square of opposition is given below.

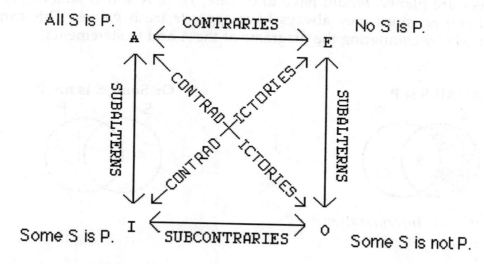

There are four logical relationships represented on the Aristotelian square of opposition holding between the four categorical statements. They are known as:

1. contradictories
2. contraries
3. subcontraries
4. subalterns

CONTRADICTORY STATEMENTS

The diagonal lines in the square connect the statements that are *contradictory*: the **A** and **O** statements, and the **E** and **I** statements. **When two statements contradict each other they will always have opposite truth-values.** That is, if the **A** statement is *true*, the corresponding **O** statement will be *false*, and if the **O** statement is *true*, the corresponding **A** statement will be *false*.

For example, assume that the **A** form statement, "All trees are plants," is *true*. Now, the corresponding **O** form statement, "Some trees are not plants," must obviously be *false*. It would be an obvious *contradiction* to assert at the same time both "All trees are plants" and "Some trees are not plants."

Similarly, if we assume that "Some trees are not plants" is *true*, then "All trees are plants" would have to be *false*. Thus, **A** and **O** statements are *contradictories*, since they always have *opposite* truth values. This can be seen clearly by comparing the diagrams of the **A** and **O** statements.

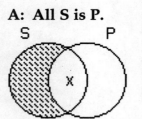

A: All S is P.

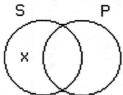

O: Some S is not P.

Aristotelian Interpretation

Notice that the **A** statement asserts just what the **O** statement denies. **A** says that every S is within P, while **O** says that there is at least one S that is not in P. If the **O** statement is true, then **A** must be false. And, as we have seen, if **A** is true, **O** must be false. In other words, since **A** and **O** are contradictory statements, they will always have *opposite* truth values.

The *contradictory* relationship also holds between **E** and **I** statements. For instance, the **I** form statement "Some houses are red things," *contradicts* the **E** form statement "No houses are red things." It should be obvious that if one of them is true then the other must be false. Again, this relation is made clear by comparing the Venn Diagrams for each statement:

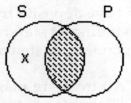

E: No S is P.

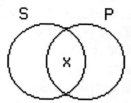

I: Some S is P.

Aristotelian Interpretation

The **E** statement asserts precisely what the **O** statement denies. The **E** statement says that there are no Ss that are Ps. In contrast, the **I** statement says that there is an S that is P. Thus, if the **E** statement is true, then the **I** statement must be false and if **I** is true, **E** must be false. In other words, **E** and **I** statements will always have *opposite* truth values.

Exercises

Part I: Complete the following statements.

1. An **A** statement is the contradictory of an _____ statement.

2. An **E** statement is the contradictory of an _____ statement.

3. When two statements contradict each other, they will always have _____ truth values.

4. When the first statement of a contradictory pair is true, the other statement will be _____.

5. When the first statement of a contradictory pair is false, the other statement will be _____.

Part II: Each of the following exercises is based upon the contradictory relation. Find the missing truth values.

1. If the **A** statement is true, the **O** statement must be _____.

2. If the **O** statement is true, the **A** statement must be _____.

3. If the **A** statement is false, the **O** statement must be _____.

4. If the **O** statement is false, the **A** statement must be _____.

5. If the **E** statement is true, the **I** statement must be _____.

6. If the **I** statement is true, the **E** statement must be _____.

7. If the **E** statement is false, the **I** statement must be _____.

8. If the **I** statement is false, the **E** statement must be _____.

CONTRARY STATEMENTS

The logical relationship holding between the **A** and the **E** statements is called the *contrary* relation. **If two categorical statements are contraries, they cannot both be true, although both of them can be false.** In other words, if an **A** statement is *true*, then the corresponding **E** statement must be *false*, and if the **E** statement is *true*, then the corresponding **A** statement must be *false*. It is also the case that the **A** statement and its corresponding **E** statement can both be false at the same time.

Consider, for example, the **A** statement, "All cars are sedans." If it is a true statement, then the corresponding **E** statement, "No cars are sedans" must be false. The Venn Diagram for the **A** and **E** statements illustrate this logical relationship:

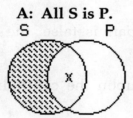

A: All S is P.

Aristotelian Interpretation

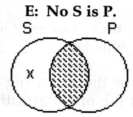

E: No S is P.

Aristotelian Interpretation

Notice that in diagramming the **A** statement we did two things. First, we shaded the "S̄P̄" area which indicates that the region representing cars that are not sedans is empty. Second, we placed an "x" in the "SP" area. That means that in addition to denying that there are any cars that are not sedans, the **A** statement also asserts that there is at least one car that is a sedan. However, the **E** statement asserts that "SP" is empty. That is, it says that there are no cars that are sedans. It cannot be true that there are cars that are sedans, asserted by **A,** and no cars that are sedans, asserted by **E.** Hence, if **A** is *true*, **E** must be *false*.

Another part of the contrary relationship is that if **E** is *true*, then **A** must be *false*. If "No cars are sedans" is true, then "All cars are sedans" must be false. Part of what **E** asserts is that there is at least one car that is not a sedan. However, **A** asserts that *all* cars are sedans. It cannot be true both that there is a car that is not a sedan and that all cars are sedans. Therefore, If **E** is *true*, **A** must be *false*. The Venn Diagram for the **A** statement indicates that the region representing cars that are not sedans is empty, while the diagram for the **E** statement indicates that the region representing cars that are not sedans has at least one member.

Although the **A** and **E** statements cannot both be true, they can both be false. This can be seen if we suppose that it is true that some cars are sedans and that some cars are not sedans. Under those conditions, the **A** statement "All cars are sedans" will be false, because some cars are *not* sedans, and the **E** statement, "No cars are sedans," will also be false since some cars *are* sedans. Thus, both **A** and **E** can be false at the same time.

Exercises

Part I: Complete each of the following statements.

1. The contrary relationship holds between the _____ and the _____ statements.

2. On the contrary relationship both of the statements can be _____, but both cannot be _____.

3. If one of a pair of contrary statements is true, the other statement must be _____.

4. If one of a pair of contrary statements is false, the other statement's truth value is _____.

Part II: Each of the following exercises is based upon the contrary relation. Find the missing truth values.

1. If the **A** statement is true, the **E** statement must be _____.

2. If the **E** statement is true, the **A** statement must be _____.

3. If the **A** statement is false, the **E** statement may be either _____ or _____.

4. If the **E** statement is false, the **A** statement may be either _____ or _____.

SUBCONTRARY STATEMENTS

The logical relationship holding between the **I** and the **O** statements is called the *subcontrary* relation. **If two categorical statements are subcontraries, at least one must be true.** In other words, corresponding **I** and **O** statements cannot both be false, although both may be true. Compare the Venn Diagrams for the **I** and the **O** statements:

I: Some S is P.

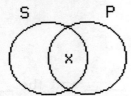

O: Some S is not P.

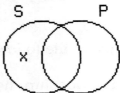

If, for example, the **I** statement "Some baseball players are intelligent persons" is false, then the corresponding **O** statement, "Some baseball players are not intelligent persons," must be true. We are, of course, assuming that there are baseball players and that it makes sense to either assert or deny the application of the concept of intelligence to baseball players. Since we are assuming that there is at least one baseball player, it will then be true either that the player is intelligent or that the player isn't intelligent. Thus, if the **I** statement, "Some baseball players are intelligent persons" is *false*, and there is at least one baseball player who is either intelligent or not intelligent, then the **O** statement "Some baseball players are not intelligent persons" must be *true*.

Moreover, if the **O** statement is *false*, then the **I** statement must be *true*. Therefore, if "Some baseball players are not intelligent persons" is false, then "Some baseball players are intelligent persons" must be true. Again, assume that there is one baseball player who is either intelligent or not intelligent. Now if the **O** statement, "Some baseball players are not intelligent persons" is *false*, then the **I** statement, "Some baseball players are intelligent persons" must be *true*. In other words, if there is not even one baseball player who is *not* intelligent, then, assuming that there is at least one baseball player, that player must be intelligent. This illustrates the claim that if **O** is false, **I** must be true.

It follows then, in the case of *subcontrary* statements, that at least one of the pair must be true. Both, however, may be true. For instance, it can be true that "Some baseball players are intelligent persons" and true that "Some baseball players are not intelligent persons." It cannot be the case, however, that both of these statements are false at the same time, on the Aristotelian interpretation of categorical statements.

Exercises

Part I: Complete the following statements.

1. The subcontrary relationship holds between the _____ and the _____ statements.

2. If two statements are subcontraries, both statements can be _____, but both statements cannot be _____.

3. If the first statement of a pair of subcontrary statements is false, the second must be _____.

4. If the first statement of a pair of subcontrary statements is true, the second statement's truth value is _____.

Part II: Each of the following exercises is based upon the subcontrary relationship. Find the missing truth values.

1. If the **I** statement is false, the **O** statement must be _____.

2. If the **O** statement is false, the **I** statement must be _____.

3. If the **I** statement is true, the **O** statement's truth value may be _____ or _____.

4. If the **O** statement is true, the **I** statement's truth value may be _____ or _____.

SUBALTERNS

The logical relationship that holds between the **A** and the **I** statements and between the **E** and the **O** statements is called the subaltern relationship. It has two parts: **(1) In the subaltern relationship, if the universal statement is true, then the corresponding particular statement of the same quality must also be true. (2) But if the particular statement is false, then the corresponding universal statement of the same quality must also be false.** For example, if the *universal affirmative* or **A** form statement "All frogs are green animals" is true, then it must certainly be true that the *particular affirmative* or **I** form statement "Some frogs are green animals" is true. This can be seen clearly if we look at the Venn Diagrams for the **A** and **I** statements:

A: All S is P.   I: Some S is P.

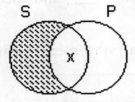   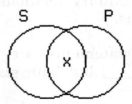

Aristotelian Interpretation

If **A** is true, then the corresponding **I** statement must also be true, since everything asserted by **I** (in the "SP" region) is also asserted by **A**. Part of what the **A** statement says, on the Aristotelian interpretation, is that there is at least one S that is a P, and this is exactly what the **I** statement asserts. Thus, the subaltern relation holds between **A** and its corresponding **I** statement. That is, if **A** is true, then **I** must be true as well.

Similarly, the subaltern relation holds between the **E** and its corresponding **O** statement. If the universal *negative* or **E** form statement, "No cats are clumsy animals" is true, then the corresponding particular *negative* or **O** form statement, "Some cats are not clumsy animals," must also be true. That is, if no cats are clumsy, then there must be at least one cat that is not clumsy. Again, this can be seen if we compare the diagrams for the **E** and **O** statements. The diagrams for the **E** and **O** statements appear at the top of the next page.

E: No S is P.

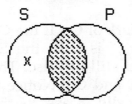

O: Some S is not P.

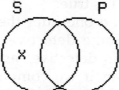

Aristotelian Interpretation

If **E** is true, then the corresponding **O** statement must also be true, since everything asserted by **O** (in the S̄P̄ region) is also asserted by **E**. Part of what the **E** statement asserts, on the Aristotelian interpretation, is that there is an S that is not a P, and that is exactly what the **O** statement asserts. Therefore, the subaltern relation holds between **E** and its corresponding **O** statement. That is, if the **E** statement is true, then the **O** statement must be true as well.

The second half of the subaltern relation is that we can infer the falsity of the universal statement from the falsity of the corresponding particular statement. Thus, for **A** and **I** statements, we can infer the *falsity* of **A** from the *falsity* of **I**. For example, if the **I** statement "Some politicians are liars" is false, then the **A** statement "All politicians are liars" must certainly also be false. That is, if there is not even one politician who is a liar, which is what the falsity of **I** entails, then the corresponding **A** form statement, "All politicians are liars," must certainly be false as well.

We can also infer the *falsity* of the **E** form statement if we know that its corresponding **O** form statement is *false*. For example, if the **O** statement "Some detectives are not police officers" is false, then the **E** statement "No detectives are police officers" must also be false. That is, if there is not even one detective who is not a police officer, which is what the falsity of **O** entails, then the corresponding **E** form statement, "No detectives are police officers," must certainly be false as well.

One cannot, however, infer the *truth* of **A** from the *truth* of **I**. If the **I** form statement, "Some politicians are liars," is true, the **A** form statement, "All politicians are liars," could still be false. Again, this can be clearly seen if we look at the diagrams for **A** and **I**. Notice that **A** asserts something more than **I**. In particular, **A** asserts that the "S̄P̄" region of the diagram is empty, while the **I** statement provides no information regarding the "S̄P̄" region. Thus, from the truth of **I** one cannot *infer* the truth of **A**. The **A** statement could still be true, of course, but we cannot *infer* its truth on the grounds that **I** is true.

Neither can one infer the *truth* of **E** from the *truth* of **O**. If the **O** form statement, "Some detectives are not police officers," is true, the **E** form statement, "No detectives are police officers," could still be false. This can be clearly seen if we compare the diagrams for **E** and **O**. Notice that **E** asserts something that **O** does not assert. Specifically, **E** asserts that the "SP" region is empty, while the **O** statement provides us with no information regarding the "SP" region. Therefore, from the truth of **O** one cannot *infer* the truth of **E**. The **E** statement, of course, *could* still be true, but we can not *infer* its truth from the truth of **O**.

Moreover, one cannot infer the *falsity* of **I** from the *falsity* of **A**. If it is false that "All ballplayers are wealthy persons," it can still be true that "Some ballplayers are wealthy persons." Similarly one cannot infer the *falsity* of **O**, from the *falsity* of **E**. Even if "No politicians are liars" is false, it can still be true that "Some politicians are liars." Looking at the diagrams for **I** and **A** and for **O** and **E** should also make this clear.

The *subaltern* relationship for the **A** and the **I** statements can be summarized as follows:

If **A** is *true*, then **I** must be *true*.

If **I** is *false*, then **A** must be *false*.

The subaltern relationship for the **E** and the **O** statements can be summarized as follows:

If **E** is *true*, then **O** must be *true*.

If **O** is *false*, the **E** must be *false*.

These are the *only* valid inferences derived from the subaltern relation. Put differently, on the subaltern relation, the *truth* of the universal statement implies the *truth* of its corresponding particular statement. Thus, the truth of **A** implies the truth of **I**, and the truth of **E** implies the truth of **O**. On the other hand, the *falsity* of the particular statement implies the *falsity* of the corresponding universal statement. So the falsity of **I** implies the falsity of **A**, and the falsity of **O** implies the falsity of **E**.

Exercises

Part I: Complete the following statements.

1. The subaltern relationship holds between the _____ and _____ statements and between the _____ and _____ statements.

2. The truth of the universal statement implies the _____ of the corresponding particular statement.

3.   The falsity of the particular statement implies the _____ of the corresponding universal statement.

4. If a particular statement is true, then its subaltern's truth value may be either _____ or _____.

5. If a universal statement is false, then its subaltern's truth value may be either _____ or _____.

Part II: For each of the following, what are we justified in inferring? If no valid inference is possible, indicate that the truth value of the second statement is unknown.

1. If **A** is true, then **I** is _____.

2. If **I** is false, then **A** is _____.

3. If **A** is false, then **I** is _____.

4. If **I** is true, then **A** is _____.

5. If **E** is true, then **O** is _____.

6. If **O** is false, then **E** is _____.

7. If **E** is false, then **O** is _____.

8. If **O** is true, then **E** is _____.

THE BOOLEAN INTERPRETATION OF THE SQUARE OF OPPOSITION

We have just examined the logical relations holding between categorical statements employing the *Aristotelian* interpretation of such statements. These relations have been represented on the Aristotelian square of opposition.

We now want to construct a square of opposition based on the *Boolean* interpretation of categorical statements. As you will recall, on the Boolean interpretation, **A** and **E** statements do not have existential import. That is, they do not imply that their subject classes have members. Thus, an **A** statement such as "All unicorns are graceful creatures" asserts only that "*If* there are unicorns, then they are graceful creatures."

The Boolean interpretation of universal categorical statements greatly limits the inferences that may be drawn from them. As a matter of fact, the only logical relation that remains on the Boolean square of opposition is the contradictory relation. It should be remembered that two statements are contradictory if they always have *opposite* truth values. The fact that the contradictory relation remains is quite clear. For the **A** statement "If there are any unicorns, then they are graceful creatures" still contradicts the **O** statement "Some unicorns are not graceful creatures." For **A** says of any possible unicorn that it must be a graceful creature, while **O** says that there is at least one unicorn that is *not* a graceful creature.

The diagrams for the **A** and **O** statements reflecting the Boolean interpretation make this clear as well.

A: All S is P.

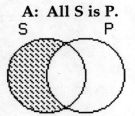

O: Some S is not P.

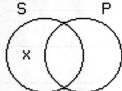

Boolean Interpretation

A says that "S̄P̄" is empty, while **O** denies this, since it asserts that "there is a S that is not P."

Similarly, the **E** and **I** statements are still contradictory. **E** says "If there are any unicorns, then they are not graceful," and **I** says "Some unicorns are graceful." Again the Boolean diagrams for the **E** and **I** statements make it clear that they remain contradictories.

E: No S is P.

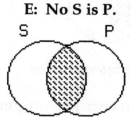

I: Some S is P.

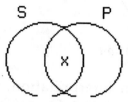

Boolean Interpretation

Notice that **E** says that "SP is empty," while **I** says that "SP has at least one member." If "SP" has a member, then it must be false that "SP" is empty. And if "SP" is empty, it must be false that "SP" has a member. Therefore, if **E** is true, **I** must be false, and if **I** is true, then **E** must be false. That is, they remain contradictories on the Boolean interpretation.

It is important to notice, however, that the *contrary* relation no longer holds between **A** and **E**. Two statements are contraries, you will recall, if both cannot be true at the same time. But on the Boolean interpretation, **A** and **E** can both be true at the same time. In order to see this, assume that there are no unicorns. The **A** form statement, "All unicorns are graceful creatures," could be true, since it asserts only that "*If* there are any unicorns, they are graceful creatures." Now if there are no unicorns, then there are none that fail to be graceful. Hence, there would be nothing to show that the **A** statement is false. But the **E** statement, "No unicorns are graceful creatures," would also be true, since if there are no unicorns, there are no graceful unicorns. Thus, "No unicorns are graceful creatures," would be true as well. But if **A** and **E** can both be true at the same time, they are no longer contraries. Hence, the contrary relation holding between **A** and **E** statements on the Aristotelian interpretation, no longer holds on the Boolean interpretation.

The fact that corresponding **A** and **E** statements are no longer contraries on the Boolean interpretation may also be seen by comparing their Venn Diagrams. Their diagrams, appearing at the top of the next page, indicate that **A** and **E** statements can both be true at the same time.

A: All S is P.

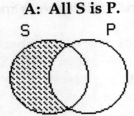

Boolean Interpretation

E: No S is P.

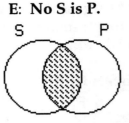

Boolean interpretation

On the Boolean interpretation, the **I** and **O** statements are no longer *subcontraries*, since **I** and **O** can both be false. This is because, on the Boolean interpretation, we are not assuming that the classes we talk about necessarily have members. Both **I** and **O** statements, you may recall, assert that the classes they talk about have members. The **I** statement, for instance, says that "there is at least one S that is a P." But suppose we talk about unicorns that are graceful. The **I** statement would then be saying, "There is at least one unicorn that is a graceful creature." But since there are no unicorns, **I** would be false. The corresponding **O** statement would assert that "There is at least one unicorn that is not a graceful creature." But, again, since there are no unicorns, the **O** statement would also be false. **I** and **O**, then, can both be false at the same time. Hence, the **I** and **O** statements are no longer subcontraries on the Boolean interpretation, because according to the subcontrary relation, either **I** or **O** must be true.

The fact that corresponding **I** and **O** statements can both be false can be seen if we look at their diagrams. Notice both diagrams assert that there is at least one member of the subject class:

I: Some S is P.

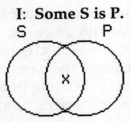

O: Some S is not P.

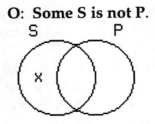

Of course, if we are talking about unicorns, it will be false that there are any members of the subject class. Because both **I** and **O** statements assert that there is such a member, both will be false. Thus, since **I** and **O**

statements can both be false, they are not subcontraries on the Boolean interpretation of categorical statements.

It should now be clear that the *Aristotelian* square of opposition depends upon two assumptions. First, as we have seen, it assumes that **A** and **E** statements either assert or imply the existence of the entities they talk about in their subject classes. Second, as our discussion of the subcontrary relation for **I** and **O** statements makes clear, the *Aristotelian* square also depends on the assumption that the entities talked about exist. That is why the subcontrary relation doesn't hold on the *Boolean* square, since on the *Boolean* interpretation of categorical statements we are not making the assumption that the classes we talk about exist.

Moreover, on the Boolean interpretation, the *subaltern* relationship no longer holds, since the truth of the **A** form statement no longer implies the truth of the **I** form statement. On the Boolean interpretation, the **A** form statement only asserts that "If there is an S, it is also a P." In other words, it no longer asserts that the S class has members. But because the **I** statement asserts that "there is at least one S that is a P," the **I** statement asserts something more than the **A** statement. Therefore, the inference from **A** to **I** no longer holds. Hence, **A** could be true and **I** false.

That the truth of the **A** form statement, on the Boolean interpretation, no longer implies the truth of the **I** form statement can be clearly seen by comparing their Venn Diagrams.

A: All S is P.

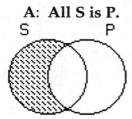

I: Some S is P.

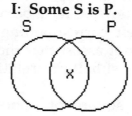

Boolean Interpretation

Notice that the **A** statement merely asserts that the $S\overline{P}$ region is empty, while the **I** statement asserts that there is at least one S that is a P. Thus, nothing asserted by **A** guarantees the truth of **I**.

Neither does the subaltern relation hold between the **E** form statement and the **O** form statement on the Boolean interpretation. Again, **O** now says something not guaranteed by **E**. **O** says that "there is an S which is not a P," while the **E** statement, on the Boolean interpretation, does not assert that there is an S. Since, given the Boolean interpretation of the **E** form statement, the **O** form statement asserts something not guaranteed by the **E** statement, the truth of **E** no longer guarantees the truth of **O**.

That the subaltern relation no longer holds may also be seen by comparing the Venn Diagrams for **E** and **O** statements. Notice that the **O** statement asserts that there is at least one S, while **E** asserts only that the "SP" region is empty.

E: No S is P.

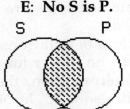

O: Some S is not P.

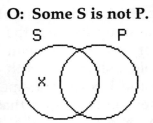

Boolean   Interpretation

The other half of the subaltern relation also fails on the Boolean interpretation of categorical statements. The falsity of the **I** statement no longer implies that the **A** statement is false. And the falsity of the **O** statement no longer implies that the **E** statement is false. **I** and **O** statements could now be false because the subject class they talk about has no members. Their corresponding **A** and **E** statements could still be true because they do not assert that the classes they talk about have members. Thus, the entire subaltern relation no longer holds on the Boolean interpretation.

The Boolean square of opposition, therefore, consists only of the *contradictory* relations holding between **A** and **O** statements and **E** and **I** statements. The three other logical relations, as we have seen, depend either on the assumption that **A** and **E** statements have existential import, or on the assumption that the subject classes one talks about in categorical statements have members. Since neither of these assumptions is being made on the Boolean interpretation of categorical statements, the contrary, subcontrary and subaltern relations no longer hold. Therefore, only the contradictory relation remains. Accordingly, the Boolean square of opposition, appearing at the top of the next page, can be represented as follows:

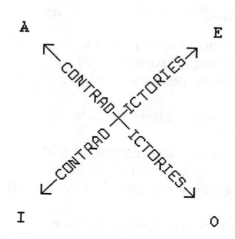

Exercises

Part I: In the exercises below, assuming that the first statement is *true*, what can be inferred about the truth value of the remaining statements? Use the *Aristotelian* viewpoint.

1. All soldiers are brave persons.

    a. Some soldiers are brave persons.
    b. No soldiers are brave persons.
    c. Some soldiers are not brave persons.

2. Some soldiers are not brave persons.

    a. No soldiers are brave persons.
    b. All soldiers are brave persons.
    c. Some soldiers are brave persons.

3. No soldiers are brave persons.

    a. Some soldiers are brave persons.
    b. All soldiers are brave persons.
    c. Some soldiers are not brave persons.

4. Some soldiers are brave persons.

    a. Some soldiers are not brave persons.
    b. No soldiers are brave persons.
    c. All soldiers are brave persons.

5. No moral judgments are matters of taste.

    a. Some moral judgments are matters of taste.
    b. All moral judgments are matters of taste.
    c. Some moral judgments are not matters of taste.

6. Some moral judgments are matters of taste.

    a. All moral judgments are matters of taste.
    b. No moral judgments are matters of taste.
    c. Some moral judgments are not matters of taste.

7. All moral judgments are matters of taste.

    a. No moral judgments are matters of taste.
    b. Some moral judgments are matters of taste.
    c. Some moral judgments are not matters of taste.

8. Some moral judgments are not matters of taste.

    a. No moral judgments are matters of taste.
    b. Some moral judgments are matters of taste
    c. All moral judgments are matters of taste.

Part II: Do the same as for **Part I**, but assume that the first statement is *false*.

Part III: Do the same as for **Part I**, but use the *Boolean* viewpoint.

Part IV: Do the same as for **Part III**, but assume that the first statement is *false*.

CHAPTER NINE

MORE IMMEDIATE INFERENCES

An immediate inference, as we have seen, is an inference made from a single premise to a conclusion. Some immediate inferences have been dealt with already in our discussion of the square of opposition in the last chapter. In this chapter we will look at some additional types of immediate inference.

CONVERSION

Conversion is a form of immediate inference which is not based upon any of the relations found on the square of opposition. The operation of conversion is performed by interchanging the subject and predicate terms of a categorical statement. The converted statement is referred to as the *converse* of the original statement. Conversion is a valid form of inference when and only when it is possible to interchange the subject and predicate terms in a categorical statement without affecting the truth value of the statement. When the truth value of the converted statement is always the same as the original statement, the two are said to be *logically equivalent*.

Consider the **E** form statement "No circles are squares." When it is converted it becomes "No squares are circles." The following Venn Diagrams show that these two statements are logically equivalent:

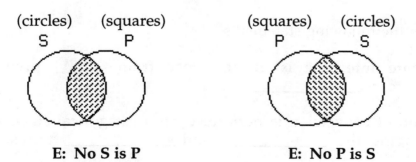

Next, consider the **I** form statement "Some flowers are pretty plants," and its conversion to "Some pretty plants are flowers." Again, Venn Diagrams show that these two statements are logically equivalent:

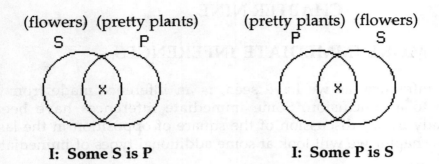

(flowers) (pretty plants)   (pretty plants) (flowers)
  S   P   P   S

I: **Some S is P**   I: **Some P is S**

Summary

Conversion is performed by interchanging the subject and the predicate terms. With **E** and **I** statements, the original statement and its converse are *logically equivalent*, that is, they will always have the same *truth values*. As we saw above, Venn Diagrams reflect the logical equivalence of the original statement and its converse.

Conversion results in logically equivalent statements only when performed on **E** and **I** form statements. As we will see, if one attempts to convert either an **A** or **O** form statement, the resulting expression will not be logically equivalent to the original. This means that the attempted conversion of an **A** or **O** form statement will not produce a valid inference from the original statement.

Exercises

Part I: Complete the following statements

1. An immediate inference is an inference from _____ premise immediately to a _____.

2. The operation of conversion is performed on a categorical statement by interchanging the _____ and _____ terms.

3. Two statements are said to be logically equivalent whenever they always have the same _____ _____.

4. Interchanging the subject and predicate terms of a categorical statement results in a valid inference only on _____ and _____ statements.

5. When the subject and predicate terms of a categorical statement are interchanged, the resulting statement is called the _____ of the original statement.

Part II: Convert each of the following categorical statements.

1. Some frogs are green reptiles.

2. No trees are animals.

3. Some birds are water fowls.

4. No televisions are radios.

5. Some novels are books.

CONVERSION OF A FORM STATEMENTS BY LIMITATION

Consider the **A** form statement "All horses are animals," and its converse "All animals are horses." Obviously, these two statements are not logically equivalent, since the first statement is true and the second is false. The following Venn Diagrams demonstrate that the two statements are *not* logically equivalent:

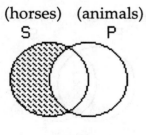

(horses) (animals)
  S   P

A: All S is P

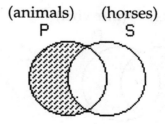

(animals) (horses)
  P   S

A: All P is S

The difference in the diagrams is clear, since they provide information about different regions. The first diagram says that the "S$\overline{P}$" region is empty, while the second diagram says that the "$\overline{P}$S" region is empty. Therefore, conversion is not a valid form of inference for **A** form statements, since the resulting statement is not logically equivalent to the original statement.

An **A** form statement can be converted, however, by a process called *conversion by limitation*. Since conversion by limitation involves moving from the truth of an **A** form statement to the truth of an **I** form statement, it is valid only on the Aristotelian interpretation of categorical statements. Conversion by limitation consists of two steps:

1. Interchange the subject and the predicate terms.

2. Change the quantity of the statement from universal to particular.

The process looks like this:

Original: All S is P.
Step one: All P is S.
Step two: Some P is S.

By using the method of conversion by limitation, the **A** form statement, "All trucks are motor vehicles," is converted to "Some motor vehicles are trucks." Notice that conversion by limitation results in an **I** form statement. Venn Diagrams illustrate the validity of this inference:

Conversion of A Form Statement by Limitation

(trucks)   (mtr vhcl)   (mtr vhcl)   (trucks)
S   P   P   S

A: All S is P   **I: Some P is S**

Aristotelian Interpretation

As the diagrams indicate, if **A** is true, that is, if "All trucks are motor vehicles," its converse by limitation, "Some motor vehicles are trucks," will also be true. The truth of the **A** statement guarantees the truth of what the resulting **I** statement asserts.

But you should notice two things. First, the original statement and its converse by limitation are not *logically equivalent*. "Some motor vehicles are trucks" could be true while "All trucks are motor vehicles" could be false. A second look at the diagrams confirms that the two statements are not logically equivalent.

Second, this inference is valid only on the *Aristotelian interpretation* of categorical statements. This is because conversion by limitation involves an inference from the truth of an **A** form statement to the truth of an **I** form statement. It is because we are assuming that the subject class must have at least one member on the Aristotelian interpretation that guarantees the "x" in the "SP" region. Without that assumption, the inference from "All trucks are motor vehicles" to "Some motor vehicles are trucks" is invalid. Accordingly, conversion by limitation is valid on the Aristotelian interpretation of categorical statements but is *invalid* on the Boolean interpretation.

A Venn Diagram reflecting the *Boolean interpretation* of categorical statements makes this clear.

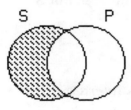

A: All S is P

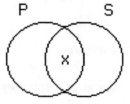

I: Some P is S

The diagram of the **I** statement indicates that there is a P that is an S, but nothing in the **A** diagram guarantees this. Thus, on the Boolean interpretation, conversion by limitation is not a valid inference. That is, the truth of **A** does not guarantee the truth of **I**.

CONVERSION OF O FORM STATEMENTS

The **O** form statement cannot be validly converted. When the subject and predicate terms of an **O** form statement are interchanged, the resulting statement is not logically equivalent to the original. Neither is the inference from an **O** statement to its converse always valid. Take, as an example, the **O** form statement, "Some athletes are not basketball players." By interchanging the subject and predicate terms we get, "Some basketball players are not athletes." Now the first statement is clearly true and the second statement is apparently false. Hence, the two statements are not logically equivalent. Moreover, the second statement cannot be inferred from the first. The following Venn Diagrams clearly show that the two statements are not logically equivalent and that the second cannot be inferred from the first.

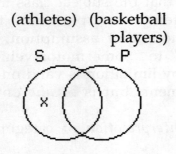

(athletes) (basketball   (basketball   (athletes)
              players)   players)
    S   P   P   S

O: Some S is not P   **O: Some P is not S**

Conversion Summary:

1. The **E** and the **I** statements can be validly converted.

2. The **A** statement can be validly converted only by limitation, and only on the traditional or Aristotelian interpretation.

3. The **O** statement cannot be validly converted at all.

Exercises

Part I: Complete the following statements.

1. Conversion by limitation can be validly performed only on an _____ statement.

2. Conversion by limitation is a valid form of inference only under the _____ interpretation of categorical statements.

3. The first step in the operation of conversion by limitation is to interchange the _____ and _____ terms.

4. The second step in the operation of conversion by limitation is to change the quantity of the statement from _____ to _____.

5. According to an **A** statement, the _____ region of the Venn Diagram is empty.

6. According to the converse of an **A** statement, the _____ region is empty.

7. Because the **A** statement and its converse make claims about different regions, the statements are not _____ _____.

8. When an **A** statement is converted by limitation, the resulting statement is an _____ form statement.

9. The statement that cannot be validly converted at all is the _____ statement.

10. When the subject and predicate terms of an **O** statement are interchanged, the resulting statement is not _____ _____ to the original, and the original statement does not _____ the truth of the resulting statement.

Part II: Find the converse or converse by limitation for each of the following statements. Indicate if a statement has no valid converse.

1. All humans are mortals.

2. Some English majors are analytical thinkers.

3. All cats are carnivores.

4. No children are drivers.

5.   Some logic professors are baseball players.

6.   Some philosophy professors are not skiers.

7.   No fish are reptiles.

8.   Some rectangles are not squares.

9.   All coats are warm articles of clothing.

10. No circles are rectangles.

OBVERSION

Another form of immediate inference is known as *obversion*. There are two steps involved in the process of obversion:

1.   Change the *quality* of the original statement.

2.   Replace the predicate term with its *complement*.

Consider the **A** form statement "All papers are combustible materials." First change the *quality* of the statement. The quality of the original statement is affirmative, so it becomes a negative statement. This involves changing the quantifier "All" to "No." The statement becomes, "No papers are combustible materials."

The second step requires replacing the predicate term with its *complement*. The complement of a class includes everything not contained in the original class. The proper way to form the complement of a class is by placing the prefix *non* in front of the predicate term. Therefore, our original statement now becomes, "No papers are *non*-combustible materials."

The *obverse* of "All papers are combustible materials" is, therefore, "No papers are non-combustible materials." The obverse of a statement is always logically equivalent to the original statement. That is, the original statement and its obverse will always have the same truth value. Since the original statement and its obverse will always have the same truth value, the inference from a statement to its obverse will always be valid. The fact that the two statements are *logically equivalent* may be seen from a comparison of their Venn Diagrams:

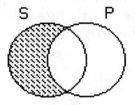

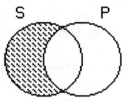

A: All S is P   **E: No S is non-P**

Both diagrams show that there is no S outside of P, or that "S$\overline{P}$" is empty.

The obverse of the **I** form statement, "Some roses are red flowers," is derived as follows. First, the *quality* is changed from affirmative to negative: (1) Some roses are *not* red flowers. Then the predicate is replaced by its *complement* class: (2) Some roses are not *non-red flowers*. Again, Venn Diagrams show that the two statements, "Some roses are red flowers," and its obverse, " Some roses are not non-red flowers," are *logically equivalent*:

Obversion of I Form Statement

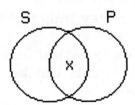

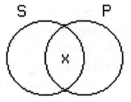

I: Some S is P   **O: Some S is not non-P**

Both diagrams indicate that there is an S that is a P. Since the original statement and it obverse are logically equivalent, the inference from the original statement to its obverse is always valid.

Now consider the **E** form statement "No newspapers are books." Through the process of obversion the statement becomes "All newspaper are non-books." We derived the obverse by changing the *quality* of the original statement from negative to affirmative, "All" to "No," and replacing the predicate term with its *complement*. The term, "books" now becomes "non-books."

Again, it is clear that the original statement, "No newspapers are books" and its obverse, "All newspapers are non-books," are logically equivalent to each other. The diagrams for the two statements are identical, showing that the statements have the same truth value.

Obversion of E Form Statements

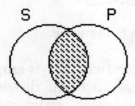   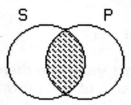

E: No S is P   **A: All S is non-P**

Both diagrams indicate that SP is empty. Since the original statement and its obverse are logically equivalent, the inference from the original statement to its obverse will always be valid.

Finally, consider the **O** form statement, "Some wines are not red beverages." Again we form the obverse by changing the *quality* of the statement, getting, "Some wines are red beverages." The predicate term is replaced with its *complement*: "Some wines are *non-red beverages*." If you do Venn Diagrams for the original and its obverse they indicate that the two statements are logically equivalent.

You should notice that, unlike conversion, *all* categorical statements can be validly obverted. Since all categorical statements can be validly obverted, there is no need for obversion by limitation.

Exercises

Part I: Complete the following statements.

1. Obversion can be validly performed on the _____, _____, _____, and _____ form categorical statements.

2. The first step in the operation of obversion is to change the _____ of the statement.

3. The second step in the operation of obversion is to replace the
    _____ _____ with its _____.

4. The complement of a class includes _____ which is not
    part of the original class.

5. The complement of a class is indicated by placing the prefix
    _____ in front of the name for the original class.

Part II: Find the obverses of the following statements.

1. No bill collectors are sensitive individuals.

2. All aestheticians are sensitive individuals.

3. Some professors are sensitive persons.

4. Some wrestlers are not sensitive persons.

5. Some vehicles are buses.

6. All rats are rodents.

7. No meter-readers are interesting conversationalists.

8. Some lawyers are not ambulance chasers.

9. All cat lovers are dog lovers.

10. Some dog lovers are not cat lovers.

Part III: Find the converse for any statements in **Part II** that can be
converted.

Part IV: Find the obverse for the statements that result from doing **Part III**.

CHAPTER TEN

CATEGORICAL SYLLOGISMS AND VALIDITY

This chapter will introduce the *categorical syllogism*. A categorical syllogism is a *deductive* argument consisting of *three* categorical statements that together refer to *three* classes. In this chapter, we will learn how to identify the three class terms used to refer to the three classes and how to represent the statements containing them in a formal manner. This will allow us to capture the *form* of a categorical syllogism. The ability to capture the form of a categorical syllogism is important because, as we shall see, the *validity* of such arguments is determined by their form. Once we have isolated the form of a syllogistic argument, we will be able to determine whether it is valid or invalid.

THE CATEGORICAL SYLLOGISM

A categorical syllogism is a deductive argument consisting of exactly two premises and a conclusion. The premises and the conclusion all consist of categorical statements. The following argument is an example of a categorical syllogism:

> Some people are vegetarians.
> <u>No vegetarians are carnivores.</u>
> ∴ Some people are not carnivores.

There are several things you should notice about the categorical syllogism. First, the syllogism has two premises and a conclusion. In our example the premises are, "Some people are vegetarians" and "No vegetarians are carnivores." The conclusion is "Some people are not carnivores." Second, these three statements together refer to exactly three classes. Every categorical syllogism will have those two characteristics. In our example, the three *classes* referred to are, "people," "vegetarians" and "carnivores." The words, "people," "vegetarians" and "carnivores" are known as *class terms*. You should also notice that each of the three class terms appears exactly twice in the argument.

MAJOR, MINOR, AND MIDDLE TERMS

Each of the three class terms of a categorical syllogism is assigned a special name in order to identify its position in the argument. They are known as the *major*, *minor*, and *middle* terms.

The procedure for determining the major, middle, and minor terms is as follows. First, one must determine which statement in the syllogism is the conclusion. In our example above, the conclusion is "Some people are not carnivores." But you should remember that the conclusion of an argument is not always stated last. You have already learned how to use indicator words and the context of an argument to determine which statement is the conclusion and which are premises, regardless of the order in which they are given.

After finding the conclusion, determining which class term is the major term and which is the minor term is not difficult. The major term will *always* be the predicate term of the conclusion. In our example, "carnivores" is the predicate term of the conclusion, so it is the *major term*. The minor term will *always* be the subject term of the conclusion. In our example, then, the term "people" is the *minor term*. The third term in a categorical syllogism is called the *middle* term. The middle term occurs once in each of the premises, but not in the conclusion. In our example, the term that appears in each premise, but not in the conclusion, is "vegetarians." The *middle term*, then, is "vegetarians."

As we have seen, the subject term of a categorical statement is labeled "S" and the predicate term is labeled, "P." In a categorical syllogism the subject term of the conclusion, or minor term, will be labeled "S" and the predicate term, or major term, will be labeled "P." We will use the letter "M" to designate the middle term.

Once the minor, major, and middle terms have been located, the form or structure of the argument can be determined. As we will see, this will allow us to use a technique to determine validity. In our example then, the form of the argument is:

Some S is M.
No M is P.
∴ Some S is not P.

Exercises

Part I: Complete the following statements.

1. A categorical syllogism is an _____ which consists of two
   _____ and a _____ all of which are
   _____ statements.

2. The three statements in a categorical syllogism refer to a total of
   _____ classes, and each class is referred to in exactly
   _____ of the statements.

3. The words used to refer to classes are called _____
   _____.

4. The three class terms of a categorical syllogism are known as the
   _____, _____, and _____ terms.

5. The statement in which the major and minor terms will always be
   found together is the _____.

6. The subject term of the conclusion is always the _____ term
   of the argument.

7. The predicate term of the conclusion is always the _____
   term of the argument.

8. The class term that appears in both of the premises but not in the
   conclusion is known as the _____ term.

9. The minor term of a categorical syllogism is designated by the letter
   _____ , the major term by the letter _____, and the middle term by
   the letter _____.

10. Determining the major, minor and middle terms and labeling them
    will allow us to represent the argument's _____.

Part II: For each of the following categorical syllogisms, determine the major, minor, and middle terms.

1. Some trees are Redwoods.
   <u>All Redwoods are unique plants.</u>

   ∴ Some trees are unique plants.

2. No hungry people are happy people.
   <u>All happy people are comfortable people.</u>

   ∴ No hungry people are comfortable people.

3. All persons who feed birds in the winter are bird lovers.
   <u>Some professors are not persons who feed birds in the winter.</u>

   ∴ Some professors are not bird lovers.

4. No dieters are underweight persons.
   <u>Some underweight persons are persons who love candy.</u>

   ∴ No dieters are persons who love candy.

5. All Christians are theists.
   <u>All theists are believers in absolute morality.</u>

   ∴ All Christians are believers in absolute morality.

FORM AND VALIDITY

As we have already indicated, the form or structure of an argument determines whether or not it is valid. We are now ready to learn how to represent the formal structure of the categorical syllogism. Let's return to our original example:

> Some people are vegetarians.
> <u>No vegetarians are carnivores.</u>
> ∴ Some people are not carnivores.

Now, in the previous section, we learned how to determine the minor, major and middle terms. You will recall that the subject term of the conclusion is the minor term, the predicate term of the conclusion is the major term and the term not appearing in the conclusion is the middle term. We also noted that the minor term, "people," is labeled "S," "the major term, "carnivores" is labeled "P" and the middle term, "vegetarians," is labeled "M." Using these labels, we represented the *form* of this argument as follows:

> Some S is M.
> <u>No M is P.</u>
> ∴ Some S is not P.

The same form or pattern can be shared by two or more arguments. To illustrate this, consider the following argument:

> Some sports are leisure activities.
> <u>No leisure activities are profitable activities.</u>
> ∴ Some sports are not profitable activities.

This argument also has the form:

> Some S is M.
> <u>No M is P.</u>
> ∴ Some S is not P.

While these arguments are composed of different statements and talk about different matters, both arguments have the same *form* or *structure*. The form of both arguments is captured by restating the argument in a fashion that reveals that common pattern or structure. Now since the validity of an argument is a matter of form, these arguments, sharing the same form, will be either both valid or both invalid.

REFUTATION BY LOGICAL ANALOGY

Since an argument's validity is determined by its form, and two arguments that share the same form are either both valid or both invalid, we can use this fact to develop a technique for demonstrating that an argument is invalid. The technique is known as *refutation by logical analogy*. When an argument is suspected of being invalid, a second argument, that is clearly invalid, can sometimes be constructed that has the same structure or form as the original argument. As we have seen, if a given argument is invalid, any argument sharing the same form will also be invalid. By constructing an obviously invalid argument that has the same form as the original argument, we can demonstrate that the original argument is invalid. In other words, we have "refuted" the original argument by constructing an obviously invalid argument having an analogous form to the original argument.

Consider the following syllogism:

> Some criminals are persons who carry guns.
> <u>Some police officers are persons who carry guns.</u>
> ∴ Some police officers are criminals.

This argument, as we will show, is invalid. One way to demonstrate the argument's invalidity is to construct another argument that is known to be invalid, but has the same *form* as the original argument. This can be done by finding an argument having the same form as the original argument, but having true premises and an obviously false conclusion. Since a valid deductive argument cannot have true premises and a false conclusion, we will know that the argument we have devised in invalid. If our original argument has the same form as the argument we have devised, then we will have shown it to be invalid. Here is an example of an argument having the same form as the original argument:

> Some men are politicians.
> <u>Some women are politicians.</u>
> ∴ Some women are men.

Both of these arguments share the same form. The form of each argument is:

> Some P is M.
> <u>Some S is M.</u>
> ∴ Some S is P.

Now the second argument has true premises and an obviously false conclusion. Therefore, the second argument is plainly invalid. And, since the original argument has the same form as the second argument, it must be invalid too. We have, then, refuted the first argument by logical analogy.

Refutation by logical analogy has two requirements. First, you must construct an argument having the same *form* as the original argument. Second, the constructed argument must have obviously *true* premises and a *false* conclusion.

Refutation by logical analogy also has two significant limitations. The first limitation is that it cannot be used to prove that an argument is valid, but can only be used to prove that an argument is invalid. Its other limitation is that it is not always possible to show that an argument is invalid using the technique of refutation by logical analogy. This is because we may not be ingenious enough to think of an invalid argument with true premises and a false conclusion that has the same form as the original argument. Therefore, our inability to devise such an invalid argument does not show that the original argument is valid.

Because of these shortcomings, we need a more general technique that will allow us to determine the validity or invalidity of any categorical syllogism. We will introduce such a technique in the next chapter.

Exercises

Part I: Reduce the following categorical syllogisms to their form. (It is essential for you to correctly identify the premises and conclusion of each argument.)

1. No philosophers are professional athletes, since some professional athletes are wealthy individuals, and no philosophers are wealthy individuals.

2. Since all parents are reliable individuals and no fifth graders are parents, no fifth graders are reliable individuals.

3. All band directors are persons who read music, thus, some guitarists are not band directors, since some guitarists are not persons who read music.

4. All true soldiers are brave persons and no brave persons are timid individuals, so no true soldiers are timid individuals.

5. All chickens are birds, so it follows that some chickens are red creatures, since some birds are red creatures.

Part II: Complete the following statements.

1. The validity or invalidity of a deductive argument is determined by its _____.

2. The form of an argument refers to its basic _____.

3. It is possible for two or more arguments to share the same _____.

4. Refutation by logical analogy is a technique used to demonstrate the _____ of an argument.

5. Refutation by logical analogy is accomplished by constructing a second argument which has the same _____ as the original argument that is being tested for validity.

6. In order to show that the original argument is invalid, the constructed argument must have _____ premises and an obviously _____ conclusion.

7. Refutation by logical analogy cannot be used to show that an argument is _____.

8. If we cannot construct an example of an invalid argument that has the same form as the original argument, that does not prove that the original argument is _____.

Part III: Determine whether the following two arguments have the same form.

1. Some white things are soft things.
   <u>All soft things are fuzzy things.</u>
   ∴ Some white things are fuzzy things.

2. Some creepy things are beetles.
   <u>All beetles are insects</u>
   ∴ Some creepy things are insects.

CHAPTER ELEVEN

CATEGORICAL SYLLOGISMS AND VENN DIAGRAMS

In this chapter we will learn how to use Venn Diagrams to determine the validity or invalidity of categorical syllogisms. We have already learned how to use Venn Diagrams to represent individual categorical statements. However, a categorical statement refers only to two classes. As we have seen, categorical syllogisms make reference to three classes. In order to diagram the categorical syllogism, that is, to represent both of its premises and its conclusion, we will need to modify our diagrams. Since the premises and conclusion of a categorical syllogism together refer to three classes, diagramming a categorical syllogism will require us to employ three circles to represent the three classes that are referred to. The three overlapping circles are drawn as follows:

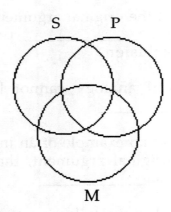

The circle on the upper left represents the S class, the circle on the upper right represents the P class, and the lower circle represents the M class. The three overlapping circles give rise to seven separate regions. Let's begin by identifying the regions of the three circles that do not overlap any of the others. We will call the region that stands for those things that are S but neither P nor M, region one. Region one, then, is labeled as $S\overline{P}\overline{M}$. $S\overline{P}\overline{M}$ is read, "S, non-P, non-M," with the bar above a letter signifying "non." Secondly, the region that stands for things that are P but are neither S nor M, we will call region two. Region two is labeled $\overline{S}P\overline{M}$ and is read "non-S, P, non-M." The region that stands for things that are M but are neither S nor P we will call region three. Region three is labeled S̄P̄M. S̄P̄M is read, "non-S, non-P, M." Here is what the diagram looks like up to this point.

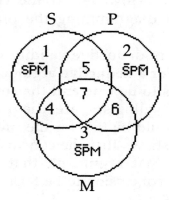

Next we will identify regions four through seven. Region four represents things that fall within the S and M classes, but are outside of the P class. It is labeled SP̄M, and is read, "S, non-P, M." Region five represents things that are S and P, but not M. It is labeled SPM̄ and is read, "S, P, non-M." Region six represents things that are P and M, but not S. It is labeled S̄PM. S̄PM is read, "non-S, P, M." Finally, region seven represents things that are S, P and M. It is labeled, SPM, and is read, "S, P, M." The completed diagram now looks like this.

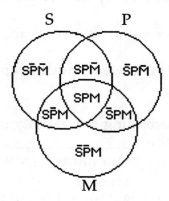

Once the seven regions of the diagram have been identified and labeled, the method for testing the validity of categorical syllogisms is straightforward. The basic procedure for determining the validity of such arguments using Venn Diagrams, is to first diagram the *premises* of the argument, and then see if the *conclusion* has been diagrammed as well. If the conclusion is diagrammed as a result of diagramming the premises, then the argument is *valid*. However, if the conclusion has not been diagrammed as a result of diagramming the premises, the argument is *invalid*.

Recalling the definition of deductive validity will help you understand how the procedure works. **For a deductive argument to be *valid*, it must be impossible for the premises to be true and the conclusion false.** When the premises of a categorical syllogism are diagrammed, they provide a representation of what it would be like for the premises to be true. Now if diagramming the premises shows that the conclusion must be true as well, then we have shown, for that argument, that it is impossible for the premises to be true and the conclusion to be false. In other words, we have shown that the argument is *valid*.

Exercises

Part I: Complete the following statements.

1. Since categorical syllogisms refer to three classes, diagramming them requires _____ circles instead of two.

2. The circle in the upper left represents the _____ class.

3. The circle in the upper right represents the _____ class.

4. The lower circle in the lower middle represents the _____ class.

5. The procedure for determining the validity of a categorical syllogism is to first diagram the _____ and then see if the _____ has been diagrammed as well.

Part II: Construct a Venn Diagram with circles representing the three classes of a categorical syllogism. Label the circles and number and label each of the seven regions. You should then study each region to make certain that you understand why each region is labeled as it is.

DIAGRAMMING ARGUMENTS WITH UNIVERSAL PREMISES

The following examples will illustrate our procedure for using Venn Diagrams to test the *validity* of categorical syllogisms. All of the examples will employ the Boolean interpretation of categorical statements unless stated otherwise.

Consider the following argument:

> All matters of taste are subjective judgments.
> <u>All moral judgments are matters of taste.</u>
> ∴ All moral judgments are subjective judgments.

Recalling our procedure for determining the minor, major and middle terms, then, "moral judgments," is the minor term or S term; "subjective judgments," is the major or P term; and "matters of taste," is the middle or M term. We can now represent the form of the argument as follows:

> All M is P.
> <u>All S is M.</u>
> ∴ All S is P.

Now recalling how **A** form statements are symbolized, the argument is symbolized as:

$$M\bar{P} = 0$$
$$S\bar{M} = 0$$
$$\therefore S\bar{P} = 0$$

The symbolization given above will assist you in diagramming categorical statements. It virtually tells you what you need to do in order to diagram a given statement. However, keep in mind that this symbolization is only an aid, and eventually you may decide to diagram statements without it.

With this in mind, let's begin by diagramming the first premise of the argument given above, "All M is P." Remember that "All M is P" is symbolized as $M\bar{P} = 0$. The diagram for "All M is P" appears at the top of the next page.

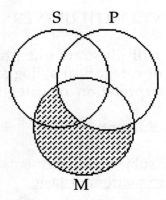

"All M is P" says that the entire class of M is *included* in the class of P. That is, there are no Ms outside of the P class, or "$M\overline{P} = 0$." We represent "All M is P" by *shading* the two M, non-P regions (regions 4 and 3) to indicate that they are empty.

The second premise, "All S is M," says that the entire S class is *included* in the M class. That is, there are no Ss outside of M, or "$S\overline{M} = 0$." We represent "All S is M," then, by shading the S, non-M regions (regions 1 and 5) of the diagram to indicate that they are empty.

Here is the diagram for the two premises of the argument:

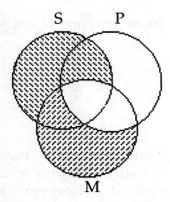

When you consult the finished diagram, you should consider what it tells us concerning the validity or invalidity of the argument. Again, our procedure is to diagram the premises and then determine whether the conclusion has also been diagrammed. If it has, the argument is *valid*. If not, the argument is *invalid*.

What does the conclusion say? It asserts that "All S is P." In other words it says that "$S\overline{P} = 0$." Now does the diagram tell us that *both* of the S non-P regions are empty? That is, are *both* of those regions shaded? Indeed, both regions 1 and 4, the two S, non-P regions, are shaded. Thus, by diagramming the premises, we have also diagrammed the conclusion. The Venn Diagram for this argument demonstrates that it is *valid*. We have demonstrated that it is *impossible* for the premises to be true and the conclusion false.

Since validity is a matter of form, we have also demonstrated that *any* argument having the same form as this argument will also be valid. That means that *if* the premises of any argument having this form were true, then its conclusion would also be true.

Now suppose we have an argument of the following form:

    No M is P.
    <u>All S is M.</u>
    ∴ No S is P.

The first premise, "No M is P" is diagrammed as follows:

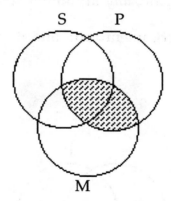

"No M is P" asserts that the entire M class is *excluded* from the P class, or, in other words, that the class of Ms which are also Ps is empty. (Remember that "No M is P" is symbolized as "MP = O.") We represent this by shading the MP regions (regions 6 and 7) to indicate that they are empty.

"All S is M," the second premise, says the entire class of S is *included* in M, or, in other words, that there are no Ss outside the M class. (Remember that "All S is M" is symbolized as "S$\overline{\text{M}}$ = 0.") We shade the S, non-M regions (regions 1 and 5) to show they are empty.

Combining the information provided by the two premises, the completed diagram looks like this:

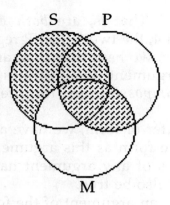

The conclusion says "No S is P," or "SP = 0." If we examine the finished diagram for this argument, we see that the *two* regions which represent Ss that are Ps (regions 5 and 7) are shaded, indicating that they are both empty. The diagram, therefore, does represent what is asserted by the conclusion, ".No S is P." Since diagramming the premises has resulted in the conclusion being diagrammed as well, the diagram tells us that this argument form is *valid*. Again, *any* argument having this form will also be valid.

Now consider another argument form and its completed diagram.

No M is P.
All M is S.
∴ No S is P.

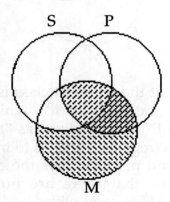

In light of the completed diagram, we must consider whether it shows that "No S is P." That is, does it show "SP = 0?" For the diagram to show that "SP" is empty, regions 5 and 7 must both be shaded. Notice that this is not the case. Since the premises provide no information about region 5, one of the SP areas, we cannot be sure that "SP = O," that is, that "SP" is empty. Because the diagram fails to show that "No S is P," diagramming the premises has failed to demonstrate that the conclusion must be true. Therefore, the argument is *invalid*.

We have now learned how to test some categorical syllogisms for validity. You may have noticed that so far we have dealt with categorical syllogisms composed of only universal statements. We will learn to diagram syllogisms employing particular statements next. Before doing so, it will be helpful to practice what we have learned up to this point.

Exercises

Find the major, minor, and middle terms and determine the form of the following arguments. Translate each argument into symbols. Then test each argument for validity using Venn Diagrams.

1. All grasses are green things.
    All green things are things pleasing to the eye.
    ∴ All grasses are things pleasing to the eye.

2. All journalists are frustrated novelists.
    No frustrated novelists are fulfilled individuals.
    ∴ No journalists are fulfilled individuals.

3. No atheists are Christians.
    All Christians are happy individuals.
    ∴ No atheists are happy individuals.

4. All articulate persons are lawyers.
    No articulate persons are trustworthy individuals.
    ∴ No lawyers are trustworthy individuals.

5. All students are persons interested in getting a good job.
    No idealists are persons interested in getting a good job.
    ∴ No students are idealists.

UNIVERSAL AND PARTICULAR PREMISES

As we indicated above, all of the arguments we have considered in this chapter up to this point have been composed solely of *universal* statements. We are now ready to learn to diagram syllogistic arguments that employ a combination of universal and particular statements. We will now consider an example of an argument form that also has particular statements:

No P is M.
<u>Some S is M</u>.
∴ Some S is not P.

Premise one says that "No P is M" or that "PM = O." We diagram this premise by shading regions 6 and 7, the regions representing things that are both P and M. By shading these regions we indicate that they are empty. The diagram for the first premise looks like this:

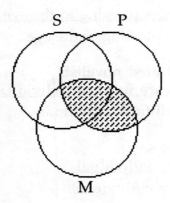

Premise two, "Some S is M," asserts the existence of at least one S that is also an M, "SM ≠ O." Since one SM region, region 7, is already declared empty, we are required to put an x in region 4, the only remaining SM region. The "x" indicates that region 4 is *not* empty, but that it has a member.

The diagram representing both of the premises for this argument form appears at the top of the next page.

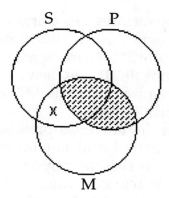

The conclusion of the argument says "Some S is not P," asserting the existence of at least one S that is not P. That is, the conclusion asserts that "$S\overline{P} \neq 0$." We can see that our diagram of the argument's premises also diagrams its conclusion. The "x" in region 4 indicates that there is an S which is not a P. Since by diagramming the premises, we have also represented the conclusion as true, this argument form is *valid*. We have shown that its premises do *entail* or *imply* the conclusion.

There is one thing you should notice about our procedure. We diagrammed the universal statement *first*. In this particular case, that is natural since the universal statement was presented first. But suppose that "Some S is M" had been given first. In attempting to diagram it first we would have had a problem. Where would we have put the "x"? Since there are *two* regions of the diagram representing Ss that are Ms (regions 4 and 7) there would have been no way to determine into which of these regions the "x" should be placed. We would have then been forced to diagram the premise as follows:

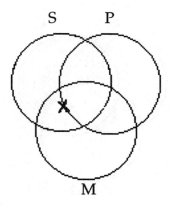

The "x" on the line between regions 4 and 7 shows there is an S which is an M. This diagrams "Some S is M." But notice that it fails to diagram the conclusion "Some S is not P." There is now no "x" that is clearly in a region which is S but not P. If we leave the "x" here, even after diagramming the other premise, "No P is M," our diagram would fail to show that the argument form is valid.

But after diagramming the universal premise "No P is M," we know that the "x" belongs in region 4 and not in region 7. Diagramming the universal statement results in shading region 7, showing that it is empty. We must then put our "x" in region 4, since region 7 has been shown to be empty. Putting the "x" in region 4 tells us that the conclusion "Some S is not P" follows from the premises. Thus, the original diagram shows that the argument is valid.

The foregoing should illustrate the importance of following the rule: **When diagramming an argument which has both a particular statement and a universal statement as premises, always diagram the universal statement first.**

Diagramming the universal premise first, however, does not guarantee that we are never forced to put an "x" on a line between two regions of the diagram. Here is an example to illustrate that point.

All P is M.
Some S is M.
∴ Some S is P.

The completed diagram for this argument form appears below:

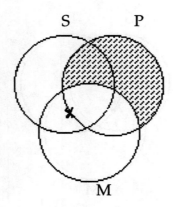

The completed diagram, appearing on the preceding page, may be explained as follows. Diagramming the first premise, "All P is M," results in regions 5 and 2 being shaded. (Remember that "All P is M" is symbolized as "P$\overline{M}$ = 0.") By shading regions 5 and 2, the regions representing "P$\overline{M}$," we indicate that they are empty.

We are told in the second premise, that "Some S is M" or "SM ≠ O." However, there are two SM regions which have not been shown to be empty, regions 4 and 7. Nothing tells us whether the SM is a P, in which case we would put the "x" in region 7, or the SM is a non-P, in which case the "x" would go in region 4. This lack of information forces us to put an "x" on the line between regions 4 and 7.

Notice that in diagramming the premises we have *failed* to diagram the conclusion. The conclusion asserts that "Some S is P." Yet our diagram doesn't show that there is an S which is clearly a P. An "x" on the line between two regions shows that *either* one *or* the other region has a member. So an "x" between regions 4 and 7 shows that *either* there is an S that is a P *or* that there is an S that is not a P. But it does not tell us definitely which is the case. Since our notion of validity requires that it must be *impossible* for the premises to be true and the conclusion false, an "x" on the line between regions 4 and 7 fails to demonstrate that the argument is valid. For the diagram to show that this argument is valid, the diagram must show that "Some S is P." That is, we need to have an "x" that is clearly in an area that is both S and P. Since there is no "x" in an area that is both S and P, this argument is invalid.

Exercises

Part I: Complete the following statements.

1. When a categorical syllogism has one premise which is a universal statement and one premise which is a particular statement, then the _____ _____ must be diagrammed first.

2. When an "x" is placed on the line between two regions, that means that either _____ or the _____ region has a member.

3. Diagramming an argument's premises represents what it would be like for the premises to be _____.

4. If an argument is valid and all of its premises are true, then its conclusion must be _____.

5. After diagramming the premises of an argument, if the diagram fails to show that its conclusion must be true, then the argument is known to be _____.

Part II: Translate the following arguments into symbols to reveal their form. Then use Venn Diagrams to determine whether they are valid or invalid.

1. Some dogs are vicious animals.
    <u>All vicious animals are dangerous animals.</u>
    ∴ Some dogs are dangerous animals.

2. All political conservatives are wealthy persons.
    <u>Some Republicans are political conservatives.</u>
    ∴ Some Republicans are wealthy persons.

3. Some suspects are not criminals.
    <u>All criminals are persons deserving of punishment.</u>
    ∴ Some persons deserving of punishment are not suspects.

4. All U. S. Senators are wealthy persons.
    <u>No wealthy persons are individuals in touch with the people.</u>
    ∴ No U. S. Senators are individuals in touch with the people.

5. All politicians are egoists.
    <u>Some egoists are likable persons.</u>
    ∴ Some likable persons are politicians.

6. All persons registered to vote are citizens.
    <u>All persons registered to vote are legal voters.</u>
    ∴ All citizens are legal voters.

7. No tourists are polite persons.
    Some polite persons are friendly persons.

    ∴ Some friendly persons are not tourists.

8. Some drunk drivers are alcoholics.
    All drunk drivers are menaces to public safety.

    ∴ Some alcoholics are menaces to public safety.

9. All insect bites are painful experiences.
    All spider bites are painful experiences.

    ∴ All spider bites are insect bites.

10. All prescription drugs are expensive items.
    Some prescription drugs are things composed of rare elements.

    ∴ Some expensive items are things composed of rare elements.

UNIVERSAL PREMISES, PARTICULAR CONCLUSION

There is only one other problem that we need to know how to deal with in using Venn Diagrams to test the validity of syllogistic arguments. This occurs when an argument has universal statements for *both* of its premises, but has a particular statement for its conclusion. Here is an example of such an argument, translated into its form.

Argument

All animals are mortals.
All cats are animals.
 ∴ Some cats are mortals.

Argument Form

All M is P.
All S is M.
 ∴ Some S is P.

The completed diagram for the argument form, "All M is P, "All S is M," therefore, "Some S is P," is as follows:

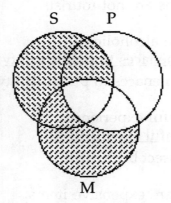

When we examine the diagram for this argument we notice that by diagramming the premises, we have not diagrammed the conclusion. The conclusion says "Some S is P" which means there is an S that is a P. In our symbols, this would be represented as "SP ≠ 0." For our diagram to represent the truth of the conclusion, "Some S is P," we need an "x" in a region representing Ss that are Ps. Although there is an unshaded region of the diagram (region 7) representing Ss that are Ps, that doesn't tell us that there is an S that is a P. It only means we have no information about that region. Now since our diagram doesn't show that there is an S which is a P, the diagram doesn't show that the argument is valid. In other words, it fails to show that it is *impossible* for the premises to be true and the conclusion false.

If we reflect on the composition of this argument, the reason the diagram of the argument indicates that the argument is invalid should be obvious. As we have seen, universal statements, on the Boolean interpretation, do not assert that the classes they refer to have members. Thus, when we diagram universal statements on the Boolean interpretation, we only shade the appropriate regions to indicate that they are empty. However, representing the truth of a particular statement, such as "Some S is P," requires that we place an "x" in an SP region of the diagram. Now since Venn Diagrams reflect the Boolean interpretation, diagramming an argument with two universal premises and a particular conclusion will always result in a diagram that shows the argument to be invalid. That is because diagramming the premises of such an argument will never result in an "x" being placed in the diagram. This explains why the diagram of the previous argument, having two universal premises and a particular statement for its conclusion, indicates that the argument is invalid.

On the Boolean interpretation of categorical statements, of course, the argument form *is* invalid. According to the Boolean interpretation, as we have seen, universal statements do not assert that the classes they refer to have members. But all particular statements do claim that the classes they refer to have members. Since all particular statements make assertions whose truth is not guaranteed by any set of universal statements, it follows that no set of universal statements implies the truth of a particular statement.

However, there are many cases where it is quite clear that when one uses universal statements, one is assuming that the class of things S stands for has members. When one says "All animals are mortals" it seems reasonable to suppose that the speaker is assuming that "there are animals." But our Venn Diagram reflects the Boolean interpretation, that **A** and **E** form statements do not assert that the classes referred to by their subject terms have members. If we are to use Venn Diagrams to diagram statements when we are assuming that the things talked about exist (the traditional or Aristotelian interpretation of categorical statements) then we must modify the diagrams.

We now know why the diagram, given earlier, does not represent what the conclusion says: "There is an S which is a P," or "SP ≠ 0." But notice that if we assume that there is an S, and we indicate that by putting an "x" in the only S region which has not been shown to be empty (region 7), then the argument has been shown to be *valid*. This is because the "x" in that region tells us that the S, whose existence we are assuming, is also a P.

It is important to see that we are not assuming that there is an S which is a P, since that would amount to *assuming* that the conclusion is true. Rather we are showing that the premises *prove* that there is an S which is also a P, provided that we *assume* that there is at least one S. Our revised diagram, appearing at the top of the next page, reflects the assumption that there exists at least one S. You should compare this diagram with the earlier one appearing on page 126. This will demonstrate the effect of the existential assumption.

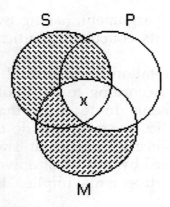

If we assume that the classes we talk about have members, that is, that at least one representative of each class we talk about exists, we can assume that "at least one S," "at least one P" and "at least one M" exist whenever we use universal statements to talk about those classes. This is to adopt the *Aristotelian* or *traditional* interpretation of categorical statements.

To take another example:

Argument Form	Symbolic Representation
All P is M.	$P\overline{M} = 0$
All M is S.	$M\overline{S} = 0$
∴ Some S is P.	∴ $SP \neq 0$

Here is the diagram for this argument when we use the Boolean interpretation of categorical statements:

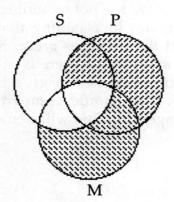

Notice, if we employ the Boolean interpretation, then the diagram on the preceding page, indicates that the argument is invalid. This is because the conclusion says that there is at least one S that is a P, or "SP ≠ 0." There is no "x" in an "SP" region of the diagram to indicate that this is the case. As the diagram indicates, on the Boolean interpretation, the argument is *invalid*.

The diagram below represents the argument using the *Aristotelian* interpretation of categorical statements. Unlike our earlier example, however, assuming that there is an S does not yield a valid argument. Neither does the assumption that there is an M. But if we assume there exists at least one P, we must put an "x" in region 7, since all of the other P regions have been shaded. With that assumption, the conclusion, "Some S is P," has been shown to follow from the premises. Hence, the argument is *valid* on the Aristotelian interpretation, since we are assuming that there is at least one P.

Aristotelian Interpretation

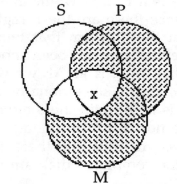

(assuming that at least one P exists.)

Now let us look at one more example:

> All P is M.
> <u>All S is M.</u>
> ∴ Some S is P.

If we diagram the premises, "All P is M" and "All S is M," we get the diagram that appears on the next page.

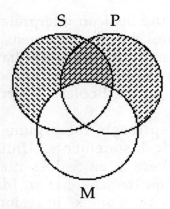

Using the Aristotelian interpretation, we can assume that there is at least one S, one P and one M. Let's begin by assuming that there is at least one S. But if we assume that there is an S, the "x" indicating this would have to be placed on the line between regions 4 and 7, since neither of these two S regions has been shaded to indicate that it is empty. Nothing in the diagram tells us that the S is a P rather than a non-P.

If we assume that there is a P, that would require us to place an "x" between regions 7 and 6, since these are the P regions that have not been shaded. There is nothing in the diagram that tells us that the P is an S rather than a non-S, since neither area has been shown to be empty.

Finally, if we assume that there is an M, we would have to place the "x" between regions 4, 7, 6, and 3, since none of the M regions has been shown to be empty. There is nothing in the diagram that tells us whether the M that exists is an S or a non-S, a P or a non-P. Once we place "x's" in the diagram to reflect the assumptions that there is at least one S, at least one P, and at least one M, the completed diagram for the argument would look like this:

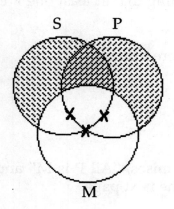

It is important to observe that in no case is an "x" placed clearly in a region which is both S and P, which is what the conclusion says. Hence, the assumption that the classes we are talking about have members does *not* allow us to represent the conclusion, "Some S is P." In this case, then, diagramming the argument's premises and assuming that each class has at least one member is insufficient to diagram the conclusion. Thus this argument is *invalid* from an Aristotelian as well as from a Boolean viewpoint.

Here are the *rules* for modifying Venn Diagrams to reflect the Aristotelian interpretation of categorical statements:

Rule One: The argument must have two universal premises and a particular conclusion. If this condition is not satisfied, do not modify the diagram. Just diagram the premises and see if that represents the truth of the conclusion.

Rule Two: If Rule One holds, then determine if it is reasonable to assume that the classes talked about have members. If it is reasonable to assume that the classes talked about have members, then go to rule three.

Rule Three: Given that Rules One and Two hold, then make the existential assumption for all three classes and place "x's" in the diagram accordingly. If following these rules forces you to put an "x" in a region that diagrams what the conclusion says, then the argument is valid from an Aristotelian perspective. If not, the argument is invalid.

Although the Aristotelian assumption allows you to assume that each of the classes talked about have members, it will generally be one particular assumption that allows you to show that an argument is valid from the Aristotelian viewpoint. Thus, for a given argument it may be, for instance, the assumption that there is an S which is the crucial assumption telling you to put an "x" in a region of the diagram that shows the argument to be valid. For another argument it may be the assumption that a P or an M exists that shows the argument to be valid. The point is that if an assumption is necessary to demonstrate that an argument is valid, you should take note of exactly what that assumption is. So, for example, if it is the assumption that at least one S exists that shows an argument to be valid, you should state that the argument is valid on the assumption that there is at least one S.

But remember that the *only* time making an assumption that a class has at least one member is appropriate is when you are diagramming an argument that has two universal statements as premises *and* a particular statement as a conclusion. If either of these conditions is not satisfied, then one is only allowed to diagram the premises and then see if that results in the conclusion being diagrammed as well. No additional step of making an assumption that classes have members is justified.

Exercises

Part I: Complete the following statements.

1. The conditions under which a Venn Diagram should be modified to reflect the Aristotelian assumption are:

    a. We must have good reason to assume that the classes we are talking about have _____.

    b. The argument must have both of the following characteristics:

        i.   Both premises are _____ statements.

        ii. The conclusion is a _____ statement.

2. From the Aristotelian viewpoint, we may assume that _____ classes referred to in a syllogism have at least one member.

3. To reflect the assumption that a class has at least one member, we put an _____ in the appropriate region of the diagram.

4. If the assumption that a class has at least one member forces us to put an "x" in a region that diagrams what the conclusion says, then the argument is _____.

5. If that assumption does not result in our being forced to put an "x" in a region that captures what the conclusion says, then the argument is _____.

Part II: Determine the validity or invalidity of the following syllogisms using Venn Diagrams. Use the Aristotelian interpretation.

1. All football players are athletes.
    No billiard players are athletes.
    ∴ Some billiard players are not football players.

2. No vegetables are foods high in cholesterol.
    All foods high in cholesterol are unhealthy foods.
    ∴ Some vegetables are not unhealthy foods.

3. All logicians are philosophers.
    All mathematicians are logicians.
    ∴ Some philosophers are mathematicians.

4. No graduate students are wealthy persons.
    All graduate students are intelligent individuals.
    ∴ Some wealthy persons are not intelligent individuals.

5. No saints are sinners.   *No m is S*
    All compassionate persons are saints.   *All P is m*
    ∴ Some sinners are not compassionate persons.   *Some S is not P*

need an x out there
no empty classes in

Part III: Use Venn Diagrams to determine the validity or invalidity of the *aristot.* following categorical syllogisms. Do the diagrams using the Boolean *since all others r* interpretation. *empty it can't be*

At least one x in class

1. All sorts of exercise are healthy activities, therefore, some healthy activities are not aerobic activities, since some sorts of exercise are not aerobic activities.

2. Some novels are great works of literature, and all great works of literature are things that enrich the spirit, so some novels are things that enrich the spirit.

3. No movie stars are paupers, because all actors are movie stars, and no actors are paupers.

4. No paupers are happy persons, and all scholars are paupers, so some scholars are not happy persons.

5. All barbers are extroverts, therefore, all barbers are entertaining persons, for all extroverts are entertaining persons.

6. Some fishermen are pirates, since all pirates are sailors, and all fishermen are sailors.

7. All friends of Dracula are unhealthy persons, thus no friends of Dracula are hearty persons, because some unhealthy persons are not hearty persons.

8. Some good things are things that come in small packages, for all expensive things are good things, and some expensive things are things that come in small packages.

9. All persons without a conscience are psychopaths, and all persons without a conscience are criminals, therefore all criminals are psychopaths.

10. Some students are scholars, since all professors are scholars, and some students are professors.

Part IV: Which of the invalid arguments in **Part III** are valid if we adopt the Aristotelian interpretation of categorical statements? Do a diagram for any of the above arguments for which the Aristotelian interpretation might make a difference.

CHAPTER TWELVE

TRANSLATING CATEGORICAL STATEMENTS I

In the previous chapters devoted to categorical logic, we have learned how to determine the validity of two basic types of inferences involving categorical statements. First, we have dealt with immediate inferences based on the square of opposition, and those involving conversion and obversion. Second, we have learned to test categorical syllogisms for validity using Venn Diagrams.

In all of these methods for determining the validity of arguments, we have been employing what are known as *standard form* categorical statements. In the real world, however, such statements are seldom employed. Does that mean, then, that our methods for determining the validity of arguments are not applicable to statements and arguments we might encounter in the real world? Not at all. It does mean that in order to apply the methods we have learned for determining the validity of arguments we must adapt statements encountered in everyday contexts to standard form categorical statements.

Fortunately, adapting such statements is not difficult. Although one does not often find standard form categorical statements outside of logic textbooks, one does often encounter statements that are, in effect, categorical statements or statements that assert something that may be captured by categorical statements. In order to use the methods we have learned for determining validity, we need only to translate these expressions into standard form categorical statements.

In the case of categorical syllogisms, we may face additional problems. For instance, in addition to finding categorical statements that are not in standard form, we may also encounter syllogisms that appear to have more than three terms because they employ synonymous expressions. In this, and the following chapter, we will learn how to deal with problems of this kind.

STANDARD FORM CATEGORICAL STATEMENTS

As we have seen, categorical logic uses four basic types of categorical statements known as **A, E, I** and **O** statements. Each standard form categorical statement has the following characteristics. First, all standard form categorical statements have a *quantifier*; "all," "no," or "some."

Second, all such statements have a *subject term* and a *predicate term*, each denoting a class. Both the subject and predicate term will be, grammatically, a noun or noun phrase. Finally, each standard form categorical statement will have a *copula*. These will be the words "are," or "are not," or "is," or "is not," which link the subject and predicate terms.

It is only when an expression conforms exactly to all of these requirements that it is a standard form categorical statement. In everyday discourse, our expressions usually don't conform exactly to these requirements. Thus, most of the time our expressions are not standard form categorical statements. However, we often do make statements that can be regarded as categorical statements even if they are not in standard form. Such statements may be asserting exactly what a standard form categorical statement asserts. What we want to learn is how to accurately translate these everyday categorical expressions into standard form categorical statements. For, once this is done, we will be able to use our techniques for deriving valid immediate inferences from such statements. And if we encounter syllogistic arguments containing statements that are not in standard form, by translating those statements into standard form, we can use Venn Diagrams to test such arguments for validity.

Exercises

Complete the following statements.

1. A standard form categorical statement will consist of four components. They are a _____, a _____, a _____, and a _____.

2. A categorical syllogism may fail to be in standard form for two reasons. The first is that it may contain categorical statements that are not in _____ _____. The second is that it may appear to have more than three terms because of _____ _____.

IMPROPER CLASS TERMS

Now that we are aware of the characteristics that constitute a standard form categorical statement, it should be relatively easy for you to tell whether a statement is in standard form. Consider the following example:

Some soldiers are brave.

We want to know if this statement is in standard form. Does it have a standard quantifier, "All," "No," or "Some?" The answer is obviously, yes. Does it have a copula? Again, the answer is yes. Does it have a subject term and a predicate term, each of which names a class? Here the answer is no. The statement has a proper subject term, "soldiers," but the predicate term does not denote a class. This non-standard predicate however, is easily made standard. Clearly the statement is meant to assert that some soldiers are included in the class of brave persons. Thus, to translate this statement into standard form we need only modify the predicate term. The statement translated into standard form becomes:

Some soldiers are brave persons.

In the above example both the subject and predicate terms are relatively simple, "soldiers" and "brave persons." But sometimes class terms can be more complicated. For example:

All persons who are musicians in large metropolitan symphony orchestras are dedicated professionals who must practice their instruments for hours each day.

This is a standard form categorical statement. Its subject class is "persons who are musicians in large metropolitan symphony orchestras" and its predicate class is "dedicated professionals who must practice their instruments for hours each day."

Exercises

Locate the improper class term in each of the following statements, then translate each statement into standard form.

1. Some of the cats are mistreated.

2. Some birds are not able to fly.

3.   All accomplished artists are talented.

4.   All of the toys are broken.

5.   No facts are easily denied.

MISSING COPULA

A different sort of problem is illustrated in the following example:

>   All cats eat mice.

The statement in this example has a standard quantifier and the subject and predicate terms refer to classes of things. The difficulty with this statement is that it lacks a copula, the words "are" or "are not." Thus, in order to translate "All cats eat mice" into a standard form categorical statement, we need to supply a copula. Our original statement becomes:

>   All cats are animals that eat mice.

You should observe that after supplying the copula, it was necessary to modify the predicate term. It is now "animals that eat mice."

Exercises

Rewrite each of the following examples by supplying the missing copula and, where necessary, the missing class term.

1.   All cows eat grass.

2.   Some students come to class late.

3.   No poor people have money

4.   Some dreams come true.

5.   All faculty may use the lounge.

NEGATIVE QUANTIFIERS

Another way in which a categorical statement can fail to be in standard form occurs when it has a negated quantifier. Here is an example:

Not all suspects are persons who have told the truth.

Statements containing negated quantifiers are more difficult to deal with since it is not always obvious what they are asserting. There is a procedure for dealing with these and other expressions whose meaning is not obvious. First, ask yourself whether the statement is *affirmative* or *negative*. If it is an affirmative statement it must be either an **A** or **I** form statement. If it is a negative statement, then it must be either an **E** or **O** form statement. This statement is quite obviously a negative statement. Thus, it is either an **E** or **O** statement. Next, we ask, is it *universal* or *particular*? It is clearly not asserting that no suspects have told the truth. Hence, it must be a particular statement. Since the statement is both negative and particular it must be an **O** form statement. Therefore, we can translate it into standard form as follows:

Some suspects are not persons who have told the truth.

We could have also inferred that this is an **O** form statement from the fact that "*Not* all suspects are persons who have told the truth" is the denial or contradictory of the **A** form statement, "All suspects are persons who have told the truth." We know from our study of the square of opposition that the negation or contradiction of an **A** form statement is an **O** form statement.

Let's now look at a similar example:

Not any suspects are persons who have told the truth.

Again, this is clearly a negative statement. That means the statement is either an **E** or **O** form statement. But is it a universal or a particular statement? If we carefully consider what the statement is saying, it is denying that *any* of the suspects have told the truth. Thus, it is referring to the entire class of suspects and is, therefore, a universal statement. Since we have already established that it is a negative statement, it follows that it is an **E** form statement. Translated into standard form it becomes:

No suspects are persons who have told the truth.

There is another way to see that "Not any" introduces an **E** statement. Ask yourself if *not any* suspects have told the truth, how many have told the truth. Clearly the answer is "none." In other words "not any S is P" says that SP is empty. So it is an **E** statement.

Exercises

Translate each of the following statements into standard form.

1. Not all cats are cuddly animals.

2. Not any cars in the parking lot are stolen vehicles.

3. Not all humans are mortal.

4. Not all of the candidates told the truth.

5. Not any witness was telling the truth.

OTHER NON-STANDARD QUANTIFIERS

Finally let's look at other sorts of non-standard quantifiers. For example:

Each of the criminals is a person who was punished.

In order to correctly translate this expression into standard form we need to ask whether it is universal or particular. It would appear that if "each" criminal was punished, then the entire class of criminals was punished. Thus, the statement is *universal*. The statement is also quite obviously *affirmative* rather than negative. That means that it is an **A** form statement. Translated into standard form it becomes:

All criminals are persons who were punished.

Another instance of a non-standard quantifier occurs when a statement appears to have no quantifier at all. Consider the following example:

Nurses are always compassionate.

Although this example appears not to have a quantifier, it is rather clear that the statement asserts that *all* nurses are compassionate. Here "always" functions as a universal affirmative quantifier. Thus, we have an **A** form statement. The other difficulty is that in this statement the predicate is not a class term. "Compassionate" does not denote a collection of things. But we have already learned how to deal with this problem. "Compassionate" becomes "compassionate persons." We can, then, translate this expression into standard form as follows:

All nurses are compassionate persons.

Now consider a slightly different example:

Nurses are not always friendly.

We may be inclined to think that if "Nurses are always compassionate" is translated as "All nurses are compassionate persons," then "Nurses are not always friendly" should be translated as "No nurses are friendly persons." But if we carefully consider what "Nurses are not always friendly" is asserting, we will see that it is the negation, or *contradictory*, of an **A** statement. In other words, it is an **O** form statement. So it becomes clear that the correct translation into standard form of "Nurses are not always friendly" is:

Some nurses are not friendly persons.

Another non-standard quantifier is illustrated by the following example:

Few professors are wealthy persons.

This statement is obviously affirmative in quality. But is it a universal or a particular statement? "Few" clearly refers to part of the class of professors. Thus, the statement is a particular affirmative or an **I** form statement. Translated into standard form it becomes:

Some professors are wealthy persons.

The following is a similar example:

Most lawyers are wealthy persons.

Again, since "most" clearly refers to part of the class of professors, this is obviously a particular affirmative statement or **I** form statement. It is translated into standard form as:

Some lawyers are wealthy persons.

There are, of course, countless other ways in which categorical statements can deviate from standard form. Some of them will be considered in the next chapter. It is obvious, however, that many of the problems of translation into standard form can be solved if we first ask whether the statement is particular or universal, and then ask whether it is affirmative or negative. Since there are only four types of standard form categorical statements, we can usually decide whether it is an **A**, **E**, **I** or **O** form statement.

Exercises

Part I: Translate each of the following statements containing non-standard quantifiers into standard form.

1. Each of the wines was red.

2. Procrastinators are always late.

3. Spider bites are not always fatal.

4. Few lies are helpful.

5. Snake bites are sometimes fatal.

Part II: Translate each of the following statements into standard form.

1. All persons who know her love her.

2. No candidates need to be residents of the city.

3. Some witnesses were not truthful.

4. Every record selling more than one million copies is a platinum record.

5. All members must pay dues.

6. Some students study hard.

7. Spider bites are often not fatal.

8. The trains are never on time.

9. Plants are sometimes poisonous.

10. Many horses are intelligent.

11. Several of the members are present.

12. Not many owls are smart.

13. Few cats are smart.

14. Many jobs pay only minimum wage.

15. Some who spoke up did not tell the truth.

16. Some plans go astray.

17. Not everything that glitters is golden.

18. Professors are not always scholarly.

19. Not any bartenders are bashful.

20. Not every tourist is impolite.

CHAPTER THIRTEEN

TRANSLATING CATEGORICAL STATEMENTS II

In Chapter Twelve we saw the need for translating statements into standard form. We also learned how to translate various non-standard categorical statements into standard form. In this chapter we will look at other ways in which categorical statements can fail to be in standard form and learn how to translate them into standard form.

MORE STATEMENTS LACKING A STANDARD QUANTIFIER

Let's begin with an example of a statement that, strictly speaking, is not a categorical statement.

> If you don't exercise, you won't be healthy.

Although there is no explicit reference to classes in this statement, classes are implicitly referred to. The classes implicitly referred to are the class of "persons who exercise" and the class of "healthy persons." We want to be able to translate expressions of this sort into categorical statements that preserve the implicit class inclusion or exclusion claims made by such statements. Once we understand the classes that are implicitly referred to in this statement, how do we translate what the statement is asserting into a standard form categorical statement?

If one thinks carefully about what is asserted by "If you don't exercise, you won't be healthy," it appears to be claiming that if you are healthy, then you must exercise. This means that "All healthy persons are included in the class of those who exercise." So we can translate the original statement into the following **A** form statement:

> All healthy persons are persons who exercise.

Other statements that deviate from standard form because they lack a standard quantifier are statements beginning with the word "only." For example:

> Only registered students may attend classes.

This example presents several difficulties. Notice that the statement has no standard copula. Moreover, the only obvious class referred to is "registered students." Upon reflection, however, we can see that the other class referred to is "persons who may attend classes." This gives us "registered students are persons who may attend classes." So we now have the two classes and the copula taken care of. The final difficulty concerns the proper order of the classes. It is tempting to think that we can now simply replace "only" with "all." In that case the statement would be translated:

All registered students are persons who may attend classes.

But this is *not* what our original statement says. Instead, "Only registered students may attend class" claims that one must be registered in order to attend classes. It does not say that if one is registered one may attend classes. There may be other requirements for class attendance aside from registration, such as paying tuition and the like. However, we can capture what the original statement is saying by reversing the order of the subject and predicate terms.

All persons who may attend class are registered students.

A general rule, when translating statements beginning with "only" to an **A** form statement, is that one must reverse the order of the subject and predicate terms. Thus, "Only contest entrants are contest winners" is translated "All contest winners are contest entrants." Similarly, "Only patients get treatment" becomes "All persons who get treatment are patients."

Exercises

Part I: Complete the following statement:

1. When translating an "only" statement, there are two steps to be followed:
   a. _____.

   b. _____.

Part II: Translate each of the following statements into standard form.

1.　If you're not pro-union, you're not pro-labor.

2.　If you don't eat a balanced diet, you won't be healthy.

3.　Only those who are apprehended will be prosecuted.

4.　Only ticketed passengers may board the plane.

5.　Only those with medical insurance can get free services.

STATEMENTS WITHOUT QUANTIFIERS

Another difficulty in translating statements into standard form arises when there is no explicit quantifier for a categorical statement. Consider the following example:

> Candidates are citizens.

The question in this case is whether we are referring to "some candidates" or "all candidates." In this example it is relatively clear that the statement is asserting that "All candidates are citizens." A similar example is:

> Spiders are not insects.

"Spiders are not insects" asserts that the entire class of spiders is excluded from the class of insects. The correct translation into standard form is, "No spiders are insects."

Other cases are not so clear. For instance:

> Lawyers are not ethical.

Is one asserting that "No lawyers are ethical individuals" or only that "Some lawyers are not ethical individuals?" It appears that the statement is intended to deny that any lawyers are ethical. Therefore, "No lawyers are ethical individuals" would *appear* to be the best translation. But since the E form statement is false, while the **O** form statement is true, interpreting the statement as an **O** form statement is more *charitable*.

Our rule, then, for handling statements lacking quantifiers, when it is unclear whether the statement is universal or particular, is as follows: If your knowledge makes it obvious that the particular statement (either **I** or **O**) is true but the universal statement (either **A** or **E**) is false, then consider it a particular statement. However, if you have no such knowledge, and the statement is offered without qualification, interpret the statement as a universal statement.

Exercises

Translate each of the following statements into standard form.

1. Bears are carnivores.

2. Children are annoying.

3. Trees lose their leaves in the fall.

4. Evergreens do not lose their leaves in the fall.

5. Computers are programmable machines.

SINGULAR STATEMENTS

Some statements that can be translated into standard form categorical statements contain references to *individuals*, as well as classes. Notice the second premise and conclusion of the following argument:

> All engineers are mathematicians.
> <u>Dan is an engineer.</u>
> ∴ Dan is a mathematician.

The second premise refers to an *individual*, rather than to a class of things. Such statements are called *"singular statements."* Singular statements assert that an *individual*, rather than a class, is included in or excluded from a class. "Dan is a mathematician," for example, asserts that the individual, Dan, is included in the class of mathematicians.

Singular statements, however, can be treated as class statements if we assume that for each individual thing there is a *unit class* containing only that individual. **A unit class is a class containing exactly one member.** Thus, "Dan is a mathematician" says that the unit class containing that member is completely included in the class of mathematicians. In other words, a singular affirmative statement is considered equivalent to an **A** form statement and is formalized as "All S is P." Hence, "Dan is a mathematician" is regarded as asserting something like "All persons identical to Dan are mathematicians."

Singular negative statements such as "Tom is not a logician," are taken to be equivalent to **E** form statements and are formalized as "No S is P." So, "Tom is not a logician" can be regarded as asserting "No persons identical to Tom are logicians."

Since singular statements are taken to be equivalent to either **A** or **E** form statements, we can use Venn Diagrams to test arguments containing such statements for validity. In the example above, the singular statement, "Dan is a mathematician" will be diagrammed as an **A** form statement, while negative singular statements will be diagrammed as **E** form statements. Because singular statements are taken to have existential import, when we translate them into **A** or **E** form statements, we will employ the *Aristotelian* interpretation for such statements.

Exercises

Part I: Complete the following statements.

1. Syllogistic statements referring to individuals instead of classes are called _____ statements.

2. A class which contains exactly one member is called a _____ class.

3. Singular statements are assumed to have _____ _____.

4. A negative singular statement is diagrammed as an _____ form statement.

5.   An affirmative singular statement is diagrammed as an _____ form statement.

Part II: Translate the following singular statements into standard form categorical statements.

1.   Jerry is married.

2.   Greg is not awake.

3.   Joan is a police officer.

4.   Spot is not a cat.

5.   Susan is a student.

EXCEPTIVE STATEMENTS

We now need to look at one other type of categorical statement having a non-standard quantifier. Some quantifiers such as "All but a few," "Not quite all" and "Almost everyone," assert what are known as *exceptive* statements. Exceptive statements assert that a statement is universally true with only a few exceptions.

For an adequate understanding of exceptive statements, we need to see that they actually assert *two* statements, not one. Exceptive statements are disguised conjunctions of two statements. Consider the following examples:

Almost everyone enjoyed the concert.

Not quite all of the professors joined the union.

All but a few defects were detected.

The first example asserts *both* that "Some persons are individuals who enjoyed the concert" *and* "Some persons are not individuals who enjoyed the concert." Similarly, the second example asserts that "Some professors are persons who joined the union" *and* "Some professors are not persons who joined the union." The third example, "All but a few defects were detected" asserts *both* that "Some defects are things that were detected" *and* "Some defects are not things that were detected."

This analysis of exceptive statements tells us that an exceptive statement is not equivalent to any single standard form categorical statement. Rather, it is a *conjunction* of an **I** and an **O** statement.

When we translate exceptive statements, such as "Almost all members voted," you may have noticed that we ignore the fact that the statement asserts that more members voted than did not. It is simply translated as "Some members are voters" *and* "Some members are not voters."

If we wish to test an argument for validity that contains an exceptive statement, our diagramming procedure must reflect the conjunction of two statements that an exceptive statement asserts. Consider the following example:

> All chickens are birds.
> <u>Almost all chickens are things that can fly.</u>
> ∴ Some birds are not things that can fly.

The exceptive statement in the second premise translates into the conjunction, "Some chickens are things that can fly" *and* "Some chickens are not things that can fly." With this in mind, we can formalize the argument as follows:

> All M is S.
> Some M is P.
> <u>Some M is not P.</u>
> ∴ Some S is not P.

In order to diagram this argument, we diagram the universal premise, "All M is S," first, as usual. This requires us to shade the "M$\overline{\text{S}}$" region (regions 3 and 6). Then we need to diagram both the second and third premises, "Some M is P" and "Some M is not P." Diagramming "Some M is P" requires us to put an "x" in the only "MP" region not already shaded (region 7). To diagram "Some M is not P," the other half of our exceptive statement, we put an "x" in the only unshaded "M$\overline{\text{P}}$" region (region 4). Once we have diagrammed the premises of the argument, we look at the diagram to determine if we have also diagrammed the conclusion. Here is the diagram for this argument:

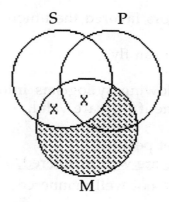

Have we, by diagramming the premises, also diagrammed the conclusion? The conclusion asserts that "Some S is not P." If you look at the diagram, you will see that there is an "x" in an S non-P region (region 4). Therefore, our diagram indicates the "Some S is not P" is true. By diagramming the premises, we have also diagrammed the conclusion. That tells us that the argument is valid.

Exercises

Part I: Complete the following statements.

1. Exceptive statements actually make _____ assertions.

2. When translating exceptive statements into standard form, we will treat them as an _____ and an _____ statement.

3. When a categorical syllogism contains an exceptive statement as a premise, both of the _____ implicit within it must be represented in the diagram.

Part II: Translate the following exceptive statements into standard form.

1. All but a few of the runners have finished the course.

2. Not quite all of the models were finalists.

3. Almost every professor voted in the union election.

4. Only some administrators favored the union.

5. Not quite every chicken can fly.

Part III: Translate the following syllogisms into standard form and use Venn Diagrams to determine if they are valid.

1. No auctioneers are quiet people.
    <u>Almost all quiet people are well mannered.</u>
    ∴ Some auctioneers are not well mannered.

2. All sneakers are items of clothing.
    <u>Only some sneakers are running shoes.</u>
    ∴ Some items of clothing are not running shoes.

SYLLOGISMS APPEARING TO HAVE MORE THAN THREE CLASSES

Sometimes an argument can fail to be in standard form because it uses synonymous expressions for some of its class terms. In such cases the argument fails to be in standard form, since by definition a standard form categorical syllogism must have exactly three terms. Consider the following example:

   No students are wealthy persons.
   <u>All students are intelligent persons.</u>
   ∴ Some rich persons are not smart persons.

This argument appears to have five terms, not three. However, this is more appearance than reality because within the argument there are synonymous expressions. Observe that the class term "rich persons" appearing in the conclusion means the same as "wealthy persons" appearing in the first premise. We can, therefore, replace "wealthy persons" in the first premise with "rich persons." Also "intelligent persons" appearing in the second premise means the same as "smart persons" appearing in the conclusion. Therefore, we will replace "smart persons" with "intelligent persons." Our argument now reads:

No students are rich persons.
<u>All students are intelligent persons.</u>
∴ Some rich persons are not intelligent persons.

The argument now has only three terms and is in standard form. If we wished, we could now test the argument for validity using Venn Diagrams.

In this chapter and the preceding one, we have learned how to translate a variety of statements encountered in ordinary English into standard form categorical statements. Once we have mastered these techniques of translation, we can greatly expand the number of arguments we can test for validity using Venn Diagrams and the principles of immediate inference.

However, as we will see, not all statements refer to classes. We want to be able to deal with arguments that do not use categorical statements. In Chapter Fourteen, we will begin to deal with some arguments of this sort.

Exercises

Part I: Translate the following statements into standard form.

1. Only the good die young.

2. Not all children are polite.

3. Not anyone who applied was hired.

4. Computers are never user friendly.

5. Few persons really know how to ski.

6. Not many leaves remain on the trees.

7. Susan is not a happy person.

8. Whales are not fish.

9. Gold is not always yellow.

10. Snails are always slow.

11. Socrates is a philosopher.

12 Not everything we say comes back to haunt us.

13. Almost all of our actions are insignificant.

14. Most quitters are unorganized.

15. All but a few medicines are expensive.

16. Whatsoever one sows, one will reap.

17. Each lie one tells gets one deeper in trouble.

18. Not all plans go astray.

19. Every barber is an extrovert.

20. If you don't enter, you won't win.

Part II: Put the following syllogisms into standard form. This will require translating some of the statements into standard form. You will also have to eliminate some synonymous terms to ensure that the syllogism has exactly three terms. After completing these steps, diagram the syllogisms to determine if they are valid. Use the Boolean interpretation of categorical statements.

1. Savings and loan companies are in financial trouble.
    <u>Organizations with money troubles need to act conservatively</u>.
    ∴ Lending organizations need to be very cautious.

2. All angels are immaterial beings.
    <u>No non-material beings are heavenly creatures</u>
    ∴ All angels are heavenly creatures.

3. Some unintentional acts are not criminal offenses.
   <u>All criminal offenses are acts that should be punished</u>.

   ∴ No intentional acts are acts that should be punished.

4. All acts of murder are intentional actions.
   <u>Some taking of human life are unintentional actions</u>.

   ∴ Some killings of humans are not murder.

5. All athletes are healthy.
   <u>Some persons who train athletes are athletic</u>.

   ∴ Some athletic trainers are persons in good health.

CHAPTER FOURTEEN

PROPOSITIONAL LOGIC

In this chapter we begin the study of propositional logic. First, we will discuss the importance of form in propositional logic. You will learn to understand and distinguish instances of simple and compound statements. Then we examine the notion of a truth-functional compound statement, and you will learn to distinguish this type of statement from other statements. Finally, you will be introduced to three different sorts of statements employed in propositional logic: conjunctions, disjunctions, and negations.

PROPOSITIONAL LOGIC: SIMPLE AND COMPOUND STATEMENTS

Like categorical logic, propositional logic is deductive. It is sometimes called symbolic logic because special *symbols* are used to represent statements and to represent truth functions. Propositional logic allows us to test arguments for validity that do not use categorical statements. The fundamental difference between categorical logic and propositional logic is that the basic units referred to in categorical logic are *classes*, while the basic units of propositional logic are *statements*.

In propositional logic you will encounter both simple and compound statements. To make a distinction between simple and compound statements, we need first to recall that every statement has a truth value. That is, each statement, including those of propositional logic, is either true or false. The test for determining whether a sentence is a statement is whether it can be true or false. Compare, for example, the following two sentences:

The table has a circular top.

Please pass the potatoes.

The first example is a statement. That is, it is either true or false. Either the table has a circular top or it doesn't. In the second example you should observe that it makes no sense to say that it is either true or false. Therefore, the second sentence is not a statement.

A *simple* **statement expresses a** *single* **state of affairs**. In other words, a simple statement is the smallest part of an expression that can still be true or false. Consequently, simple statements cannot be broken down any further and still be statements. That is, they cannot be broken down into a smaller unit that is still true or false. Consider the following examples of simple statements:

> The sun is shining.

> It is cloudy outside.

> Cats are agile animals.

> Border Collies are clever animals.

Each of these examples is a statement, that is, a sentence that is either true or false. None of them can be broken down into a smaller statement that is still true or false. For instance, neither "the sun" or "shining" is either true or false. Thus, each of the above examples is a *simple* statement. However, whether a statement is simple or not has little or nothing to do with its length. Long and seemingly complex sentences can also be simple statements. Here are two examples:

> The magnificent black stallion stood motionless before the spellbound multitude of spectators.

> No one without proper identification will be allowed into the designated restricted area.

Both of these statements, although seemingly complex, are *simple* statements. That is, neither of them can be broken down into smaller or simpler parts that are still true or false. Each of the above statements makes one and only one assertion.

COMPOUND STATEMENTS

A compound statement is made up of *two* **or** *more* **simple statements**. Compound statements, of course, are also either true or false. Consider the following examples of compound statements:

The sun is shining or it is cloudy outside.

Cats are agile and they are clever.

What makes these examples compound statements, rather than simple statements, is that they can be broken down into simpler units that are each either true or false. In the first example, "The sun is shining or it is cloudy outside" there are two simple statements:

"The sun is shining" *and* "It is cloudy outside."

Notice that "The sun is shining" is itself either true or false. The same holds for "It is cloudy outside." "The sun is shining or it is cloudy outside," therefore, is a *compound* statement, since it is made up of two simple statements. The second example is also composed of two simple statements. "Cats are agile" is either true or false, and "They are clever" is either true or false. Thus, "Cats are agile and they are clever" is a *compound* statement.

Exercises

In this exercise identify the simple and compound statements. Place an "S" in front of simple statements and a "C" in front of compound statements.

_____ 1.   Roger's car failed to start last night.

_____ 2.   There are many Republican liberals.

_____ 3.   Phyllis is here now but Mary has left.

_____ 4.   The advertising budget is in bad shape.

_____ 5.   Although Sue was in love with Jim, she refused to marry him.

_____ 6.   Karen comes from a wealthy family.

_____ 7.   While Mark is popular, Karen is very intelligent.

_____ 8.   Happiness is a cold drink on a very hot day.

_____ 9.   The little white chapel standing between Williams and Shatzel Hall is very old.

_____ 10.   Either we can win, or we can't.

TRUTH-FUNCTIONAL COMPOUND STATEMENTS

As we have already seen, propositional logic employs both simple and compound statements. We must now discuss an important feature of the compound statements employed in propositional logic. Such compound statements are *truth-functional*. What does that mean? **A compound statement is truth-functional if its truth or falsity is determined *solely* by the truth or falsity of the statements contained within it.** Consider the following example of a truth-functional compound statement and its component simple statements:

The car has been washed and it is parked in the garage.

Notice that in this example, if *both* of the simple statements are true, then the compound statement which they comprise will also be true. That is, if it is true that "The car has been washed" and it is true that "It is parked in the garage," then the entire compound statement will be true. However, if either one of the simple statements is false, the compound statement as a whole will be false. In other words, the truth value of the entire compound statement is determined *solely* by the truth values of the two simple statements of which it is composed. When that is the case, we say that the statement is *truth-functional*.

So, the truth or falsity of a truth-functional compound statement is determined *solely* by the truth or falsity of its component parts. Or, put differently, the truth or falsity of the compound statement is a *function* of the truth or falsity of its component statements. That explains the term, *truth-functional*.

There are also compound statements in which the truth or falsity of the statement is *not* determined solely by its component parts. This is because these statements assert something more than the truth or falsity of their component parts. For example:

Bob didn't go out last night *because* he had a cold.

The truth or falsity of this compound statement is *not* determined solely by the truth or falsity of its component parts. This is because the two component statements, "Bob didn't go out last night," and "Bob had a cold," could both be true and yet the compound statement could still be false. You should observe that the statement, "Bob didn't go out last night because he had a cold," in addition to asserting the truth of its component statements, makes an additional assertion, namely, that Bob didn't go out last night *because* he had a cold. Thus, it makes a causal assertion. For the compound statement to be true it must be the case not only that "Bob didn't go out last night" and that "He had a cold," but also that he didn't go out *because* he had a cold. In other words, the causal claim made by the statement must be true also, if the statement compound is to be true. We will call statement compounds whose truth depends, in part, on the truth of such casual claims, *causal compounds*.

Causal compounds, of course, are statements. They are either true or false. However, since their truth or falsity is not determined *solely* by the truth or falsity of their component parts, they are not truth-functional statement compounds.

Another sort of compound statement, whose truth or falsity is not determined solely by the truth of falsity of its components, is known as a *temporal compound*. Here is an example:

The plane took off *after* the storm had ended.

Again, the truth or falsity of this compound statement is not determined solely by the truth or falsity of its component parts. It may be true that "the plane took off," and it may also be true that "the storm ended." However, that is not sufficient for the statement to be true. It must also be true that the plane took off *after* the storm ended. Notice that the statement asserts that the events, the plane taking off and the ending of the storm, took place in a certain temporal order That the events took place in that order must also be true for the compound statement to be true. In other words, the *temporal* claim made by the statement must be true as well.

Since temporal compounds are statements, they, like all statements, are either true or false. But since their truth or falsity is not determined *solely* by the truth or falsity of their components, temporal statement compounds are not truth-functional. This, as we will see, has implications for how we will deal with such statements.

As we have already seen, propositional logic deals with compound statements that are truth-functional. This raises a question about whether we can deal with compound statements that are not truth-functional in propositional logic. The answer is that we can deal with both causal and temporal compounds. However, when we encounter such statements we must treat them as if they were truth-functional statements. That is, we will *ignore* the additional causal or temporal claims that they make. In effect, then, we will treat them as truth-functional.

For example, when we encounter a statement such as "Bob didn't go out last night because he had a cold," we will simply ignore the casual claim implicit in the statement. Instead, we will treat the statement as though it says:

Bob didn't go out last night *and* he had a cold.

The same will be true of temporal statement compounds. That is, we will treat the statement "The plane took off *after* the storm ended" as though it says:

The plane took off *and* the storm ended.

This convention will allow us to represent both causal and temporal compounds within propositional logic. Of course, we will have to remember that the original statement is saying *more* than we are representing it to say.

Exercises

Which of the following are truth-functional compounds? Place a "TF" before those statements that are truth-functional compounds; place a "C" before causal compounds and a "T" before temporal compounds.

_____ 1. When I was twenty-one, I heard a wise man speak.

_____ 2. I am twenty-two and I know that what he said was true.

_____ 3. George Washington served two terms as President, but John Adams served only one.

_____ 4. All was in silence; there was no need for words.

_____ 5. Robert and Cindy are coming.

_____ 6. After she got the message, she reconsidered her position.

_____ 7. Because the rain was pouring, we moved into the shelter.

_____ 8. It was sunny outside and I got a sunburn.

_____ 9. I got a sunburn because it was sunny outside.

_____ 10. As a result of my sunburn, I slept very little last night.

CONJUNCTIONS

We will begin our consideration of truth-functional compound statements by looking at conjunctions. Conjunctions are constructed by placing the word "and," or a similar word, between two simple statements. For example:

> Margy is bright and she is a hard worker.

Notice that this statement is composed of two simple statements connected by the word "and." The simple statements making up the conjunction are called *conjuncts*. In this case the first conjunct is "Margy is bright," and the second is "she is a hard worker." A conjunction asserts that *both* of its conjuncts are true. Thus, in order for a conjunction to be a true statement, both of its conjuncts must be true. In other words, if either conjunct is false, the entire expression will be false. "Margy is bright and a hard worker" will be a true statement, therefore, only if it is true that "Margy is bright" and also true that "she is a hard worker."

It will be useful for us to be able to represent conjunctions symbolically. We can begin to do this by introducing a symbol to replace the word, "and." Our symbol for conjunction is called the *dot*. Thus, in our example, it functions as follows:

> Margy is bright • she is a hard worker.

We can complete the symbolization by using the letter "p" to stand for "Margy is bright" and the letter "q" to stand for "she is a hard worker." The complete translation of this conjunction into symbols looks like this:

p • q

The symbolic expression "p • q" is read, "p dot q," or "p and q," or "both p and q."

Although we have used the lowercase letters, "p" and "q" and the "•" to stand for a particular conjunction, "Margy is bright and she is a hard worker," "p • q" can be used to represent *any* conjunction containing two simple statements. We will call these lower case letters *variables*, because they can be used to represent *any* simple statement. So, "p," for example, does not represent a *particular* statement but can be used to represent *any* simple statement. The same will be true of all of the other statement letters we use.

We now adopt the *convention* of using the lower case letters from the middle of the alphabet to stand for individual simple statements. Thus, we will use the letters, "p," "q," "r," "s," and "t" as our statement variables. Within the context of a given passage, we will always use "p" to stand for the first simple statement, "q" for the second, "r" for the third and so on. This will help guarantee that the translations we make will be consistent.

The "•" is called a *logical connective*, because it connects the simple statements, or conjuncts, into the statement compound known as a conjunction. Since a conjunction is a truth-functional compound statement, the dot symbol is a *truth-functional connective*. That is, the truth of falsity of "p • q" is determined solely by the truth or falsity of its components.

There are four possible combinations of truth or falsity for a conjunction containing two simple statements. Both simple statements can be true or both can be false, or the first simple statement can be true and the second false, or the first simple statement can be false and the second true. We can represent these possibilities most clearly by means of a truth table.

p	q	p • q
T	T	T
T	F	F
F	T	F
F	F	F

The first line represents the case in which "p" and "q" are both true. In that case, the conjunction, "p • q" will be true, since a conjunction asserts that both of its conjuncts are true. The second line represents the situation in which "p" is true and "q" is false. Since a conjunction asserts that both conjuncts are true, if "p" is true and "q" is false, "p • q" will be false. In line three, "p" is false and "q" is true, and in line four both "p" and "q" are false. In both of these cases, "p • q" will be false, because, again, a conjunction asserts that both of it conjuncts are true.

The truth table provides a complete truth-functional definition of the logical connective "•." That is, it tells us under every conceivable circumstance when "p • q" will be true and when it will be false.

Notice that a conjunction will be true only if both of its conjuncts are true. This should not be surprising, since a conjunction, such as "p • q," asserts that *both* "p" and "q" are true. Thus, if either of its conjuncts is false, then the conjunction will be false. Keeping this in mind should make it easy to remember how to construct truth tables for conjunctions.

Exercises

For the following conjunctions *assume* that "p" and "s" are *true* and "q" and "r" are *false*. Then determine the truth value for the entire statement, placing a "T" before those statements that are true and an "F" before those statements that are false.

_____ 1. p • q

_____ 2. s • p

_____ 3. r • s

_____ 4. q • r

_____ 5. p • s

DISJUNCTIONS

We continue our discussion of truth-functional statement compounds by looking at disjunctions. Here is an example:

Either Margy is rich or she is a hard worker.

Notice that this compound statement is made up of two simple statements, "Margy is rich" and "she is a hard worker." The simple statements making up a disjunction are called *disjuncts*. The most common way of asserting a disjunction is with the words, "*either . . . or . . .*" or sometimes with just the word "*or.*"

Unlike conjunctions, which assert that *both* of its conjuncts are true, disjunctions assert that *at least one* of its disjuncts is true. In our example, then, we are asserting that *either* it is true that "Margy is rich" *or* that it is true that "Margy is a hard worker." For our statement to be true, therefore, it must be the case that at least of one these simple statements is true. If *both* disjuncts are false, then a disjunction will be a false statement.

However, suppose that *both* disjuncts are true. That is, suppose that it is true that "Margy is rich" and "she is also a hard worker." How does that affect the truth value of our disjunction? Well, since the disjunction says that at least one of the disjuncts is true, the disjunctive statement will still be true. In other words, if Margy is rich and a hard worker, it will be the case that at least one disjunct is true. Thus, if both disjuncts are true, the disjunctive statement will be true as well.

We can more easily represent the conditions under which a disjunction is true or false by first introducing the symbol for disjunction. The symbol, known as the *wedge*, looks like this: "v." If we let "p" stand for "Margy is rich" and "q" stand for "she is a hard worker," we can symbolize this disjunctive statement as follows:

p v q

The expression, "p v q," is read, "either p or q" or "p wedge q" or sometimes as simply "p or q." The symbol, "v," is a *logical connective* since it connects the simple statements making up the statement compound.

We can summarize the conditions under which a disjunction will be true or false by means of the following truth table:

p	q	p v q
T	T	T
T	F	T
F	T	T
F	F	F

The first line represents the case where both "p" and "q" are true. Relating this to our example, this would represent the case where it is true that "Margy is rich" and also true that "she is a hard worker." Since for a disjunction to be true it need only be true that one of its disjuncts is true, it follows that when both disjuncts are true, "p v q" will be true.

The second line represents the case in which "p" is true and "q" is false. Again, in our example, this represents the case in which it is true that "Margy is rich" but false that "she is a hard worker." Since the disjunction asserts only that at least one of these is true, the disjunction, "p v q," will be true when "p" is true and "q" is false.

The third line represents the case in which "p" is false and "q" is true. In our example, this is the case in which it is false that "Margy is rich," but true that "she is a hard worker." Again, since a disjunction asserts only that at least one of these is true, our disjunction, "p v q," will be true.

The fourth line represents the case in which "p" is false and "q" is also false. In our example, this is the case in which it is false that "Margy is rich," and false that "she is a hard worker." Under those conditions, our disjunction will be false, since disjunctive statements assert that at least one of their disjuncts is true, and in this case neither disjunct is true.

Notice then, that disjunctions are true in every case except when both disjuncts are false. Thus, in order to remember the truth table for disjunction, you only need to remember that the only time disjunctions are false is when both disjuncts are false. Otherwise, the disjunction is true.

What we have discussed so far captures what is called *inclusive disjunction*. An inclusive disjunction asserts that at least one of its disjuncts is true and it allows for the possibility that both of its disjuncts are true. So when I assert that "Either Margy is rich or she is a hard worker," I do not exclude the possibility that she is both rich *and* a hard worker. In other words, I assert that at least one disjunct is true, but allow for the possibility that both are true. This is the sort of disjunction that the wedge symbolizes.

However, there is another sort of disjunction that we should be aware of. This second sense of disjunction is known as *exclusive disjunction*. Here is an example of exclusive disjunction:

Either you will be fired or you will get a raise.

Someone who says this is not likely to mean that it is possible that you would *both* be fired and that you would get a raise. In other words, although this statement asserts that either "you will be fired" or "you will get a raise," it seems to deny that it could be that case both "you will be fired" and "you will get a raise." Since it rules out or *excludes* the possibility that both of its disjuncts are true, it is called *exclusive disjunction*.

Thus, in the case of exclusive disjunctions, if both disjuncts are true, an exclusive disjunction as a whole will be false. An exclusive disjunction will also be false if both of its disjuncts are false, since it asserts that exactly one of its disjuncts will be true.

Although there are many examples of exclusive disjunctions, we will focus on *inclusive disjunctions*. We will refer to inclusive disjunction simply as disjunction, and employ the wedge to symbolize only inclusive disjunction. Thus, "disjunction" will, for our purposes, mean "inclusive disjunction." However, when it becomes necessary, we will be able to translate expressions asserting exclusive disjunctions and to evaluate arguments containing such expressions. The correct way to translate exclusive disjunctions will be dealt with later in this text.

For now it is sufficient to remember, in the case of disjunctions, that they will be true provided at least one of their disjuncts is true. That means that disjunctions will also be true if both of their disjuncts are true. In other words, the only situation in which a disjunction will be a false statement is when both of its disjuncts are false. The complete set of conditions under which a disjunctive statement will be true or false has already been illustrated by the truth table for disjunction provided earlier in this section.

Since the truth or falsity of a disjunction is determined solely by the truth or falsity of the simple statements out of which it is composed, it follows that disjunctions are truth-functional statement compounds. The wedge, used to symbolize disjunction, is therefore a truth-functional connective.

Exercises

In the following statements *assume* that "p" and "r" are true and that "q" and "s" are false. Then indicate the truth value of the entire statement by placing a "T" before any statements that are true and an "F" before any statements that are false. The exercises begin on the next page.

_____ 1. p v s

_____ 2. q v r

_____ 3. s v q

_____ 4. p v r

_____ 5. q v s

NEGATION

In everyday language we often use negations. They are used to *deny* the truth of some assertion. For example, consider the following assertion:

>   Bob is going to be promoted.

If we want to *deny* that Bob is going to be promoted we can say:

>   Bob is *not* going to be promoted.

There are, of course, other ways to deny our original assertion. We could say, for example:

>   It is not the case that Bob is going to be promoted.

The important thing to see is that the negation of a statement results in a statement having the *opposite* truth value of the original statement. So, if "Bob is going to be promoted" is true, then "Bob is not going to be promoted" is false.

The logical operator that we will use to symbolize a negation is called the *tilde*: "~." If we use "p" to stand for "Bob is going to be promoted," we can translate "Bob is *not* going to be promoted" as follows:

>   ~p

Since a given statement, say "p," has only two possible truth values, true or false, we can represent the effect of the logical operator, "~," in the truth table at the top of the next page.

p	~p
T	F
F	T

The first line represents the case in which "p" is true. If "p" is true, then "~p" will be false. The second line represents the case in which "p" is false. If "p" is false, the "~p" will be true. This truth table can be thought of as defining the logical operator, "~."

In this chapter, we have introduced the dot, the wedge and the tilde, and defined each of them by means of a truth table. All of three are logical *operators*, since they affect the truth value of the statement. However, the tilde differs from the dot and the wedge, because the tilde is *not* a logical connective. That is, it does not connect simple statements, as do the dot and the wedge, but since it does affect the truth value of statements, it is a logical operator.

Exercises

Part I: For the following, assume that "p" and "q" are *true* and "r" and "s" are *false*. Indicate the truth value of the entire statement by placing a "T" before the statements that are true and an "F" before the statements that are false.

_____ 1.   ~r

_____ 2.   ~p

_____ 3.   ~s

_____ 4.   q

_____ 5.   ~q

Part II: Translate each of the following into symbols. Remember to use "p" for the first statement component and "q" for the second and so on.

1.   The radio is too loud and so is the stereo.

2. It's false that the radio is too loud.

3. The radio is not too loud, but the stereo is.

4. Either the radio is too loud or the stereo is.

5. Either the radio is not too loud or the stereo is not too loud.

6. The car is in the garage.

7. Before eating breakfast, Joan went jogging.

8. Because it was sunny outside, Bill got a sunburn.

9. Either the Reds or the Phillies will win the pennant.

10. The Reds and the Yankees will both win pennants this year.

11. Either the Yankees or the Tigers will not win the pennant.

12. The Yankees won't win the pennant.

13. The Reds will win, but the Phillies won't

14. Either the Reds will win or they won't.

15. The Tigers will win.

Part III: For the examples in Part II, if we assume that "p" is true and "q" is false, which statements are true and which are false?

CHAPTER FIFTEEN

UNDERSTANDING CONDITIONALS

In Chapter Fourteen you learned the functions of three of the logical operators of propositional logic: the "dot" that symbolizes conjunction, the "wedge" that symbolizes disjunction, and the "tilde" or negation symbol. In this chapter we will introduce the remaining two logical operators and their functions: the *horseshoe*, used to symbolize conditional statements, and the *triple-bars*, used to symbolize biconditional statements. They are both logical connectives used to symbolize truth-functional compound statements. As was the case with the previous logical operators, both of these operators will be defined by a truth table. Finally, we will discuss the use of *punctuation* in propositional logic.

CONDITIONALS

The standard way of stating a conditional is by using "If . . . then . . ." to introduce the simple statements contained in the statement compound. For example:

> *If* Sara did her homework, *then* she went to the concert.

In this compound statement, the first statement unit, "Sara did her homework," is called the *antecedent*. The second statement unit of the compound, "she went to the concert," is called the *consequent*. A conditional statement asserts that *if* its antecedent is true, *then* its consequent is also true.

It is important to understand that conditional statements do not assert the truth of their antecedents. So, in our example, we are not asserting that it is true that "Sara did her homework." Rather, we are saying that *if* it is true that she did her homework, *then* the consequent will be true. Moreover, the conditional statement does not assert the truth of its consequent. Instead, it says that the consequent, "she went to the concert," will be true *if* the antecedent is true.

Since a conditional statement asserts that if its antecedent is true, then its consequent will also be true, a conditional statement as a whole will be true provided that it is true that "Sara did her homework" and also true that "she went to the concert." More generally, the conditional statement will be true if both its antecedent and consequent are true.

Now suppose it is true that "Sara did her homework" but false that "she went to the concert." In that case, the conditional statement will be plainly false. For we have asserted that "If Sara did her homework, then she went to the concert." However, if Sara did her homework, but did not go to the concert, then the conditional statement is obviously false. Since conditional statements assert that if their antecedents are true then their consequents will also be true, conditional statements are false when their antecedents are true and their consequents are false.

We have now covered two of the four possible combinations of truth or falsity that can hold for a conditional statement. When both the antecedent and the consequent are true, as we saw, the conditional statement is true also. When the antecedent is true and the consequent is false, the conditional statement is false.

Let us now suppose that it is false that "Sara did her homework," but true that "she went to the concert." Is the conditional statement true or false under those conditions? Well, notice that the conditional statement does not say that Sara went to the concert *only if* she did her homework. So if she goes to the concert even though she didn't do her homework, that doesn't show that the conditional statement is false. We will therefore regard a conditional statement with a false antecedent and a true consequent as a true statement.

That leaves only one other possibility. This is the case in which both the antecedent and the consequent are false. In our example, that would be the case in which it is false that "Sara did her homework" and false that "she went to the concert." Now remember that the conditional states that "If Sara did her homework, then she went to the concert." Therefore, if she didn't do her homework, it would be only natural to suppose that she did not go to the concert. Hence, if both the antecedent and the consequent are false, the conditional statement should be regarded as true.

The results of our discussion of the truth values for the conditional can be summarized as follows. The only time a conditional statement will be false is when the antecedent is true and the consequent is false. In all other cases, the conditional will be true.

We now introduce a new *logical connective* to symbolize conditional statements. It is called the horseshoe, which looks like this: "⊃." The conditional statement: "If Sara did her homework, then she went to the concert" is symbolized as:

$$p \supset q$$

The expression, "p ⊃ q" is read, "If p, then q," or "p implies q," or "p horseshoe q." We can now define the "⊃" using a truth-table that summarizes the conditions under which a conditional statement is true or false.

p	q	p ⊃ q
T	T	T
T	F	F
F	T	T
F	F	T

Each line of the truth-table for the conditional statement can be explained using the following example:

If you are to win the contest, then you must enter it.

The first line of the truth-table represents the case in which it is true that you win the contest and it is also true that you enter it. As we have seen, under those conditions, when the antecedent is true and the consequent is true, the conditional statement is true. This is, essentially, what the conditional asserts. If the antecedent is true, then the consequent is also true.

The second line represents the case in which it is true that you win the contest, but it is false that you enter it. Under those conditions, when the antecedent is true and the consequent is false, the conditional statement is false.

On the third line, it is false that you win the contest, but true that you entered it. Since the conditional does not say that if you enter then you will win, the conditional statement is true when its antecedent is false and its consequent is true.

The fourth line represents the case in which it is false that you win the contest and false that you entered the contest. Given what the conditional statement says, this is just the outcome one would expect. So when both the antecedent and consequent of the conditional statement are false, the conditional statement will be true.

Again, all of this information can be easily summarized as follows: The only situation in which a conditional statement is *false* is when the antecedent is true and the consequent is false. Otherwise, the conditional is true.

Exercises

Part I: Complete the following statements.

1. The first simple statement in a conditional is known as its _____.

2. The second simple statement in a conditional is known as its _____.

3. A conditional statement is false only when its antecedent is _____ and its consequent is _____.

4. Conditional statements assert that _____ their antecedents are true, _____ their consequents are true as well.

5. Conditional statements do not assert that either their antecedents or their consequents are _____.

Part II: Determine the truth values of the following by assuming that "p" and "r" are true and "q" and "s" are false. Write "T" before true expressions and "F" before false expressions.

_____ 1. p ⊃ q

_____ 2. q ⊃ r

_____ 3. p ⊃ r

_____ 4. q ⊃ s

_____ 5. p ⊃ s

BICONDITIONALS

A biconditional statement, as the name implies, is really two conditionals rolled into one. Here is an example:

> The car will run if and only if the mechanic fixed the engine.

This statement is really equivalent to the two conditionals: "If the mechanic fixed the engine, then the car will run" *and* "If the car will run, then the mechanic fixed the engine." A biconditional statement asserts that one of its components is true if and only if its other component is true. In other words, it asserts that both of its components have the *same* truth value.

We will now introduce the symbol for the *logical connective*, the triple-bars, to represent the biconditional. Our example, "The car will run if and only if the mechanic repaired the engine" is translated as follows:

$$p \equiv q$$

Now consider another example of a biconditional:

> You will win the contest if and only if you enter.

Under what conditions will this statement be true and when will it be false? Suppose that it is true that you win the contest and also true that you entered it. In that case it is clear that the biconditional statement is true, since it asserts that you will win the contest if you enter it. Next, suppose that you don't enter the contest and that you didn't win it either. Since the biconditional says you will win the contest only if you enter it, that is just what one would expect given what the biconditional says. Thus, if it false that you win the contest and false that you entered, the biconditional is true.

However, now imagine that somehow it is true that you won the contest even though you did not enter it. Clearly, under those conditions, the biconditional is false. After all, it said that you could win only if you entered. Finally, suppose that it is false that you won the contest, but true that you entered it. Again, the biconditional will be false, since it asserts that if you entered you would win. We can summarize these results in the following truth-table:

p	q	p ≡ q
T	T	T
T	F	F
F	T	F
F	F	T

Line one represents the case in which both "p" and "q" are true. As we have seen, in that case the biconditional is true. Line two represents the case in which "p" is true and "q" is false. Since a biconditional asserts that "p" will be true if and only if "q" is also true, the biconditional "p ≡ q" is false when "p" is true and "q" is false. In line three, "p" is false and "q" is true. Since the biconditional says that "q" can be true if and only if "p" is true, the biconditional will be false under those conditions. Line four represents the case in which both "p" and "q" and false. Again, the biconditional asserts that "p" can be true if and only if "q" is true. Since "q" is false, the biconditional says that "p" is false as well. Line four, then, represents exactly what the biconditional says, and is therefore true.

Both our truth-table and our discussion show that a biconditional statement is true if and only if both of its simple statements have the *same* truth value. This is represented by lines one and four of the truth-table. However, when the simple statements of a biconditional conditional have different truth values, the biconditional is false. This is represented by lines two and three of the truth-table. All of this information can be easily remembered if one recalls that the biconditional is true when and only when the two simple statements have the same truth value.

Exercises

Part I: Complete the following statements.

1. Biconditionals are really two _____ rolled into one.

2. When the components of a biconditional have the same truth value, the biconditional is a _____ statement.

3. When the components of a biconditional have a different truth value, the biconditional is a _____ statement.

4. The symbol for a biconditional is a logical operator known as the
_____ _____ .

5. Biconditionals assert that their components have the same
_____ _____ .

Part II: Determine the truth values of the following by assuming that "p" and "r" are true and "q" and "s" are false. Place a "T" before true expressions and an "F" before false expressions.

_____ 1. $p \equiv q$

_____ 2. $s \equiv r$

_____ 3. $q \equiv s$

_____ 4. $p \equiv r$

_____ 5. $q \equiv r$

PUNCTUATION

All the logical operators used in propositional logic have now been introduced. These logical operators allow us to determine under what conditions a given statement is true or false. However, up to this point we have been dealing with relatively simple compound statements. If we want to represent more complex statements in our symbolic language, we find that we immediately run into a problem. Here is an example to illustrate what I mean:

$$p \cdot q \vee q$$

The problem is that this statement is *ambiguous*, since it can be interpreted in these two different ways:

1. $(p \cdot q) \vee q$

2.   p • (q ∨ q)

According to the first interpretation, the statement is a *disjunction*. That is, "p • q" is the first disjunct, and "q" is the second. On the second interpretation, the statement is a *conjunction*; "p" is the first conjunct and "q ∨ q" is the second conjunct.

This is an important problem for two related reasons. The first is that when we translate from English into our symbolic language, we want to be able to clearly express what the original English statement is asserting. This is impossible if some of our symbolic expressions are ambiguous. The second reason that this is an important problem is that if some of our translations are ambiguous, we will be unable to determine their truth-value. We can see this clearly if we suppose, for instance, that "p" is a false statement and "q" is a true statement.

If "p" is false and "q" is true, what is the truth value of the first interpretation of our original statement?

1.   (p • q) ∨ q

Since, according to this interpretation, we are dealing with a disjunction, it will be a true statement. This is because even if the left side of the disjunction, "p • q," is false, the fact that the right side of the disjunction, "q," is true, is sufficient to make the entire statement true. You will recall that a disjunction is false only when *both* of its disjuncts are false. Hence, using this interpretation, the original statement is true.

According to the second interpretation, the original statement is a conjunction:

2.   p • (q ∨ q)

Under this interpretation, the original statement is false. Because, if "p" is false, then the first conjunct is false. That is sufficient to make the entire statement false, given that conjunctions are true only when *both* of their conjuncts are true.

It should be easy to see the importance of eliminating ambiguity from our symbolic expressions. The truth or falsity of the original statement depended upon which interpretation we adopted of our original expression. There could hardly be a more important difference! What allowed us to arrive at a statement that was not ambiguous, was the use of punctuation. Thus, we have demonstrated the importance of punctuation in our symbolic language.

Shorter statements can also be ambiguous. Here is an example:

~p v q

This statement can be interpreted two different ways:

1. (~p) v q

2. ~(p v q)

The first says "not p, or q." In other words it says that either "p" is false or "q" is true. The second statement says "It's false that either "p" or "q" is true." If we assume that "p" is true and "q" is true, then the statement would be true on the first interpretation and false on the second interpretation. The first statement would be true, on the first interpretation, because although "~p" would be false, the other disjunct, "q" would be true. If at least one disjunct is true, then the entire disjunction will be true. However, on the second interpretation the original statement would be false. This is because if both "p" and "q" are true, then "p v q" would be true. Since the statement, on the second interpretation is the negation of "p v q," it would be false. Again, we see the importance of punctuation is our symbolic language.

However, to simplify our punctuation, we adopt the following convention: *We interpret the "~" to apply to the smallest part of an expression that the punctuation allows.* Thus, in our example, the expression "~p v q" will be interpreted to mean, "(~p) v q." It will follow, then, that "~p v q" is no longer ambiguous, since by convention it means the same as "(~p) v q." But if we want the "~" to negate the entire expression, we will write "~(p v q)."

To further illustrate our convention, here is another example:

~((p ⊃ r) • (~q v s))

You will notice that there are two tildes in this expression. The second one negates only the "q." However, the first tilde negates the entire expression. So whatever the truth value of "(p ⊃ r) • (~q v s)," given the first tilde, the expression "~((p ⊃ r) • (~q v s)" will have the opposite truth value. In other words the first tilde applies to the entire expression, while the second tilde applies only to the truth value of "q."

Exercises: For the following statements, assume that "p" and "r" are true and that "q" and "s" are false. Determine the truth value for each expression, placing a "T" before each statement that is true and "F" before each statement that is false.

_____ 1. r ⊃ s   _____ 11. ~(q v r) • p

_____ 2. ~r v p   _____ 12. (p • s) ⊃ r

_____ 3. p • ~q   _____ 13. ((p • r) v q) • p

_____ 4. q ⊃ s   _____ 14. (p • s) v ~r

_____ 5. p ≡ q   _____ 15. ~(p v ~q)

_____ 6. q ≡ ~p   _____ 16. (p • s) ≡ (r • s)

_____ 7. p v ~r   _____ 17. (p v s) • (q • r)

_____ 8. p • (q • p)   _____ 18. ((p ≡ q) • r) ⊃ s

_____ 9. p ⊃ (~q v s)   _____ 19. ~(~(p v q) • r) ⊃ p

_____ 10. s ≡ (q • p)   _____ 20. ~((p • ~q) v (r ≡ s))

main connectives

CHAPTER SIXTEEN

TRANSLATING PROPOSITIONAL STATEMENTS I

In the two preceding chapters, we introduced all the basic elements of the symbolic language for propositional logic. In this chapter you will learn to translate ordinary English statements into this symbolic language. Translating such statements into symbolic language will enable you to represent their truth-functional structure, and more easily determine their truth or falsity. This will pave the way for testing arguments containing truth-functional statements for validity.

TRANSLATING CONJUNCTIONS

We already know how to translate simple conjunctions. Here is an example:

> Sue is a lawyer and Bill is a doctor.

This statement is translated:

> p • q

The purpose of this chapter is to assist you in translating less straightforward examples. As it turns out, there are several ways of expressing conjunctions in English, and some of them do not appear, on the surface, to be conjunctions. By learning to deal with such examples, you will increase your ability to translate from English into the symbolic language of propositional logic.

Consider the following statement:

> Bob and Dave are going to the game.

It may be tempting to take this as a simple statement and thus to translate it simply as "p," since there are not obviously two statements here to be connected by a conjunction. This is because, in English, we do not always fully express the components of a conjunction. However, if you ask yourself what the statement is actually saying, you will see that it is asserting the following conjunction:

Bob is going to the game and Dave is going to the game.

So, the correct translation is:

p • q

Another difficulty results from the fact that when a conjunction is expressed, a word other than "and" may be used to connect the components. Here are some examples:

Although it is raining, it is not very cold.

The book is long, but very interesting.

Even though she was tired, she continued to study.

She was firm, yet compassionate.

It was cool, though humid.

While the mountains were majestic, they were foreboding.

Both of us are flying to Denver today.

The expression, "She was firm, yet compassionate," for example, is asserting that "She was firm *and* she was compassionate." The expression, "It was cool, though humid" is asserting the conjunction, "It was cool *and* it was humid." "Both of us are flying to Denver today" is saying "You are flying to Denver today *and* I am flying to Denver today." Since each of the above examples asserts a conjunction, each is translated:

p • q

There is one other potential difficulty that should be mentioned. You may recall that, in Chapter Fourteen, we talked about causal and temporal compound statements. You should now remember that we are ignoring the temporal or causal characteristics of such statements and treating them as conjunctions. That means that examples such as the following are also conjunctions:

> The morning air was cool when we arrived at the lake.

> Because he is a fast runner, he won the race.

Such examples are also translated:

> p • q

What all of these examples have in common is that they are all saying what a conjunction fundamentally says. That is, they all assert that *both* of their component statements are true. So it will help you to remember that if a statement is asserting that both of its components are true, that is, both p and q are true, then it should be translated as a conjunction.

TRANSLATING DISJUNCTIONS

We have already learned how to translate straightforward disjunctions into symbols. Here is an example:

> Either it will rain today or the sun will shine.

As we have seen, we translate this sort of expression as follows:

> p ∨ q

However, disjunctions present many of the same difficulties we encountered with conjunctions. For example:

> Either Ralph or Bill called.

Again, it might be tempting to think that this is a simple statement, since there appears to be only one claim that is either true or false. Nevertheless, upon reflection, you should be able to see that "Either Ralph or Bill called" is actually asserting:

Either Ralph called or Bill called.

Here there are clearly two statement components, "Ralph called" and "Bill called." The correct translation, then, of "Either Ralph or Bill called" is the following disjunction:

p ∨ q

We have noted, in the case of conjunctions, that they are not always formed by using the word "and." Similarly, disjunctions are sometimes formed by using words other than "either-or." Here is an example:

The game will begin on time, unless it rains.

Now you might wonder why this is a disjunction. To see that it is, it is helpful to recall exactly what it is that a disjunction is saying. Remember that disjunctions assert that at least one of their component statements is true. Notice that this is precisely what is being asserted by "The game will begin on time, unless it rains." It is saying either it is true that the game will begin on time or it is true that it will rain. Therefore, the statement is saying that at least one of its disjuncts is true. The key to recognizing this statement as a disjunction is to see that it is making this claim.
Thus, "The game will begin on time, unless it rains," is translated:

p ∨ q

To further solidify your understanding of what a disjunction says, consider another example:

At least one of us will accept her invitation.

If there are two of us, you and me, then "At least one of us will accept her invitation" means "Either you will accept her invitation, or I will accept her invitation." In other words, one way of understanding a disjunction is to see that it is asserting, "at least one . . ." That is, either p is true, or q is true. Thus, "At least one of us will accept her invitation," is translated:

p ∨ q

TRANSLATING NEGATIONS

We have already learned how to translate expressions containing negations. For instance:

Bob has not studied for the test.

This, as we have seen, is translated:

~p

We have also learned how to translate more complicated expressions involving negations:

It is false that both Sue and Karen are coming to the party.

In this example, the words, "It is false that," negate the entire conjunction that follows them, rather than just the "p." So the correct translation for this negation is:

~(p • q)

Although it is relatively easy to translate expressions having negations as one of their components, there are two basic sorts of problems that can arise. The first concerns "neither/nor" expressions. Consider the following example of a neither/nor statement:

Neither his reputation nor his money could save him from going to prison.

At first glance the most natural translation for this statement might appear to be "~p v ~q." However, that would be a mistake. We can see that this is a mistake if we read back the translation. The translation, "~p v ~q," says that "Either his reputation won't save him from going to prison or his money won't save him from going to prison." In other words, it says that a least one of them won't save him from prison, leaving open the possibility that the other will. Observe, however, that the original statement denies that *either* could save him from prison. That means that "~p v ~q" does not capture what the original statement says.

So, how do we capture what the original statement says? There are two ways this can be done. First, if we want to preserve the apparent disjunctive nature of the original statement, then we can translate it as "~(p v q)." This says "It is not the case that either his reputation or his money can save him from going to prison. Translating "Neither his reputation nor his money could save him from going to prison" by the symbolic expression, "~(p v q)," captures what the original statement asserts.

Or, we can translate the statement as a conjunction: "~p • ~q." This says that his reputation will not save him from prison *and* his money will not save him from prison. This translation also preserves what the original statement asserts, namely, that it is false that *either* his reputation or his money will keep him from going to prison.

As it turns out, "~(p v q)" and "~p • ~q" are logically equivalent. We will see later that this means that they will always have the same truth value. Since the two expressions are fundamentally saying the same thing, it doesn't matter which translation we select.

The other difficulty regarding the translation of negations occurs when we encounter an expression containing several negations. The following is an example:

It is not the case that neither Linda nor Janet will win the race.

The tendency with such a statement is to be confused by the negatives. If we have difficulty understanding what the original English statement is asserting, we will also have difficulty in correctly translating the expression into our symbols.

It is helpful to break such statements into two parts. This allows us to do the translation in two steps: First, translate the part of the statement that says ". . . neither Linda nor Janet will win the race." You should easily recognize this part of the statement as a neither/nor statement. It can be translated as "~p • ~ q." In English this says "Linda will not win the race and Janet will not win the race."

The second step is to translate the part of the statement that says "It is false that. . ." This is a negation, and it is translated as a tilde: "~." Combining the two steps results in the following translation:

~(~p • ~q)

In the exercise that appears below you are being asked to translate a number of conjunctions, disjunctions and negations. If you encounter difficulties with any of the translations, you should consult the relevant section from this chapter.

Exercises

Part I: Translate each of the following into symbolic notation. (Remember to use "p" for the first statement component in English, "q" for the second, "r" for the third, and so on.)

1. Either Professor Plum was in the library, or he was in the kitchen.

2. It is false that it is raining.

3. It is raining and it is very cold.

4. Lucy and Bradley ran past the house.

5. Unless you pay me, I will repossess the car.

6. When the music ended, the dancers quit dancing.

7. Either you will wake up and smell the coffee, or your life will pass you by.

8. Neither Ronald nor George voted for Bill.

9. Its false that neither Bill nor Steve will win.

10. Even though he was hungry, William kept to his diet.

11. The post office will be open, unless it is a holiday.

12. It is not true that Sue did not go to the game and that Tom did.

13. Sue did not go to the game and Tom didn't either.

14. Tom is either at home or at the office, and Sue is not here.

15. Although he wanted to lose weight, he simply did not have the will power to do so.

16. Unless it stops raining, the game will be canceled.

17. Because it is raining, the game will not be played.

18. It is false that either Paul or Valerie is sick.

19. I finally went to sleep, after the alarm went off.

20. Either we get approval for the design, or engineering and research will have to make major changes.

21. She was happy, though tired.

22. It's not true that Tom is either at home or at the office, and Sue is not here.

23. I will study hard, but either I will need a quiet room or a seat in the library.

24. I will be there at 5:00 or 6:00 p.m.

25. It's not the case that this is the last logic example you will see.

Part II: If we assume that "p" is true, "q" is false and "r" is true, which of the statements in **Part I** are true and which are false.

CHAPTER SEVENTEEN

TRANSLATING PROPOSITIONAL STATEMENTS II

In Chapter Fifteen, we learned how to translate relatively straightforward conditionals into symbolic language. In this chapter you will learn to translate conditionals that are less straightforward. To assist you in learning to translate conditionals, we will introduce the distinction between *necessary* and *sufficient conditions*. Finally, we will work on improving your skills for translating biconditionals and learn how to distinguish them from conditionals.

TRANSLATING CONDITIONALS

There are several ways of stating a conditional in English. The most straightforward way is captured in the following example:

If it continues to rain, then the dam will break.

Notice that this example has the standard, "If . . . then . . ." form. But we want to look at other ways of expressing conditionals. For example, the word "then" is sometimes left out.

If it continues to rain, the dam will break.

Sometimes, the "if" appears in the middle of the statement, rather than at the beginning.

The dam will break, if it continues to rain.

The words "if" and "then" need not occur at all in a conditional. Here are several examples:

Seeing the blood stains implies that there has been foul play.

He will go to the game, in case the tickets arrive on time.

Receiving the call means that she will be here.

She will win the spelling bee, should she spell this word.

Provided she does the training, she will win the race.

He will pass the exam, provided he studies for it.

Each of the preceding statements expresses a conditional. Each is asserting that if its antecedent is true, then its consequent is also true. Being able to see that this is what each of these statements is saying is an important step in learning to translate conditionals.

Although all of the above are examples of conditional statements, some of them are more easily translated into the symbolic notation for conditionals than others. In this chapter, we will focus on those ways of expressing conditionals that cause us the most difficulties for translation.

Most difficulties regarding the translation of conditionals arise from the problem of determining which component statement is the antecedent and which is the consequent. This presents no difficulty with straightforward conditionals. For example:

She will win the spelling bee, should she spell this word.

Obviously, "the car starts" is the antecedent and "it has fuel" is the consequent. The translation is then:

$$p \supset q$$

But suppose the statement is the following:

The car will start, if it has fuel.

In this case, "it has fuel" is the antecedent and "the car will start" is the consequent, since the word "if" which introduces the antecedent, is in the middle of the statement. If we remember our rule which says that the first component in English is given the letter, "p," and the second, "q," and so on, then "p" will stand for "the car will start" and "q" for "it has fuel." Since "q" is standing for the antecedent and "p" for the consequent, the correct translation is:

$$q \supset p$$

It is important to take note of the fact that to correctly translate, "The car will start, if it has fuel" we had to reverse the order of "p" and "q." The reason for this is that when the word "if" occurs by itself in a conditional statement it always introduces the *antecedent* of that conditional. Since the "if" occurs in the middle of the English expression, it introduces the second component, "q," as the antecedent of the conditional. To capture this in our symbolic notation we have to invert the order of "p" and "q."

Now consider a slightly different example:

The car will start only if it has gas.

This statement is correctly translated:

p ⊃ q

The reason we translate this expression "p ⊃ q," is that the words "only if" introduce the *consequent* of a conditional statement. Since the statement component "it has gas," symbolized as "q," is the consequent, the correct translation is "p ⊃ q."

As we have already seen, there are a variety of ways of expressing conditionals in English. Consequently, there are a number of other ways of introducing *antecedents* and *consequents* for conditionals. Let's look at some of our earlier examples and discuss the correct translation for each.

Seeing the blood stain implies that there was foul play.

If we remember that one way of reading "p ⊃ q" is "p implies q," then the translation for this example should be relatively obvious. Since the word "implies" introduces the *consequent* of a conditional, the correct translation is "p ⊃ q."

He will go to the game, in case the tickets arrive on time.

In this example, the words "in case" function like the word "if" and therefore introduce the *antecedent* of the conditional. Because we must use "p" for "He will go to the game" and "q" for "the tickets arrive on time," then we must reverse the order in which the statements appear in English. The correct translation, therefore, is "q ⊃ p."

Receiving the call means that he will be there.

The word "means" does the same work as "implies" and, therefore, introduces the *consequent*. The correct translation is "p ⊃ q."

She will win the spelling bee, should she spell this word.

Notice that the word "should" functions logically like the word "if." It introduces the *antecedent*. Because the antecedent comes second in the example, we must reverse the order of the two simple statements. The correct translation is "q ⊃ p."

Provided she does the training, she will win the race.

"Provided" here does the same work logically as the word "if." That is, it introduces the *antecedent*. Thus, it is not necessary to reverse the order of antecedent and consequent as they occur in English. Therefore, the correct translation for "Provided she does the training, she will win the race" is "p ⊃ q."

He will pass the exam, provided he studies for it.

Again, "provided" does the same work as "if." However, "provided" occurs in the middle of this statement, introducing as the *antecedent* the component, "he studies for it." That means that the correct translation is "q ⊃ p."

It should be clear that it is extremely important when translating conditionals that we determine which component statement is the antecedent and which is the consequent. To assist in your translations, here is a partial listing of the words that introduce either the antecedents or consequents of conditionals:

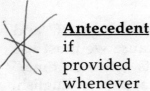

Antecedent	**Consequent**
if	then
provided	only if
whenever	it must be true
in case	it will be the case
should	implies

Exercises

Translate each of the following statements into symbolic notation.

1. If the weather holds, the game will be played.

2. I'd quit this job now, if I could find another one.

3. When the opportunity arises, I am going to take it.

4. Seeing the clouds implied that it was going to rain.

5. Provided she tries, she will win.

6. Only if it rains, will the picnic have to be canceled.

7. I will answer the phone, should it ring.

8. I will answer the phone only if it rings.

9. I will answer the phone provided it rings.

10. I will answer the phone if it rings.

11. The Reds will win provided that they get good pitching.

12. The Tigers will win, only if the Blue Jays collapse.

13. In case you loan me the money, I will go out tonight.

14. If he is the killer, then he's dangerous.

15. You can translate conditionals, if you try.

NECESSARY AND SUFFICIENT CONDITIONS

Conditional statements express two different sorts of conditions. They are known as *necessary* and *sufficient* conditions. Understanding the necessary and sufficient condition distinction will help you understand three things about conditionals. First, it will help you understand *why* conditionals are translated as they are. This should also improve your ability to perform the translations. Second, understanding the distinction between necessary and sufficient conditions will help you distinguish the antecedent from the consequent of conditionals. Finally, understanding the necessary/sufficient condition distinction will assist you in understanding why conditional statements are either true or false.

A condition is said to be *necessary* if without it something cannot be the case. For instance, being at least 35 years of age is a necessary condition for being President of the United States. This means that if one is not at least 35 years old, one cannot be President of the United States.

A condition is said to be *sufficient* if when it is satisfied, something must be the case. Being a horse, for example, is sufficient for it to be an animal. In other words, if something is a horse, then it must be true that it is an animal.

Notice, however, that being a horse is *not* a necessary condition for being an animal. That is, something can be an animal without being a horse. Being a horse, then, is a sufficient, but not a necessary condition, for being an animal. Also, being at least 35 years of age is *not* a sufficient condition for being President of United States. One can be at least 35 years of age and not be President. Thus, being at least 35 years old is a necessary, but not a sufficient, condition for being President.

In order to apply this distinction to our understanding of conditionals, consider the following example:

If the light is on, then there is electricity present.

This statement is asserting that having the light on is *sufficient* to guarantee that there is electricity present. Thus, knowing that the antecedent, "the light is on," is true, is sufficient for us to know that the consequent, "there is electricity present," is true as well. As we have seen, we would translate this statement: "p ⊃ q."

Here is a slightly different example:

The light is on only if there is electricity present.

This statement says that the presence of electricity is a *necessary* condition for the light bulb being on. So, for the antecedent, "The light is on," to be true, it is necessary that "there is electricity present." Now, as we have seen, this "p only if q" statement would also be translated, "p ⊃ q."

We are now in a better position to understand *why* these translations are correct. As we said earlier, every conditional statement expresses both a necessary and sufficient condition. The simple statement making up the *antecedent* of a conditional is always a *sufficient* condition for the truth of its consequent. Therefore, in the example, "If the light is on, then electricity is present," the statement is saying that the truth of the antecedent, "the light is on," is sufficient for the truth of the consequent. In other words, "If p is true, then q is true."

Similarly, the second example tells us that the *consequent* of a conditional statement is always a *necessary* condition for the truth of its antecedent. So, in the example, "The light is on only if electricity is present," we are being told that the truth of the consequent, "electricity is present," is necessary for the truth of the antecedent, "the light is on." In other words, "p is true only if q is true."

Any conditional, therefore, is asserting that its antecedent is sufficient for the truth of its consequent *and* that its consequent is necessary for the truth of its antecedent. If we let the letter "S" stand for "sufficient condition," and the letter "N" stand for "necessary condition," we can represent this as follows:

$$\underline{S} \supset \underline{N}$$

This means that whatever statement occupies the *antecedent* position is asserted to be a *sufficient* condition for the statement that occupies the consequent position. That is, the conditional statement asserts that *if* its antecedent is true, then its consequent is also true. It also means that whatever statement occupies the *consequent* position is a *necessary* condition for the statement that occupies the antecedent position. That is, the conditional statement asserts that its antecedent can be true *only if* its consequent is true.

You should now understand why we have translated the two examples examined so far as we have. With that in mind, let's look at some other examples:

The light is on if there is electricity present.

In this example, we are being told that "there is electricity present" is *sufficient* for the truth of "the light is on." Again, let "p" stand for the first statement component, "the light is on" and "q" stand for "there is electricity present." Since sufficient conditions are always placed in the antecedent position, represented by "q" in this case, that means this statement is translated:

   q ⊃ p

This translation is just what we should expect, if we remember from the previous section that "if" introduces the *antecedent*. Put differently, "if" introduces a sufficient condition.

   Here is another example:

   The light is on provided that there is electricity.

This statement asserts that the presence of electricity is a sufficient condition for the light being on. "Provided q is true, p is true." It is translated:

   q ⊃ p

   Consider another example:

   Provided the light is on, there is electricity.

This statement is saying that "the light is on" is sufficient for it being true that "there is electricity." That is, "if p is true, then q is true." The correct translation is:

   p ⊃ q

   You should now have a better understanding of why words like "if" and "provided" introduce the antecedents of conditionals. It is because such words carry with them the notion of a *sufficient* condition. On the other hand, words such as "only if" and "must" introduce the consequents of conditionals, because they carry with them the notion of a *necessary* condition. Given that sufficient conditions always occupy the antecedent position, and that necessary conditions always occupy the consequent position, we should be able to make sense of our symbolic translations of conditionals. It will be helpful, at this point, for you to study all of the examples presented in this section with this in mind.

The distinction between necessary and sufficient conditions also sheds light on why the conditional is false only when the antecedent is true and the consequent is false. The conditional claims that the truth of "p" is *sufficient* for the truth of "q," that is, "if "p" is true then "q" is true." So, we should be able to understand that if "p" is true and "q" is false, the conditional will be a false statement.

Exercises

Translate the following statements into symbolic notation.

1. If the lights are on, then someone is at home.

2. The lights are on only if there is someone at home.

3. You can ride in the car if you wear a seat belt.

4. In case you want to ride, buckle your seat belt.

5. Buckling your seat belt implies that you want to ride.

6. If the class is open and you have your student I.D., then you can register.

7. If you don't have your student I.D., then you cannot register.

8. It's false that if you don't have your student I.D., then you can register.

9. Were I to try, I could do this.

10. If you don't want to cook, then you will eat out or pick something up.

11. If you neither want to cook nor eat out, you may have to do without.

12. You can start the car, provided that it has gas and the battery is not dead.

13. The car will start, only if it has gas and its battery has been charged.

14. Were it to rain, either the picnic or the game would be called.

15. Having chicken pox implies that she has a fever.

TRANSLATING BICONDITIONALS

We have already learned how to translate straightforward examples of biconditionals. Here is an example:

The boat will sink if and only if the hull is ruptured.

This biconditional is translated:

p ≡ q

However, biconditionals are not always expressed using the words "if and only if." Other expressions that amount to the same thing are the following:

The boat will sink just in case the hull is ruptured.

The boat will sink when and only when the hull is ruptured.

The boat will sink exactly when the hull is ruptured.

Each of these examples would be translated:

p ≡ q

Translating biconditionals is not, for the most part, very difficult. There are two things, however, to keep in mind. The first is to be certain that you know exactly what a biconditional asserts. A biconditional asserts that its two components have the same truth value. That is, "p is true if and only if q is true." Fundamentally, a biconditional should be understood as two conditionals rolled into one. Taking a look at another example of a biconditional will help us to see that this is so.

She will graduate if and only if she passes her finals.

This statement asserts that "She will graduate, *if* she passes her finals" and "She will graduate *only if* she passes her finals." This means that the biconditional could be translated:

$$(p \supset q) \bullet (q \supset p)$$

Symbolically, this is what a biconditional asserts. The assertion is that "p" is both *necessary* and *sufficient* for "q," and "q" is both *necessary* and *sufficient* for "p." This is why it is called a biconditional. It is simply two conditional statements combined into a single expression. Although the above translation is perfectly adequate as a translation of a biconditional, we will continue to use the shorter:

$$p \equiv q$$

The second thing to keep in mind is that one must be careful not to confuse: "p only if q" with "p if and only if q." The first is a conditional, not a biconditional. It is translated "$p \supset q$." The second is a biconditional and is translated "$p \equiv q$."

Exercises

Translate the following statements into symbolic notation.

1. The car will start, if and only if, it has gas.

2. The roof leaks, when and only when, it rains.

3. The Pistons will win only if they win all of their remaining games.

4. The plane will be on time exactly when it leaves on time.

5. I will work harder just in case I get a raise.

6. The Pistons will win, if and only if, they win all of their remaining games.

7. If the roof leaks, then it is either raining or snowing.

8. The car will start, if and only if, it has gas, provided that the battery is not dead.

9. If the roof is not leaking, then it is neither raining nor snowing.

10. If you have your student I. D. then you can register, if and only if, you have not flunked out.

11. If you have your student I. D. you can register, only if you have not flunked out.

12. Either you study hard or you will fail, if and only if, you don't already know the material.

13. You will graduate and succeed in life just in case you either work hard or you are very lucky.

14. Neither you nor your parents can know what lies ahead, when and only when, neither you nor your parents are psychic.

15. If you don't know what you are doing then you shouldn't act so smart, only if you don't want to be found out.

CHAPTER EIGHTEEN

CONSTRUCTING TRUTH TABLES

We have already used truth tables to define the truth functional operators that were introduced earlier. Now we want to develop a more complete account of the truth table and its uses. As we will see, truth tables are designed to provide a complete account of the conditions under which a given symbolic expression is either true or false. Since we have now learned to translate truth functional statements from English into symbolic notation, we will be able to use truth tables to determine, in every case, when such an expression is true and when it is false.

Truth tables can be used for a variety of purposes. In this chapter, we will learn to construct truth tables and to use them to determine when an expression is a tautology, contradiction or a contingent statement. In Chapter Nineteen, we will also learn how to use truth tables to determine when two expressions are logically equivalent and to test arguments for validity.

TRUTH TABLE CONSTRUCTION

As we mentioned above, truth tables are designed to provide a complete account of the conditions under which a given truth functional statement is either true or false. Since any statement has only two possible truth values, true or false, it follows that for a statement form having only one *variable*, a truth table representing that expression will require two rows, one representing the case when the variable is true and the other the case when the variable is false. Suppose we begin with the expression:

p ∨ p

This expression, a disjunction, has one variable, "p." We know that "p" is either true or it is false. The truth table for "p v p" will require two rows to represent the *two* possibilities. As we have seen, a disjunction is false only when both of its disjuncts are false. The truth table for "p v p," appears at the top of the next page.

p	p v p
T	T
F	F

The first row under "p" represents the case in which "p" is true. In that case "p v p" is true, since both disjuncts are true. (In this example both disjuncts happen to be the same variable.) The second line represents the case in which "p" is false. Since both disjuncts are false in line two, the expression "p v p" will be false. The truth table shows *all* the possibilities of truth and falsity that can hold for "p v p," since this expression has only one variable. A truth table for *any* expression having only one variable will contain exactly two rows.

Now let's look at an expression containing two variables. Consider the following expression:

   p • q

Since this expression has two variables, "p" and "q," it will require a truth table of four rows. This is because there are *four* possible combinations of truth or falsity that can obtain for "p" and "q." Both "p" and "q" could be false or both could be true. Or, "p" could be true and "q" false, or "p" could be false and "q" true. The truth table below represents these *four* possibilities. Now since the expression is a conjunction, we know that it will be true only when *both* of its conjuncts are true. Here is the truth table for "p • q:"

p	q	p • q
T	T	T
T	F	F
F	T	F
F	F	F

The first row represents the case where both "p" and "q" are true statements. When both of its conjuncts are true, "p • q" is true. The second row represents the case in which "p" is true and "q" is false. Since a conjunction is true only when both of its conjuncts are true, notice that in row two, "p • q" is false. In row three, "p" is false and "q" as true. Because one conjunct is false, "p • q" will be false. Finally, in row four, both "p" and "q" are false. The conjunction, "p • q," is false in that case as well.

This truth table provides a complete picture of the conditions under which "p • q" is either true or false since it lists all the possible combinations of truth and falsity for the two variables, "p" and "q." It will *always* be the case that an expression with two variables will require a truth table containing four rows.

We can now state a general rule regarding the number of rows required by a given expression for truth tables. The rule is that each time we add a variable to an expression the number of rows required for the truth table doubles. So, if an expression has only one variable, it requires a truth table having two rows. An expression having two variables requires a truth table with four rows. If an expression has three variables, its truth table must have eight rows and so on.

Let's look at another example:

$(p \supset q) \bullet r$

Notice that this expression has three variables, "p," "q" and "r." Using the rule given above, that means we will need a truth table of *eight* rows. Below, the left side of the table is presented, but the truth values for the expression, "(p ⊃ q) • r," have not been determined.

p	q	r	$(p \supset q) \bullet r$
T	T	T	
T	T	F	
T	F	T	
T	F	F	
F	T	T	
F	T	F	
F	F	T	
F	F	F	

Again, the truth values under "p," "q" and "r" represent all the possible combinations of truth or falsity that can hold for the three variables. Notice that in the first row all the variables are represented as true and in the last row, all are represented as false. Between the first row and the eighth row are all the other possible combinations of truth and falsity for the three variables.

There is a standard way of generating the truth values for the different variables. For the last variable we always use the pattern "T-F," with the pattern repeating as many times as necessary to reach the required number of rows. In the example above, "r" is the last variable and the "T-F" pattern is repeated until we reach eight rows. The next to last variable, "q," has the pattern, "T T F F," with the pattern repeating as many times as needed. The first variable, in this case, "p," has the pattern "T T T T F F F F." (If we have a truth table with four variables, say "p," "q," "r" and "s," the table would have sixteen rows and the letter "s" would have the "T-F" pattern repeated until we reached the required number of rows. The first variable, "p" would have the pattern of eight "Ts" and then eight "Fs.")

To fill in the values for "(p ⊃ q) • r" we must notice, first of all, that it is a conjunction. The left conjunct is "(p ⊃ q)" and the right conjunct is "r." To find the truth values for our expression, we must first determine the truth values for the left conjunct. Then we determine the truth values for the right conjunct, "r." Here is the truth table with those values filled in:

p	q	r	(p ⊃ q)	•	r
T	T	T	T		T
T	T	F	T		F
T	F	T	F		T
T	F	F	F		F
F	T	T	T		T
F	T	F	T		F
F	F	T	T		T
F	F	F	T		F

Because the left conjunct of our expression is a conditional, we look at the truth values under the "p" and the "q," and we find that the only cases of a true antecedent and a false consequent are in rows three and four. Since those are the only conditions under which a conditional is false, in all the other rows "p ⊃ q" will be true. That explains the truth values under "p ⊃ q." The right side of the conjunct is "r." To derive the truth values for "r" we only need to copy them from the "r" column of the truth table. Once we have the values for "p ⊃ q" and for "r," we are ready to complete our truth table. We look under the column for "p ⊃ q" and the column for "r" to determine the truth values for the complete expression, "(p ⊃ q) • r." The final truth table appears at the top of the next page:

p	q	r	(p ⊃ q)	•	r
T	T	T	T	**T**	T
T	T	F	T	**F**	F
T	F	T	F	**F**	T
T	F	F	F	**F**	F
F	T	T	T	**T**	T
F	T	F	T	**F**	F
F	F	T	T	**T**	T
F	F	F	T	**F**	F

The truth values for the entire expression, "(p ⊃ q) • r," are given under the "•" in bold type. In this case, the "•" is the *main logical connective*. That is what makes this expression a conjunction. The column of truth values under the "•" is known as the *final value column* of the truth table. The truth values under the other columns of a truth table are only preliminary to the final value column.

There is a general lesson to be learned from this example. When doing truth tables for an expression containing parentheses, it is necessary to determine the truth value for the part of the expression in parentheses before you can determine the truth values for the entire expression. When there is more than one set of parentheses, begin with that part of the expression within the innermost parentheses. Notice that we have to know the truth values of "p ⊃ q" before we can determine the truth values for the complete expression.

Now we can explain how we arrived at the truth values for the final value column of our truth table. Since a conjunction is true only if both of its conjuncts are true, we get the truth value of true only in rows one, five and seven of the final value column of the truth table. In all other rows you should notice that either "p ⊃ q" is false or "r" is false or they are both false.

Here is one final example:

~(~p • q)

Let's begin by doing the truth table for the part of this expression contained *within* the parentheses, "~p • q." The truth table for this part of the our expression appears at the top of the next page.

p	q	~	(	~p	•	q)
T	T			F	F	T
T	F			F	F	F
F	T			T	T	T
F	F			T	F	F

The values have been filled in for "~p" and for "q." They were obtained by *negating* the values for "p" and by simply copying the values for "q" from the left side of the truth table. The column under the "•" represents the values for the expression "(~p • q)." However, you should notice that the table is not complete, since the expression we are dealing with is "~(~p • q)." Below is the completed table, *omitting* the truth values under "~p" and "q."

p	q	~	(~p	•	q)
T	T	T		F	
T	F	T		F	
F	T	F		T	
F	F	T		F	

Given the way this expression is punctuated, the entire expression is within the scope of the outermost "~." That means that it is the *main logical operator* in this expression. Therefore, the truth values under the outermost "~" are the *final value column* of the truth table. The final value column will always be under the logical operator not contained within any parentheses. It is the final value column of the truth table that tells us under what conditions the expression, "~(~p • q)," will be true or false.

Exercises

Part I: Complete the following statements.

1. The number of rows in a truth table is determined by the number of _____ in the statement.

2. A statement with only one variable requires a truth table with _____ rows.

3. A statement with two variables requires a truth table with
    _____ rows.

4. A statement with three variables requires a truth table with
    _____ rows.

5. Each additional variable requires the number of rows in a truth table to
    _____.

6. A statement with four variables requires a truth table with
    _____ rows.

7. When there is more that one logical operator in a statement, you
    should begin determining the truth values for the part of the
    expression contained in the _____ parentheses.

8. The truth values under the logical operator that describes the truth
    values for the entire expression are called the _____
    _____ column of the truth table.

9. Truth tables provide a complete account of all the possible
    combinations of _____ and _____ that can hold
    for the variables represented.

10. Consequently, truth tables provide a complete picture of the conditions
    under which an expression is either _____ or
    _____.

Part II: Do a truth table for each of the following statement forms.

1. p ⊃ q

2. p • q

3. p ≡ q

4. p ∨ q

5. ~p v q

6. ~(~q ⊃ ~p)

7. p v (~r • q)

8. (q ≡ r) v ~(p • ~r)

9. (p • p) ⊃ (r ≡ p)

10. (r v s) ⊃ ~q

TAUTOLOGOUS, CONTRADICTORY AND CONTINGENT STATEMENTS

Most of the statements we make in everyday conversation are capable of being either true or false. They are called *contingent statements*. However, not all statements have the possibility of being true and not all statements have the possibility of being false. Statements that cannot possibly be false are called *tautologies*. Statements that cannot possibly be true are called *contradictions*.

1. Tautologies

Tautologous expressions often strike us as rather strange. For example, suppose you ask me if this class requires a term paper and I reply, "Either it requires a term paper or it doesn't." I think you would correctly conclude that I haven't really given you any information regarding class requirements. If we analyze this statement we will see that each of its components is either true or false. "It requires a term paper" is either true or it is false and "It doesn't require a term paper" is either true or false. However, if you reflect on the complete statement, you should be able to see that it cannot possibly be false since at least one of the disjuncts must be true. Remember that a disjunctive statement is true provided that at least one of its disjuncts is true. That the statement, "Either it requires a term papers or it doesn't," must always be true can be demonstrated clearly if we symbolize the statement and do a truth table for it.

The statement is symbolized as "p v ~p." The truth table for "p v ~p" appears at the top of the next page.

p	p v ~p
T	T
F	T

In the first row, where "p" is true, "p v ~p" will be true because if one disjunct is true, the entire disjunction will be true. In row two, where "p" is false, "~p" will be true. Because one of its disjuncts is true, the disjunction, "p v ~p," will be true. The truth table tells us, then, that there are no possible conditions under which "p v ~p" will be false. If "p" is true, "p v ~p" will be true, and if "p" if false, "p v ~p" will also be true. The presence of all "Ts" under the main logical operator tell us that this expression is a tautology. Sometimes tautologies are referred to as *necessarily true* statements.

Although "Either p or not p" is a rather obvious tautology, some tautologous expressions are not so obvious. Consider the following example:

$$p \supset (q \supset p)$$

A truth table reveals that this expression is also a tautology.

p	q	p	⊃	(q ⊃ p)
T	T		T	T
T	F		T	T
F	T		T	F
F	F		T	T

In the truth table presented above, we have only filled in the truth values for "q ⊃ p" and for the complete expression "p ⊃ (q ⊃ p)." Again, the presence of all "Ts" in the final value column tells us that the expression is a tautology. That means that there are no conceivable circumstances under which an expression having this form can be false.

2. Contradictions

Although we are more familiar with contradictory statements than we are with tautologies, contradictory statements may also strike us as strange. Suppose you ask me again if there is a term paper required for this class. Imagine that my answer is "There is a term paper required and there isn't."

Again, I have failed to provide you with any real information regarding class requirements. The expression, "There is a term paper and there isn't a term paper" can be symbolized as "p • ~p." A truth table for this statement looks like this:

p	p • ~p
T	F
F	F

Under the final value column, you will notice that there are only "Fs." This is because in the first row, where "p" is true, "p • ~p" will be false, since the second conjunct, "~p," is false. As you know, in the case of conjunctions, they are true only if *both* of their conjuncts are true. However, if "p" is false, which is represented by the second row, "p • ~p" will also be false, since the first conjunct is false. This tells us that the expression, "p • ~p," will be false in every possible circumstance. The presence of all "Fs" under the final value column means that this statement is a contradiction. Sometimes contradictions are called *necessarily false* statements.

It should now be obvious why it is considered a criticism when we say of a statement, "That's a contradiction." It is because such statements cannot possibly be true. Thus, when one utters a contradiction, we know that, necessarily, it must be a false statement.

Sometimes a statement can be a contradiction without it being so obvious. The expression, "p • (p ⊃ (q • ~p))," for example, is a contradiction as the truth table below demonstrates:

p	q	p •	(p ⊃	(q • ~p))
T	T	F	F	F
T	F	F	F	F
F	T	F	T	T
F	F	F	T	F

Notice that there are only "Fs" in the final value column of the truth table for "p • (p ⊃ (q • ~p))." This tells us that the expression is a contradiction.

3. Contingent Statements

Most of the statements that we make in our everyday lives are *contingent* statements. Unlike tautologies, which have all "Ts" in the final value column of their truth tables, and contradictions, which have all "Fs" in the final value column, a contingent statement will have a least one "T" and at least one "F." This is because contingent statements are true under some conditions and false under other conditions. For example, "~p v q," is a contingent statement, as the truth table below shows:

p	q	~p v q
T	T	T
T	F	F
F	T	T
F	F	T

The truth table for "~p v q" demonstrates that there are some conditions under which "~p v q" is true, and some under which it is false. The presence of a combination of "Ts" and "Fs" in the final value column of the truth table tells us that this expression is a contingent statement.

Exercises

Part I: Complete the following statements:

1. A tautology is a statement that is always _____, regardless of the truth values of its component statements.

2. A truth table for a tautology will have all _____ in its final value column.

3. A contradiction is a statement that is always _____, regardless of the truth values of its component statements.

4. A truth table for a contradiction will have all _____ in its final value column.

5. A contingent statement will sometimes be _____ and will sometimes be _____.

6. A truth table for a contingent statement will have at least one _____ and at least one _____ in its final value column.

7. Tautologies are sometimes called _____ _____ statements.

8. Contradictories can be called _____ _____ statements.

Part II: Use truth tables to determine which of the following are tautologies, contradictions or contingent statement forms.

1. p ⊃ p

2. ~p • p

3. p v ~q

4. (p • q) • ~q

5. p ⊃ (p • q)

6. (p • q) ⊃ p

7. (p ⊃ q) • ~(~p v q)

8. ~(p • q) ≡ (~p v ~q)

9. (p ⊃ q) v q

10. ~(p v q)

11. (p ⊃ ~q) ⊃ ~(p • q)

12. ~(p ⊃ q) ≡ (~q ⊃ ~p)

13. p ⊃ (p v q)

14. (p • q) v r

15. (p • (q • r)) ⊃ r

16. p v (q v r)

17. (~p • ~q) ≡ (p v q)

18. ~(p • ~q) ⊃ (~p v q)

19. p ⊃ (p v r)

20. (p v r) ≡ (q v p)

CHAPTER NINETEEN

TRUTH TABLES AND VALIDITY

In Chapter Eighteen, you learned how to construct truth tables and how to use them to determine whether an expression is a tautology, a contradiction or a contingent statement. One of the things you will learn in this chapter is how to use truth tables to determine if two statements are logically equivalent. You will also learn how to use truth tables to test arguments for validity.

LOGICAL EQUIVALENCE

Two statements are logically equivalent if they *always* have the same truth value regardless of the truth value of their component statements. Expressions can be logically equivalent even though they may seem to be very different. Consider the following two statement forms:

$$p \supset q \qquad \sim p \lor q$$

These statement forms, at first glance, certainly do not appear to be logically equivalent. Fortunately, we have a method for determining whether two statement forms are logically equivalent through the use of truth tables. The method is as follows: First, we do a truth table for each expression. Then, we connect the two statement forms with the triple bars. If the resulting expression is a *tautology*, then the two statement forms are logically equivalent. Here is the truth table for: "$p \supset q$" and "$\sim p \lor q$."

p	q	$p \supset q$	$\sim p \lor q$
T	T	T	T
T	F	F	F
F	T	T	T
F	F	T	T

To show that the two expressions are logically equivalent, we connect them with the triple bars and do a truth table for the resulting expression. If we get all "Ts" under the final value column, then the two expressions are logically equivalent. The truth table showing that "p ⊃ q" and "~p v q" are logically equivalent is given below.

p	q	(p ⊃ q)	≡	(~p v q)
T	T	T	T	T
T	F	F	T	F
F	T	T	T	T
F	F	T	T	T

This truth table demonstrates that "p ⊃ q" and "~p v q" are logically equivalent. This is because two statements are said to be logically equivalent when the expression of that equivalence is a tautology. The formal expression of equivalence is made by connecting the two expressions with the triple bars. The presence of all "Ts" under the triple bars tells us that the expression, "(p ⊃ q) ≡ (~p v q)," is a tautology. Thus, "p ⊃ q" and "~p v q" are logically equivalent.

You may recall that in Chapter Sixteen we said that there were two correct ways of translating "neither-nor" statements. The two correct translations are either "~p • ~q" or "~(p v q)." The justification for claiming that either translation is acceptable is that the two expressions are logically equivalent. We can now demonstrate that equivalence. First, here is a truth table for the two expressions:

p	q	~p • ~q	~(p v q)
T	T	F	F
T	F	F	F
F	T	F	F
F	F	T	T

To show that the two statements are logically equivalent, we connect them with the triple bars and then do a truth table for the resulting expression. Here is the final truth table:

p	q	(~p • ~q)	≡	~(p v q)
T	T	F	T	F
T	F	F	T	F
F	T	F	T	F
F	F	T	T	T

Since the truth table shows that the statement of their equivalence is a tautology, "~p • ~q" and "~(p v q)" are shown to be logically equivalent.

In Chapter Seventeen we pointed out that "p ≡ q" is a shorter way of expressing "(p ⊃ q) • (q ⊃ p)." That is, we claimed the logical equivalence of "p ≡ q" and "(p ⊃ q) • (q ⊃ p)." To demonstrate that these two expressions are logically equivalent, we first do a truth table for the two statement forms:

p	q	p ≡ q	(p ⊃ q)	•	(q ⊃ p)
T	T	**T**	T	**T**	T
T	F	**F**	F	**F**	T
F	T	**F**	T	**F**	F
F	F	**T**	T	**T**	T

Then, using the values under "p ≡ q" and "(p ⊃ q) • (q ⊃ p)," we connect the two expressions with the triple bars:

p	q	(p ≡ q)	≡	((p ⊃ q) • (q ⊃ p))
T	T	T	**T**	T
T	F	F	**T**	F
F	T	F	**T**	F
F	F	T	**T**	T

Notice that the truth values for the final value column of our truth table are all "Ts." That means the expression of the equivalence of the two statements is a tautology. Hence, the two expressions are logically equivalent.

Exercises

Part I: Complete the following statements.

1. The first step in determining whether two expressions are logically equivalent is to do a _____ _____ for the two statements.

2. The second step is to connect the two expressions with the _____ _____ .

3. The third step in determining whether two expressions are logically equivalent is to do a truth table for the _____ statement.

4. When the resulting truth table has all _____ in the final value column of the truth table, the two expressions are shown to be _____ _____.

5. When two statements are logically equivalent, the statement of their equivalence is a _____.

Part II: Use truth tables to determine which of the following pairs of statement forms are logically equivalent.

1. "~q ⊃ ~p" and "~p v q"

2. "~(p • ~q)" and "(p ⊃ q)"

3. "~p • q" and "p v ~q"

4. "(~p v ~q)" and "~(p • q)"

5. "p" and "~ ~p"

6. "p ⊃ q" and "p v ~q"

7. "p ≡ q" and "(~p • ~q) v (p • q)"

8. "(p • q) v (r • p)" and "p • (q v r)"

9. "(p ⊃ q) v r" and "(p v q) ⊃ r"

10. "~(p • q)" and "~p v q"

VALIDITY

Truth tables provide us with a method for testing the validity of arguments composed of truth functional statements. The rationale for the method is quite simple. As you will recall, a *valid argument* cannot have true premises and a false conclusion. Since a truth table provides every possible combination of truth and falsity that can hold for a given statement, the truth table tells us under every conceivable circumstance when a statement will be true or false. If we do a truth table for each statement in an argument and there are no cases in which all the statements serving as premises are true and the statement serving as the conclusion false, we will know that the argument is *valid*. However, if there is even a single case of all true premises and a false conclusion, then the argument is *invalid*.

Consider the following argument:

If I get the job, I will buy a new car. I got the job. Therefore, I will buy a new car.

We must first translate the argument into its symbolic form. Using "p" for "I get the job" and "q" for "I will buy a new car," the argument is symbolized as follows:

p ⊃ q
p
∴ q

Once the argument is translated, we then do a truth table for the two statements functioning as the premises and the statement functioning as the conclusion.

		1	2	C
p	q	p ⊃ q	p	q
T	T	T	T	T
T	F	F	T	F
F	T	T	F	T
F	F	T	F	F

The truth table shows that this argument is *valid*. If you look at the columns that represent the two premises, "p ⊃ q" and "p," you will see that both premises are true only in the first row. Notice, that in row one, the conclusion, "q," is also true. There are no instances, then, in which both of the premises are true and the conclusion is false. Since the truth table represents every possible combination of truth and falsity for each of the statements making up the argument, we have shown that it is impossible for the premises to be true and the conclusion false. It follows, therefore, that the argument is valid.

When we use truth tables to determine the validity or invalidity of arguments, what we are looking for is a single instance in which all of the premises are true and the conclusion false. If we find such an instance, the argument is invalid. If there is no case in which all of the premises are true and the conclusion false, then the argument is valid.

Here is an example of another argument:

Either you will win the game or you won't qualify for the tournament. You will win the game. Therefore, you will qualify for the tournament.

This argument can be translated as follows:

p v ~q
p
∴ q

We can now do a truth table to determine if the argument is valid. Remember we are looking for the possibility of all true premises and a false conclusion.

		1	**2**	**C**
p	q	p v ~q	p	q
T	T	T	T	T
T	**F**	**T**	**T**	**F**
F	T	F	F	T
F	F	T	F	F

If you look at the second row of this truth table, shown above in bold type, you will see that both of the premises are true and that the conclusion is false. Since it is impossible for a valid argument to have true premises and a false conclusion, the truth table shows that this argument is *invalid*.

We can now summarize our procedure for using truth tables to test arguments for validity:

1. Translate all the statements of the argument into symbolic notation.

2. Construct a truth table representing each statement in the argument.

3. Examine each row of the truth table to determine if there is a row in which all the premises are true and the conclusion false.

4. If there is a row in which all the premises are true and the conclusion is false, then the argument is *invalid*.

5. If there is no row in which all of the premises are true and the conclusion is false, the argument is *valid*.

Here is one final example:

I will go to the game if I finish my homework and do my chores. So, I will be going to the game, since I finished my homework and chores.

First, to translate the statements into symbolic notation, we must assign statement letters to each of the simple statements in the order in which they occur in English. Thus, "p" will stand for "I will go to the game" and "q" for "I finished my homework" and "r" for "I do my chores."

The first statement will be translated: "(q • r) ⊃ p." Because the "if" is in the middle of the statement, "I finish my homework and do my chores," it must be placed in the antecedent position. The second part of the statement, "I will be going to the game," is translated as "p." The last statement, "I finished my homework and chores," is translated "q • r."

There is one further thing to notice about our example. The second statement, "I will go to the game," is the conclusion of the argument. In this case the word, "so" indicates that it is the conclusion. Our final translation, then, is:

(q • r) ⊃ p
q • r
∴ p

We are now ready to test the argument for validity. Again, we will do a truth table for each statement of the argument and then examine the table to see if there is any case in which all of the premises are true and the conclusion is false. If there is such a case, the argument will be invalid. If no instance of true premises and a false conclusion occurs, then the argument is valid. Here is the truth table for the argument:

			1	2	C
p	q	r	(q • r) ⊃ p	q • r	p
T	T	T	T	T	T
T	T	F	T	F	T
T	F	T	T	F	T
T	F	F	T	F	T
F	T	T	F	T	F
F	T	F	T	F	F
F	F	T	T	F	F
F	F	F	T	F	F

When you examine this truth table, you will see that there are no cases in which all the premises are true and the conclusion is false. That tells us that this is a valid argument. Since the validity of an argument is determined by its form, any other argument sharing this form will also be valid.

By applying the techniques developed in this chapter, you should be able to test any argument composed of truth functional statements for validity.

Exercises

Part I: Complete the following statements:

1. When an argument is valid, it is impossible for there to be true premises and a _____ conclusion.

2. If a truth table has no row in which all the premises are true and the conclusion is false, then the argument is _____.

3. A truth table shows an argument to be invalid if there is even one case of all true premises and a _____ conclusion.

4. An argument form containing two statement variables requires a truth table having _____ rows.

5. An argument form containing four statement variables requires a truth table having _____ rows.

Part II: Use truth tables to determine the validity or invalidity of each of the following argument forms.

1. p v q
   ~q
   ∴ p

2. ~q ⊃ ~p
   p
   ∴ q

3. p ⊃ q
   ~p
   ∴ ~q

4. ~p v q
   q
   ∴ p

5. p • q
   ∴ p

6. p ⊃ q
   q
   ∴ p

7. (p ≡ q) v r
   ~r
   ∴ p ≡ q

8. (~p v q) ⊃ (q v r)
   ~(~p v q)
   ∴ ~(q v r)

9. p ⊃ q
   q ⊃ r
   ∴ p ⊃ s

10. (p • q) ⊃ (r • s)
    p v ~r
    r ≡ q
    ∴ p v s

Part III: Translate the following arguments into symbolic notation. Then use truth tables to test each argument for validity.

1. I will pass this course if and only if I study hard. Therefore, If I don't study hard, I won't pass this course.

2. We can go fishing today only if the fog lifts. The fog has lifted. It follows that we can go fishing today.

3. If I get the call, then I will get the job. If I get the job, I will get the car. Hence, I will get the car if I get the call.

4. Either she got the call and is not interested or she didn't get the call. She is not interested. So, she must have gotten the call.

5. You will win the lottery if and only if you enter. You entered. Therefore, you won.

6. It's false that he was both too busy and too tired to come. We know he wasn't too tired. Hence, he must have been too busy.

7. Either Ted is in love with Ellen or he is simply having a bad day. If Ted is in love with Ellen, then he will want to see her. So, either Ted is having a bad day or he will want to see Ellen.

8. Laura is a judge. For, Laura is a judge only if she is a lawyer. But she is a lawyer unless she is a doctor. And we know that she isn't a doctor.

9. Bill will either be here or at the office. If he is at the office, he will call us. So, provided he calls us, he is at the office.

10. Either the Mayor must resign or face criminal charges for his conduct. He will not go to jail only if he does not face criminal charges. Therefore, either he must resign or he will go to jail.

11. Susan will run for office if and only if student council approves. Student council will approve unless there is a conflict of interest. Thus, Susan will not run for office if there is a conflict of interest.

12. If Tom invests in bonds, then if interest rates rise, he will lose money. Interest rates are going to rise. Hence, Tom will lose money if he invests in bonds.

13. Life is worth living, provided life has a meaning, or you are having fun. So, life has a meaning only if life is worth living.

14. Either he was in the room at the time or someone else committed the murder. He was in the room at the time only if he is capable of running very fast. He is not a fast runner. Therefore, someone else committed the murder.

15. Susan will run for office if she gets the endorsement, provided that she is still interested. It follows that she didn't get the endorsement. After all, she is still interested even though she didn't run.

CHAPTER TWENTY

QUANTIFICATION THEORY

This chapter introduces the *language* and the *symbols* of elementary *quantification theory*. One purpose of this chapter is for you to learn how to translate English statements into the symbols used in quantification theory. You will also learn how some quantified statements are logically related to others on the square of opposition.

The techniques employed in propositional logic have allowed us to deal with arguments employing truth functional statements. However, propositional logic does not allow us to evaluate arguments that do not employ truth-functional statements. To illustrate this, consider the following argument:

> All mammals are warm blooded animals.
> <u>All whales are mammals.</u>
> ∴ All whales are warm blooded animals.

Using the technique of Venn Diagrams from categorical logic, we can show that this is a *valid* argument:

> All M is P.
> <u>All S is M.</u>
> ∴ All S is P.

However, if we symbolize this argument using the methods of propositional logic, it appears to be *invalid*. For example, we can assign the variable "p" to the first statement, the variable "q" to the second premise and "r" to the conclusion. The argument would then be symbolized:

> p
> q
> ∴r

A truth table for this argument form is obviously going to show it to be invalid, while we can demonstrate that the original argument is valid. It is clear, then, that the traditional sort of propositional translation does not capture the form of the argument. Since the whole point of symbolizing arguments is to represent their form correctly, it should be obvious, therefore, that the techniques of propositional logic are not applicable to this kind of argument.

The problem in translating arguments composed of statements that are not truth functional into the symbolism of propositional logic, arises from the fact that the form of this argument does not depend upon the manner in which the simple statements are arranged. Here the form depends upon a different kind of logical structure. As we have seen, that structure can be captured in the **A**, **E**, **I**, and **O** statements of categorical logic.

The method of symbolism, called quantification, that we are going to introduce in this chapter, will handle not only the propositions of categorical logic, but will also allow us to handle a wide variety of additional types of statements as well. It is therefore a much more powerful and flexible method of symbolization than that employed in categorical logic. We will begin our introduction to quantificational logic with what are called *singular statements*.

SINGULAR STATEMENTS

Consider the following statement: "Jim is an athlete." This is called a *singular statement*. It asserts that Jim has the *property* or *attribute* of being an athlete. Because it asserts that Jim has a certain property, in this case the quality of being an athlete, it is an *affirmative* singular statement. There are also *negative* singular statements. For example, "Jim is not an athlete," denies that Jim has the property or attribute of being an athlete.

In *singular affirmative statements*, the subject term refers to an individual thing while the predicate term refers to some characteristic or attribute that the individual thing possesses. In *singular negative statements*, the subject term refers to an individual thing and the predicate term refers to some attribute that the individual thing does not possess. Here are examples of affirmative and negative singular statements:

Bob is a graduate student.

Donna is a professor.

Henry is not a cat.

Because singular statements refer to individual things and their properties, we will introduce two sorts of symbols:

1. Lowercase letters, a-w, to stand for individual things.

2. Uppercase letters, A-Z, to stand for properties or attributes.

When symbolizing singular statements, we will place the uppercase letter representing a property first and the lowercase letter representing an individual thing after the property letter. For example, to symbolize "Jim is an athlete" we write:

Aj

Here are some other examples of *affirmative singular statements* and their translations:

Bill is a teaching assistant: Tb

Donna is a professor: Pd

Kant is a philosopher: Pk

Tampa is warm: Wt

A *negative singular statement* such as "Jim is not an athlete" is symbolized:

~Aj

It should be noted that the lowercase letters denoting individuals will be regarded as *constants*. Within a given context each lowercase letter will be used to stand for a particular individual or thing each time it is used in that context. So, for example, within the context of the argument, "All athletes are fit, Jim is an athlete, so Jim is fit" the letter "j" will refer to the same individual, Jim, throughout the argument. Thus "j" functions as a *constant*.

A single individual can possess several properties. For example, we might say that Sue has the property of being a civil engineer (Cs), a mother

(Ms), a volunteer (Vs), etc. On the other hand, several individuals can share the same property. For example, three different people might share the common property of being married: Bob is married (Mb), Joan is married (Mj), and Paul is married (Mp).

This distinction can be set out as follows:

Same Individual, Different Properties

Sue is a civil engineer.   Cs

Sue is a mother.   Ms

Sue is a wife.   W s

Different Individuals, Same Property

Bob is married.   Mb

Joan is married.   Mj

Paul is married.   Mp

Exercises

Part I: Complete the following statements.

1. A statement that attributes a specific property to an individual or thing, is called a _____ _____ _____.

2. A statement that denies a specific property to an individual or thing, is called a _____ _____ _____.

3. A singular statement attributes a specific _____ to a single individual or object.

4. In a singular statement the lowercase letters a - w are used to stand for _____.

5. In a singular statement the uppercase letters A - Z are used to stand for _____.

Part II: Symbolize each of the following singular statements.

1. Don is tired.   _____

2. Robert is not hungry.   _____

3. Kentucky is hilly.   _____

4. Cindy is not lazy.   _____

5. Cathy is the president of the student body.   _____

VARIABLES AND PROPOSITIONAL FUNCTIONS

As we have seen, the same property can be shared by several individuals. We can capture this notion in our symbolization. To do this, we write a capital letter "M" standing here for the property of being married, and a small letter "x," or "Mx." In "Mx," the small letter "x" is an *individual variable.* It does not refer to any *particular* thing, person, or individual. In "Mx," "x" is a place holder that can be replaced by a *constant*, such as "b" or "j," that stands for a particular individual.

The distinction between variables and constants is extremely important. Constants are used to make statements. Thus, "Mb," "Mj," and "Mp" are all either true or false, since they assert that a particular individual has the property of being married. On the other hand, "Mx" does not symbolize a statement. So it is neither true nor false. The symbolization, "Mx," is called a *propositional function*. A propositional function can *become* a statement when its variable "x," is replaced by a constant.

Specifically, the propositional function, "Mx," becomes a statement when we replace the variable "x" with a constant referring to an individual person or thing. For example, if we replace the variable "x" with the letter "j" referring to Joe, we get the singular statement, "Mj," which symbolizes "Joe is married." Unlike the propositional function, "Mx," "Mj" is a statement and is, therefore, either true or false.

QUANTIFIERS

We have now learned how to translate singular statements like "Larry is angry." There are also general statements like "Everything is broken" and "Something is rotten." Neither of these statements makes a reference to a particular individual thing or object. However, in these statements, properties are seemingly attributed to "everything" and to "something."

Translating general statements requires us to *quantify* the thing or things we are referring to. This allows us to specify whether we are talking about *all* things possessing a particular property or only *some* things that possess a particular property. We can represent this distinction by employing two different types of quantifiers: a *universal quantifier* and an *existential quantifier*. We will begin with the universal quantifier used to symbolize general universal statements.

UNIVERSAL QUANTIFICATION

It will be helpful to begin our discussion of universal quantification with an example. Consider the statement:

Everything is broken.

This, obviously, is a *universal* statement, since it claims that *everything* is broken. Notice that it does not refer to any individual thing. To translate this, we first introduce the *universal quantifier*, "(x)." This is read, "for any x," "for all x," or "given any x." We already know how to represent attributes with capital letters. As we have seen, the attribute "broken" can be represented by the letter "B." Since the statement is not referring to any individual, we will use the variable, "x," rather than a letter representing a constant. Therefore, we can symbolize "Everything is broken" as follows:

(x) Bx

This can be read, "For all x, Bx." Since we know in this case that "Bx" stands for "x is broken," we can read "(x) Bx" as "For all x, x is broken" or, of course, "Everything is broken."

EXISTENTIAL QUANTIFICATION

Now consider the general statement:

> Something is rotten.

Notice that this says that *some* things are rotten or *at least one* thing is rotten. It is, therefore a *particular* statement. It is also a general statement since it does not refer to any individual thing. To translate this statement, we introduce the *existential quantifier*, "(∃x)." The existential quantifier is read, "there exists an x." In this case, we will use the capital letter, "R," to stand for the property of being "rotten," and since we are not referring to any individual, we will use the variable, "x," rather than a constant. We can symbolize "Something is rotten" as follows:

> (∃x) Rx

This is read, "There exists an x, Rx." Since "Rx" stands for "x is rotten," we can read "(∃x) Rx" as "There exists an x, such that x is rotten."

Since "(x) Bx" is the translation of "Everything is broken," "(x) Bx" is a statement and is, therefore, either true or false. Similarly, "(∃x) Rx," which translates, "Something is rotten," is a statement and is, therefore, either true or false.

This means that there are two different ways in which a propositional function such as "Hx" or "Gx," can become statements. The first is by replacing the variable of a propositional function with a constant. For example, the propositional function "Hx," where "H" refers to the attribute "happy," becomes a statement if we replace the "x" with a constant representing an individual, say George. This gives us, "Hg," which translates, "George is happy." "Hg" is, accordingly, either true or false. The process of replacing a variable of a propositional function with a constant, is called *instantiation*.

The second method is called *generalization*. It occurs when a quantifier, "(x)" or "(∃x)," is placed before a propositional function. Consider, for example, the propositional function "Gx," where "G" stands for the property of being good. If we quantify it by placing the universal quantifier, "(x)," before it we get the statement, "(x) Gx" which stands for "Everything is good." If we quantify it by placing the existential quantifier,

"(∃x)," before it we get the statement, "(∃x) Gx," which translates, "Something is good."

Although we have been concentrating on affirmative general statements, the method of generalization also holds true for negative general statements. For example:

"Nothing is working" is symbolized: (x) ~Wx.

"Something is not working" is symbolized: (∃x) ~Wx.

We have introduced the four sorts of general statements, universal affirmative, universal negative, particular affirmative and particular negative, and how to symbolize them. As a result, we can now set up a square of opposition for the four general sorts of statements. In order to make the square of opposition perfectly general, we will use the Greek letter, "Φ," to stand for *any* property whatsoever.

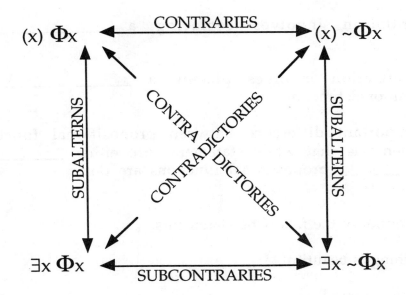

These four general statements have the same logical relations that hold for categorical statements on the Aristotelian square of opposition. The universal affirmative statement is the contradictory of the particular negative statement. Similarly, the universal negative statement is the contradictory of the particular affirmative statement. The universal affirmative and universal negative statements are contraries and the particular affirmative and particular negative statements are subcontraries. The subaltern relation holds between the universal affirmative and particular affirmative statements and between the universal negative and particular negative statements. For more information regarding the significance of these logical relations, see Chapter Eight.

Exercises

Part I: Complete the following statements.

1. Because they are not statements, propositional functions are neither _____ nor _____.

2. The two methods by which propositional functions can become statements are called _____ and _____.

3. Instantiation involves replacing a _____ with a _____ .

4. Generalization involves placing a _____ before a propositional function.

5. An important difference between propositional functions and statements is that while statements are either _____ or _____, propositional functions are not.

Part II: Symbolize the following statements.

1. Everything is beautiful.

2. Nothing is sacred.

3. Something is fishy.

4. Something is not right.

5. Carol is an accountant.

6. Nothing matters.

7. Sue is not at home.

8. Everything is relative.

9. Something is not material.

10. Something is good.

SYMBOLIZING CATEGORICAL STATEMENTS

Although the four types of general statements can be represented on a square of opposition, they are not exactly like the statements of categorical logic. Unlike the general statements we have learned to symbolize so far, categorical statements make reference to two classes. However, categorical statements can be translated into the symbolic notation of quantification theory. Consider the following **A** form categorical statement:

All horse races are rigged events.

In translating categorical statements into quantificational logic, it is important to note that we will be using the *Boolean* interpretation of categorical statements. According to the Boolean interpretation, "All horse races are rigged events," says:

If there are any horse races, then they are rigged events.

In other words, a universal affirmative statement, on the Boolean interpretation, is equivalent to a *conditional* statement. To capture the universal character of the statement, we will use the universal quantifier, "(x)." We will use "Hx" to stand for "horse races" and "Rx" to stand for "rigged event." Building on what we have learned in translating general statements, our translation of "All horse races are rigged events," will be:

$(x) (Hx \supset Rx)$

This can be read, "For all x, if it is a horse race, then it is a rigged event." Suppose our statement, however, is the **E** form categorical statement:

No horse races are rigged events.

On the Boolean interpretation, this says, "If there are any horse races, then they are not rigged events." The translation for this statement is:

(x) (Hx ⊃ ~Rx)

The translation can be read: "For all x, if it is a horse race, then it is not a rigged event."

Particular affirmative, or **I** form statements, and particular negative, or **O** form statements, can also be translated. For example:

Some politicians are lawyers.

This **I** form statement says, "There exists at least one politician who is a lawyer." Since it is a particular statement, we will use the existential quantifier. Using "Px" to stand for "politicians" and "Lx" to stand for "lawyers," the statement is translated:

(∃x) (Px • Lx)

This is read: "There exists an x, such that it is a politician and a lawyer." However, suppose that our statement is:

Some politicians are not lawyers.

Since this is a particular negative statement, or **O** form statement, it will be translated as follows:

(∃x) (Px • ~Lx)

This can be read: "There exists an x, such that it is a politician and not a lawyer." Here is a summary of the translations for **A**, **E**, **I** and **O** form statements:

Statement	Translation
A: All horse races are rigged events.	(x) (Hx ⊃ Rx)
E: No horse races are rigged events.	(x) (Hx ⊃ ~Rx)
I: Some horse races are rigged events.	(∃x) (Hx • Rx)
O: Some horse races are not rigged events.	(∃x) (Hx • ~Rx)

Using the Greek letters, "Φ" and, "Ψ," to stand for *any* properties whatever, we can then construct the following Boolean square of opposition. Since the symbolized **A** and **E** statements in our square of opposition reflect the Boolean interpretation, the only logical relation that holds is the contradictory relationship between **A** and **O**, and **E** and **I**, statements. The Boolean square of opposition appears below.

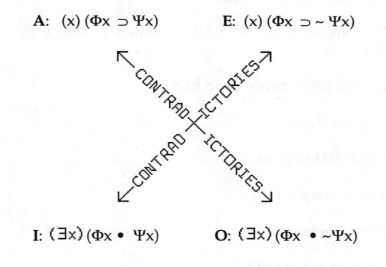

A: (x) (Φx ⊃ Ψx)   **E**: (x) (Φx ⊃ ~ Ψx)

I: (∃x) (Φx • Ψx)   **O**: (∃x) (Φx • ~Ψx)

Exercises

Part I: Translate the following statements into the symbolic notation of quantification theory.

1.   All sparrows are birds.

2. Some cars are limousines.

3. No judges are criminals

4. Some birds are singers.

5. Not all cars are diesels.

6. Some baseball players are athletes.

7. Every physical object is extended in space.

8. Not every law is just.

9. No things that swim are things that fly.

10. A few laws are unconstitutional.

Part II: Below are several sorts of statements. Select the appropriate translation for each.

1. Some baseball pitchers are good hitters.

2. Everything is great.

3. Socrates is a philosopher.

4. Something is wrong.

5. Nothing is forever.

6. All that glitters is not gold.

7. Susan is a lawyer.

8. Some dogs are animals with fleas.

9. Pat is not a doctor.

10. Not all Christians are saints.

11. Arizona is not cold.

12. California is shaky.

13. Nothing was lost.

14. Some politicians are conservatives.

15. Tigers have stripes.

16. Only freshmen are eligible.

17. Bob is a fisherman.

18. None but the good die young.

19. Something is not on sale.

20. All basketball players are athletes.

CHAPTER TWENTY-ONE

EVALUATING INDUCTIVE ARGUMENTS

In our discussions of categorical and propositional logic, we have been concerned with deductive arguments. Deductive arguments, it will be recalled, are arguments that make the claim that if their premises are true, then their conclusions must be true as well. In other words they claim that their premises imply or entail their conclusions.

Not all deductive arguments satisfy this claim. Deductive arguments whose premises fail to imply or entail their conclusions, as we have seen, are called invalid. Some deductive arguments do satisfy this claim. Deductive arguments whose premises do imply or entail their conclusions are called *valid*. A valid deductive argument having all true premises must have a true conclusion as well. Such arguments are called *sound*.

In Chapter Five we introduced what are known as inductive arguments. Inductive arguments do not make the claim, either explicitly or implicitly, that their conclusions follow with necessity from their premises. In other words, they do not claim that their premises imply or entail their conclusions. Inductive arguments make a more modest claim for themselves. **An inductive argument claims that its premises strongly support its conclusion or make its conclusion probably true.** In fact, an argument is considered an inductive argument precisely because it claims that the truth of its premises makes its conclusion probably true.

It is the nature of inductive arguments that they make assertions in their conclusions that go beyond anything their premises can guarantee. With an inductive argument, it is never the case that if its premises are true, then its conclusion *must* be true. In other words, no inductive argument is ever valid. So, with inductive reasoning, regardless of how careful we are, our conclusions can never follow from our premises with certainty.

Since no inductive argument is ever valid, it might be tempting to draw the conclusion that all inductive arguments are invalid and are, therefore, worthless. Drawing such a conclusion, however, would be a mistake. Although inductive arguments can never establish the truth of their conclusions with necessity, they can render the truth of their conclusions *highly probable*. As we shall see, arguments capable of establishing their conclusions with high probability are extremely important for our everyday reasoning.

Even though inductive arguments are never valid, they can be evaluated as good or bad. Whether an inductive argument is a good or bad argument must be determined in light of the claim that all inductive arguments make for themselves. Because inductive arguments claim that their premises *strongly support* their conclusions or make them *highly probable*, we must assess inductive arguments in terms of this claim. Since inductive arguments do not claim that their premises imply or entail their conclusions, it is inappropriate to call them either valid or invalid. If the premises of an inductive argument succeed in making its conclusion highly probable, then it is a good inductive argument. On the other hand, if the premises of an inductive argument fail to make the truth of its conclusion highly probable, then it does not live up to its claim and is, therefore, not a good inductive argument. So, just as we evaluate deductive arguments in light of the claims they make for themselves, we do the same with inductive arguments.

There are two factors that together determine whether an inductive argument succeeds in making its conclusion highly probable. The first concerns the strength of the connection between the premises and the conclusion. This can be determined by asking, "If the premises of the argument were true, would they make the conclusion probably true?" We are raising here the question of *logical correctness* which concerns the logical connection between the premises and the conclusion. You may recall from our earlier discussion of inductive arguments that we use the term *justified* for logically correct inductive arguments. The second factor concerns the question of whether the premises are true. If all the premises of an inductive argument are true and the logical connection between the premises and the conclusion is such that the premises strongly support the conclusion, then it is a *sound* inductive argument. Therefore, **a sound inductive argument is one that is both justified and has all true premises.** A sound inductive argument succeeds in making its conclusion highly probable.

One reason it is important to study inductive arguments is because so many of our everyday beliefs about the world are based on inductive reasoning. Basic beliefs, from "The sun will rise tomorrow," or "Drinking water will quench one's thirst," to more specific beliefs about which brand of car is likely to be more reliable, rest upon the foundation of inductive reasoning. The same is true of many of our most sophisticated scientific views.

Some of our beliefs about the world may be based on justified inductive arguments and some on unjustified ones. But given that so many of our beliefs rest upon inductive reasoning, the ability to distinguish justified from unjustified inductive arguments is obviously important. That's why we want to study inductive arguments.

TYPES OF INDUCTIVE ARGUMENTS

There are several types of inductive arguments. One important type, that is frequently encountered, is known as *Inductive Generalization*. Here is an example:

> I have observed hundreds of swans and each one has been white. I conclude, therefore, that, probably, all swans are white.

Notice that the premise of my argument refers to *observed* instances of swans and notes some characteristic true of each observed instance. My conclusion, however, is about *all* swans. So, on the basis of what I have observed, I have *generalized* about the entire class of swans. You should note that the conclusion claims that all swans are white; it is not simply about the particular swans I have observed. In other words, I have *generalized* from the swans I have observed, to a claim about all swans. That explains the term "inductive generalization."

Since the conclusion of my argument goes well beyond anything that can be guaranteed by my premise, even if my premise is true my conclusion could still be false. All inductive arguments share this limitation. By carefully considering the nature of this argument you should be able to see how it differs from a deductive argument and why the conclusion of an inductive generalization can never be established with more than probability.

In the above example we generalized from a premise that talked about observed instances to a conclusion about all instances of a given class. Inductive generalizations, however, need not talk about all the members of a class. Consider the following inductive argument:

> In a recent survey, 61% of those contacted favor raising taxes to provide for improved education. Therefore, 61% of the people favor raising taxes to improve education.

The sort of reasoning contained in the above example is one that we often confront as we read the newspaper or watch the news on television. The inductive reasoning used in public opinion polls is an example of what is known as *statistical generalization*. In this example, which is typical of such arguments, perhaps a few thousand people are asked their opinions concerning the issue of raising taxes to improve the quality of education. Based on the results of the opinion poll, one generalizes to a conclusion about the percentage of people who favor raising taxes for the purpose of improving education.

Again, notice that the claim made in the conclusion, that 61% of the people favor raising taxes to improve the quality of education, goes beyond anything that the premise can guarantee. The conclusion generalizes from what we know about the people surveyed to a conclusion about a percentage of all the people in the country. Therefore, even if the premise is true and even if the argument is justified, the conclusion could still be false. This, as we have seen, is the case with any inductive argument. Inductive arguments do not establish their conclusions with necessity. Whether this is a good inductive argument depends, then, on whether the argument makes its conclusion highly probable, rather than on whether it establishes its conclusion with necessity.

INDUCTIVE ANALOGY

One of the most important types of inductive reasoning is known as analogical reasoning or *argument by analogy*. Many of our common beliefs about the world are based on analogical reasoning. For example, suppose that you have eaten lunch at a certain local restaurant several times and in each case the food and service have been outstanding. Thus, you reason that the next time you eat at that restaurant the food will probably be good. Or you might infer that a snowball will be cold to the touch, since other snowballs you have touched have felt cold.

In these cases you are reasoning from some *analogy* or *similarity* between an observed instance to a conclusion about a future or unobserved instance. Here is an example of such an argument:

> The snowball I see now is similar to those I have seen in the past.
> <u>Snowballs I have touched in the past have felt cold.</u>
> ∴ If I touch this snowball, it will feel cold.

In this example I am reasoning that because the snowballs I have touched in the past have all been cold, the snowball I am about to touch will also feel cold. But how can I justify my conclusion? The conclusion is justified by appealing to the *analogy* or *similarity* between observed instances of snowballs (snowballs I have touched) and the future or unobserved instance (the snowball I am about to touch). Since the snowball I am about to touch is *similar* in all observed respects (white, round, etc.) to those I have already touched, I conclude that they will be similar in one additional respect: the snowball I am about to touch will also feel cold.

Although this example of an analogical argument is relatively simple, it does adequately illustrate the basic nature of arguments from analogy. Let us now look at an example that is somewhat more complex.

Suppose over the past few years I have taken my car into Goren's Auto Repair for service three times. All three times, the repairs have been of a minor nature and they have all involved the car's engine. Each time the quality of the repair was good. Now, my car needs to be repaired again. I reason that if I take my car into Goren's for repair then most likely the quality of the repair will be good.

My argument has the following form:

> Instances 1, 2 3 and 4 share properties P through R.
> <u>Instances 1, 2 and 3 also have property S.</u>
> ∴ Instance 4 will probably have property S.

The first line of the schema points out that the three auto repairs I have had done (1, 2, 3 and the one I intend to have done, instance 4, share certain properties. All three repairs were done by Goren's Auto Repair, the repairs were of a minor nature and all were performed on the car's engine (properties P through R). The schema's second line calls attention to the fact that in each of the three past instances the quality of the repair was good (characteristic S). The third line, which represents the argument's conclusion, asserts that the quality of the repair I am now concerned with will probably be good (4 probably will have characteristic S).

The argument rests on the similarities or analogies between the past instances of auto repair and the future one that I now contemplate. Since the past cases of auto repair and the future one share these properties, I reason that they will probably share an additional property as well. That is, that the quality of the repair will be good.

The question now arises: "How strong is this argument?" Well, the above argument, it seems to me, is pretty good. However, it might turn out that when I take my car into Goren's Auto Repair the quality of the repair will not be good. This doesn't necessarily mean that the argument is not a good one. As we have seen, with any inductive argument it is always possible for the premises to be true and the conclusion false.

CRITERIA FOR EVALUATING ANALOGICAL ARGUMENTS

To adequately assess analogical arguments we need to be aware of several criteria that are relevant to the strength of such arguments. Rather than relying on a simple intuitive estimate of an argument's strength, we may consider the following six points:

1. Number of Instances

In general, the more instances we have as evidence to reason from, the stronger the argument. After all, in the above argument we are reasoning from observed instances, the times I have taken my car to Goren's Auto Repair in the past, to a conclusion about the likely result of a future visit. Obviously, if I had taken my car to Goren's ten times and in every case the quality of repair performed on my car was good, my argument about the likely outcome of my future visit is strengthened. That is, I now have better grounds for believing that the conclusion of my argument will be true, because the increased number of instances makes it more likely that my experience at Goren's is typical of the work they do. Therefore, increasing the number of instances makes my argument stronger. Since this is an inductive argument, clearly, my conclusion could still be false. This would be true even if I had taken my car to Goren's fifty times and in each case the quality of the repair had been good. Nevertheless, the general point still holds. The *more* instances we have to reason from, the *stronger* is our argument.

But suppose that I had taken my car to Goren's only once rather than three times. Although the quality of the repairs made on my car was good, the argument would now be *weaker*. The reason is that I am now reasoning from *fewer* instances and, therefore, I have less reason to believe that my experience with Goren's Auto Repair is typical of the other repairs they perform. This provides me with weaker grounds for believing that the future repair will also be good. So, in general we can say that the *fewer* number of observed instances we are reasoning from, the *weaker* our argument will be. Conversely, the *greater* the number of observed instances, the *stronger* our argument will be.

2. Number of Similarities

The more similarities that hold between the past or observed instances from which I am reasoning, and the future instance I am reasoning about, the stronger the argument will be. Imagine, for example, that the past repairs have not only been at Goren's, all minor and on the engine, but also that all were on a specific part of the engine, the valves. Suppose also that the repair I am going to have done at Goren's is also minor and has to do with a specific part of the engine, the valves. These modifications to our original example will make the argument *stronger,* since there are more points of analogy or similarity between the past repairs and the one I am now considering. I now have a stronger argument for my conclusion that the quality of repair is likely to be good.

It will also be true that if there are *fewer* points of analogy or similarity between past cases and the future case I am reasoning about, my argument will be *weaker.* If, for instance, I only know that my car requires repairs, but I don't know whether they are minor or major, nor whether they concern the engine or transmission, then I have less reason to think my conclusion will be true. The reason my argument is weaker is that there are fewer points of similarity or analogy between the past cases I am reasoning from and the future case I am reasoning about.

So, in summary, the *greater* the number of similarities between past instances I am reasoning from and the future instance I am reasoning to, the *stronger* my argument will be. Conversely, the *fewer* the similarities between the past instances and the future instance, the *weaker* my argument will be.

3. Strength of the Conclusion

The strength of any analogical argument rests upon the evidence contained in the premises when compared to the nature of the claim made in the conclusion. The *stronger* or *more sweeping* the claim made in the conclusion, the *weaker* or *less probable* the argument will be. On the other hand, if the conclusion makes a *weaker* or less sweeping claim, the argument will be *more probable.*

Notice that my conclusion in the original argument is that the quality of the repairs to be made at Goren's Auto Repair will probably be *good*. Suppose, instead, that my conclusion is that the repairs will be of *excellent* quality. Now, since my conclusion makes a stronger claim, it is less likely to be true. However, if I inferred that the quality of the repairs would be only fair, then my conclusion is more likely to be true than the conclusion of the original argument. This is because the sort of claim being made by the conclusion is more easily supported.

We can understand why this is so if we think of the conclusion of an argument as something the premises have to support. If we make the conclusion more weighty or heavy, it is more difficult for the premises to support it. The argument is, consequently, less probable. On the other hand, if we make a less sweeping or lighter claim in the conclusion, it is easier for the premises to support it. Hence, the argument is more probable, that is, it is more likely that the conclusion will be true.

The general principle is, therefore, that the *stronger* the claim made in the conclusion, the *less likely* it is that the conclusion will be true, and thus, the argument is less probable or weaker. Conversely, the *weaker* the claim being made in the conclusion, the *more likely* it is that the conclusion will be true, and therefore, the argument will be more probable or stronger.

4. Disanalogies Between Observed and Unobserved Instances

Another factor affecting the strength of an analogical argument concerns the number of *disanalogies* or *differences* between the instances referred to in the premises and the instance I am reasoning about referred to in the conclusion. Imagine that as I drive my car the engine seems to explode and the car will not run at all. I am told by the head mechanic at Goren's that my car will require major repair. Since, in the past all the repairs at Goren's were minor in nature, this is a significant *disanalogy* between the past instances and the future instance I am reasoning about. All of my evidence about the quality of auto repairs at Goren's is based on my experience with minor repairs. Thus, the conclusion of my argument is less probable than the conclusion of the original argument. This is because of the *disanalogy* or *dissimilarity* between the past cases I am reasoning from and the future case I am reasoning about.

Arguments from analogy rest upon the respects in which there are similarities or analogies between the observed instances and the instance I am reasoning about. Thus, the more *dissimilarities* between the past or observed instances mentioned in the premises, and the future instance mentioned in the conclusion, the *weaker* the argument.

5. Dissimilarities Among Instances in the Premises

We have just seen that dissimilarities holding between instances talked about in the premises and the instance mentioned in the conclusion weakens an analogical argument. However, dissimilarities or disanalogies don't always weaken the argument. If the disanalogy occurs only among the instances mentioned in the premises, the argument will be made stronger.

In the original argument we have been considering, all the repairs made to my car have been minor and all have been performed on the engine. Imagine, however, that in other respects the previous repairs were very different from each other. One repair was on the carburetor, one on the valves and one on the timing belt. Now, despite the variety of repairs done at Goren's, in each case the quality of the repair was good. This dissimilarity or disanalogy holding among instances mentioned in the premises makes my argument stronger.

The explanation is that it is now less likely that the quality of the repairs done at Goren's in the past was because the repairs were done on some aspect of engine repair at which Goren's is particularly adept. If the past repairs were very different from each other, this suggests that Goren's does good work regardless of the nature of the repair. Therefore, I have better grounds for believing the repairs I now contemplate having done at Goren's will be of good quality. Accordingly, the argument is stronger.

In general, then, the more dissimilarities among instances mentioned in the premises, the stronger the argument.

6. Causal Relevance

In the example we have been considering, we have argued on the basis of analogies or similarities between the cases talked about in the premises and the one talked about in the conclusion. That, of course, is what makes an argument analogical. Now we have been making a very important assumption about those similarities. That assumption is that the similarities holding between instances referred to in the premises and the instance mentioned in the conclusion are *causally relevant* to the inference arrived at in the conclusion.

In more concrete terms, the argument we are considering claims that the past three instances of having my car repaired, and the future instance I am now contemplating, have certain properties or characteristics in common. All are at Goren's Auto Repair, all of a minor nature and all on the engine of my car. The analogies or similarities between these past instances and the future instance I am reasoning about, we are assuming, are relevant to the probability of the conclusion being true. The argument asserts that since the past three repairs were of good quality, we have reason for supposing that the repair I am now considering will be of good quality also. In other words, I am arguing that since the past instances share certain properties with the future instance, they will probably share an additional property as well: the quality of repair will be good.

This means that it must be plausible for us to believe that those similarities between the past instances and the future instance play a role in *causing* the property in question. That is, the fact that all the past repairs were done at Goren's, were of a minor nature and all performed on the engine of the car, played a role causing the good quality of the repair. Thus, if the same characteristics are true of the future repair, that gives us some justification for inferring that the future repair will be of good quality as well.

However, if the similarities between the past instances and the future instance are *not* causally relevant to the property I am inferring will be true, then regardless of how many similarities might exist, they would play no role in determining the strength of the argument. Suppose, for example, that the similarities were only that the repairs were done on Wednesday, were done in the same city, and in each case I was promised a loaner car to use while the repairs were being performed. Now since none of these common properties between past and future instances could plausibly be said to causally affect the quality of the repair, they have little or no relevance in determining the quality of the repair. In a word, these similarities would not be relevant.

It follows, therefore, that when assessing arguments from analogy, it is important to look at something more than the number of analogies or similarities holding between instances mentioned in the premises and the instance talked about in the conclusion. These analogies, or similarities, mean little if they do not play a causal role in producing the quality we are interested in.

Exercises

Part I: Several inductive arguments are presented below. Identify them either as inductive generalizations or analogies. Which are good arguments and which are not? Why?

1. Three out of four dentists surveyed who chew Sticky gum, recommend it for their patients who chew gum. Thus, Sticky gum is favored by three out of four dentists.

2. My brother, my sister, my mother and father are all going bald. I conclude that I too will probably go bald.

3. Nearly everyone on my block opposes the new tax levy for our district. It follows that it will be defeated.

4. Judy has written four successful plays. She has just completed her fifth play. I infer that it will probably be successful too.

5. Last week I met one of Bill's friends. He was boring. Today, I met another of Bill's friends. She was boring too. I bet all of his friends are boring.

6. I know three people who smoked all of their lives. Each died from lung cancer. Joe smokes as well. It is likely that he will also die from lung cancer.

7. Every peanut I have tasted has been salty. It seems probable, then, that all peanuts are salty.

8. Since eighty percent of those surveyed favor having prayer in public school, it must be the case that eighty percent are in favor of having it.

9. I have read one textbook and found it fascinating. I think, therefore, that it is probable that all textbooks are fascinating.

10. I have eaten at Joe's diner four times. Each time I had vegetable soup, and it was always delicious. Today, I plan to have the vegetable soup at Joe's again. It is likely that it will be delicious.

Part II: Several analogical arguments are presented below. After the argument is presented, a number of changes are proposed for each argument. Using the criteria for assessing analogical arguments, decide in each case whether the change strengthens or weakens the original argument. Provide a reason for your answer by appealing to the appropriate criterion.

1. Bob has previously gone out on three blind dates arranged by Mike. Bob has enjoyed being with each date. Mike has just arranged another blind date for Bob. Bob anticipates (reasoning by analogy) that he will enjoy being with the new date as well.

   a. Suppose that Bob had previously gone out with five blind dates arranged by Mike, rather than three.

   b. Suppose that Bob infers that he will find the new date highly enjoyable.

   c. Suppose that all three of Bob's past dates were with lawyers and Bob's new date is also with a lawyer.

   d. Suppose that Bob infers that his new date will be at least pleasant, if not enjoyable.

   e. Suppose that one of Bob's dates was with a doctor, another was with a waitress, and that one was with a teacher, but that Bob doesn't know the occupation of his new date.

2. Joan has been attending college for three semesters. She has had difficulties with all of her courses. Next semester she has signed up for English Literature 320. She infers that she will find this course difficult as well.

   a. Suppose that all of Joan's courses have been in the sciences.

   b. Suppose that all of Joan's past courses have been in very different areas and that she doesn't know what her new course is about.

   c. Suppose Joan has been in college for only two semesters.

    d.   Suppose Joan knows that English Literature 320 will be taught by a professor with whom she has already taken two classes.

3.   Bill has read and enjoyed four historical novels of John Jakes, all of which have dealt with American History. Bill has learned that a new novel by John Jakes has just appeared. He infers (reasoning by analogy) that he is likely to enjoy this novel as well.

    a.   Suppose that Jakes' past novels were about many different subjects and that Bill is unsure of the theme of the new novel.

    b.   Suppose Bill learns that the new book is science fiction rather than an historical novel.

    c.   Suppose that Bill has read seven historical novels by Jakes instead of four.

    d.   Suppose that instead of predicting that he will enjoy Jakes' new novel, Bill predicts that he won't be completely bored by it.

    e.   Suppose Bill learns that the new Jakes' novel is also about American History.

4.   Sue has owned three Toyota automobiles. She had driven each about 80,000 miles and all have given good service. Sue is contemplating buying another Toyota and reasons that it will probably provide good service as well.

    a.   Suppose that Sue has owned five Toyotas, instead of three.

    b.   Suppose that one Toyota was a Camry, one a Corolla and one a Tercel. She is unsure which model Toyota she will buy next time.

    c.   Suppose that all of her past Toyotas were red but that this time she intends to buy a silver one.

    d.   Suppose that Sue infers that her new Toyota will give excellent service, instead of just good service.

e.   Suppose that all of her past Toyotas were Camrys and that the new one will also be a Camry.

5.   Lynn has eaten at Founder's three times since arriving on campus. Each time she has had the roast beef with mashed potatoes and gravy. She has enjoyed all of her meals at Founders. Now she intends to have the roast beef with mashed potatoes again. She reasons that she will likely enjoy her meal.

a. Suppose she infers that she will not only enjoy her meal, but that it will be the best meal of her life.

b. Suppose that she decides to have the stir fry, rather than the roast beef and mashed potatoes.

c. Suppose she learns that the same cook prepared the roast beef and mashed potatoes as the other three times.

d. Suppose the silverware and dishes have all been replaced, since her last visit.

e. Suppose that she had eaten here only once before rather than three times.

f. Suppose that instead of having only roast beef in the past that she had enjoyed a variety of dishes on her past three visits.

CHAPTER TWENTY-TWO

FALLACIES

The term "fallacy" is often used to denote a false or mistaken belief. For example, the belief that walking under a ladder brings bad luck, is said to be a "fallacy." In logic, however, the term "fallacy" refers not to false beliefs, but to *mistakes in reasoning*.

Any mistake in reasoning could be called a fallacy. But the term is more appropriately employed for errors in reasoning that have two characteristics. Fallacies are arguments that exhibit common patterns of mistaken reasoning. Moreover, these common types of mistaken arguments are deceptive. That is, they have the ability to deceive us. It is because fallacies have these characteristics--they involve common mistakes in reasoning and they are deceptive--that it is important for us to study them. Consequently, logicians have identified these common patterns of deceptive reasoning and have given them names.

Because fallacies generally have the appearance of being instances of correct reasoning, people are often taken in by them. Since we are interested in improving our reasoning, being aware of such commonly occurring mistakes in reasoning is clearly something worthy of our attention.

In fact, you should be aware that fallacies occur everywhere. They may be encountered in advertising, political speeches, newspaper editorials, conversations among friends and even in textbooks written by professors. Since fallacies occur so frequently in our everyday lives, and they can mislead us about important matters, we need to be aware of them. More specifically, there are at least two reasons for studying fallacies:

1. By being aware of fallacies, we will be less likely to commit them in our own thinking.

2. Studying the fallacies will make it less likely that we will be taken in by them when they occur in the reasoning of others.

There may be other reasons for studying the fallacies. The ancient Greek Sophists claimed to be able to teach their students how to make the weaker argument appear to be the stronger. So, as some of my former students have pointed out, one could use the fallacies to confuse or mislead one's enemies or even one's friends. Or, they could even be used as a weapon against our parents. However, I am confident that you would never think of putting your knowledge to such purposes. In any case, our purpose in studying the fallacies is to sharpen and improve our thinking, not to confuse or mislead others.

THE STRAW PERSON FALLACY

To get an idea of what a fallacy is, it may be helpful to begin by looking at a couple of concrete examples. A very commonly discussed fallacy is known as the "straw man" fallacy. We are revising the name a bit by calling it the "straw person" fallacy.

The general idea of the straw person fallacy involves a situation in which one attacks another person's argument. Now, of course, there is nothing fallacious in attacking another person's argument. However, if as part of one's attack on another's argument, one first misrepresents that argument to make it easier to attack, then one is not really attacking the opponent's argument. Rather than attacking a "real person," one is said to be attacking a "straw person," or knocking over a "straw man."

The straw person fallacy essentially involves attacking a weakened version of an opponent's argument, instead of the opponent's real argument, and then claiming to have refuted the opponent's argument. As we are using the term, the straw person fallacy occurs when:

1. There are several reasons for an opponent's argument.

2. One destroys one of those reasons.

3. One claims that the opponent's argument has been refuted.

As an example of the straw person fallacy, consider the following. Suppose that Jill, in applying to law school, argues that she should be accepted because of her outstanding academic record, her leadership qualities, her strong desire to become a lawyer, and the fact that she is a member of an ethnic minority.

Imagine that the law school admissions personnel, in responding to her application, argue that they are unable to accept her because simply being a member of an ethic minority does not justify admission to law school. Now, clearly, the admissions personnel have badly misrepresented Jill's actual argument. She did not argue that she should be admitted only because she is a member of an ethnic minority. That was but one reason along with several others. Thus, the admissions personnel have not attacked Jill's real argument, but only a much weaker version of it. In short, they have attacked a "straw person" instead of the real thing. Put differently, they have committed the straw person fallacy.

Another example of the straw person fallacy is the following:

> **Teenage Daughter:** "Dad, I really need to have my own car. I need it to go to my job each day, to get to school and go out on dates."

> **Father:** "Sorry, but we can't afford to buy you a car just so you can go out on dates."

In this example, the father has not dealt with his daughter's actual argument, but has attacked a weaker version of her argument. She has provided several reasons designed to establish that she needs a car. Rather than dealing with her argument, her father sets up a much weaker argument to attack. Having, in his mind, demolished that weaker argument, he pretends to have refuted her original argument. In short, he has committed the straw person fallacy.

If you reflect on the nature of the straw person fallacy, as exemplified in the examples provided above, you will probably recognize that it is a very commonly committed logical mistake. Calling it a mistake, however, doesn't mean that it isn't sometimes committed deliberately. One reason it is so tempting to misrepresent an opponent's position is that it makes it easier to refute. Often different people may hold two or more plausible, though, incompatible positions. The arguments for each position may also be plausible. Consequently, it is sometimes difficult to show that your position is right and the other positions are mistaken. It is in such situations that the straw person fallacy is likely to be committed. Since you can't demonstrate that your opponent's argument is wrong, you attack a weakened version of that argument, a straw person, and then claim that you have refuted your opponent's position. But, instead, you have committed the straw person fallacy.

Implicit in the straw person fallacy may be the assumption that if one of one's reasons for a position is inadequate to support that position, then the argument as a whole fails to establish the desired conclusion. But this is clearly a false assumption. Jill's argument, in fact, is a good one. Attacking only one of her reasons for her position does not show that her actual argument has been refuted. Instead, what has been destroyed is a straw person, not Jill's real argument.

THE FALLACY OF MISDIRECTED ARGUMENT

Another common fallacy is known as the Fallacy of Misdirected Argument. Unlike the straw person fallacy, which results from ignoring some of the reasons provided for a conclusion, the Fallacy of Misdirected Argument is the result of altering the conclusion being argued for. More specifically, the Fallacy of Misdirected Argument occurs when one indicates that he or she is arguing for a given conclusion, but in fact argues for a *different* conclusion than the one originally indicated.

Politicians are often masters of this sort of argument. They may be asked about a position they have taken which is unpopular. To avoid talking about that issue, they will instead talk about a related issue on which they hold a more popular view. Here is an example:

> **Reporter:** "Senator, why do you support the housing bill currently being debated in Washington? Even members of your own party admit that paying for the bill will be difficult and the sort of housing provided in the bill will not go to those who really need it."

> **Senator:** "Well, in fact that housing bill is a good one. After all, it is the right of all Americans to have decent housing and participate in the American dream. Every right-thinking politician ought to be in favor of providing good housing for our citizens. Therefore, we should see to it that they get it."

Notice that the Senator is asked why she supports a particular bill designed to provide additional housing, despite its high costs, and the fact that those who will receive the housing are not the most needy. The Senator indicates that she is going to argue that the bill is a good one. But instead she argues only that people have a right to housing and that, therefore, the Congress has an obligation to provide it. The problem is that she said she was going to prove one thing, but ended up arguing for and concluding something different.

This example exhibits the classic pattern of the Fallacy of Misdirected Argument. The person presenting the argument indicates:

1. I'm going to argue for *p* (where *p* is a statement).

2. But the person argues for and concludes something other than *p*.

The Senator says she is going to argue that a particular bill is a good one, *p*, but argues for and concludes that Congress has an obligation to provide housing for its citizens (something other than *p*). Thus, the Senator commits the Fallacy of Misdirected Argument.

Another place in which the Fallacy of Misdirected Argument commonly occurs is in advertising. Consider the following ad.

> Announcing new Torch gasoline with Perk. It is the best gasoline you can buy! Here's why. These two cars are identical in every way, except that car A has Torch with Perk. Car B has the same amount of Torch without Perk. Now in test after test, car A goes farther on a gallon of gas than Car B. Buy new Torch with Perk.

In this ad, the claim is made that Torch is the best gasoline one can buy. Apparently, this is what the ad sets out to prove. But, in fact, it argues for a different conclusion, apparently, that Torch with Perk is better than Torch without Perk. Assuming that the test referred to in the ad was conducted fairly, the ad makes a pretty good case for that conclusion. But one may fail to notice that it does little, if anything, to prove its intended conclusion, that it is the best gasoline one can buy. There are, for example, no comparisons with other brands of gasoline. It's clear, then, that the argument contained in the commercial was not directed to proving the conclusion it was supposed to prove. Therefore, it commits the Fallacy of Misdirected Argument.

It would be a mistake to conclude from our discussion that the Fallacy of Misdirected Argument is committed only by politicians or in commercials. The fallacy occurs in many different contexts. It appears to be motivated by the following consideration: sometimes it is easier to prove a different conclusion from the one originally intended. The temptation is to offer an argument for a slightly different conclusion that is easier to support and then pretend to have established the original conclusion. If someone listening to the argument fails to notice the shift, then that person may go away thinking that the original conclusion has been established. This is clearly what is going on in the gasoline commercial discussed above.

Now that we have looked at a couple of specific fallacies, you should have a better idea of what a fallacy is. In the chapters to come, we are going to study many of the standard fallacies that logicians have identified. Such fallacies are classified according to the sort of mistake in reasoning they commit. For example, some fallacies are known as fallacies of *relevance*. That is, their premises are not really relevant to establishing the truth of their conclusions. Other fallacies rest upon unstated *false assumptions*. They are somewhat like enthymemes, with a missing premise. In this case, however, the missing premise required to make them logically correct, turns out to be false. Other fallacies, as we will see, are the result of *unclear language*.

Regardless of the type of fallacy with which we are dealing, it is important to remember that all fallacies are arguments. Thus, a passage should not be identified as committing a fallacy unless it clearly contains an argument. Once it is clear that we are dealing with an argument, then we can determine whether that argument commits a fallacy.

Exercises

Part I: Which of the following are true and which are false?

1. All fallacies are arguments.

2. Fallacies, as logicians use the term, are mistaken beliefs.

3. Fallacies occur only in academic settings.

4. All arguments are fallacies.

5. A fallacy is a mistake in reasoning.

Part II: Identify the following either as Straw Person or Misdirected Argument. Be prepared to justify your answer.

1. **Salesperson:** "You really should buy these books for your children. They are completely current, written in language your children can

understand and they contain information vital to your children's academic success. Moreover, just look at the handsome binding. These books will look great in your den."
Parent: "Unfortunately, I can't afford to buy books simply because they will look good in my den."

2. I wish to prove that raising taxes will not cause damage to our economy. Taxes are the fuel that allows government to work. With more revenue just think of what we can provide for our citizens. Therefore, raising taxes will allow us to do more of the things government is supposed to do.

3. Here's proof that the Cord is the best car. At Cord, we have been improving the reliability of our cars for the last 10 years. In fact, we have improved our quality more than any other car. Thus, you ought to buy a Cord, because it is the most improved car.

4. **Student:** "Please, you must let me out of my lease. I have lost my job and can no longer afford the rent. Moreover, my apartment is too far away from my new job. Also, my new neighbors are very noisy."
Landlord: "I'm sorry but if I let everybody out of his lease just because of a few noisy neighbors, I would go broke. It's out of the question."

5. Fluffy is the largest selling pillow. This can be seen by considering the following fact: over the last five years the sale of Fluffy pillows has increased faster than any other brand of pillow. So, you can see that Fluffy is the fastest growing brand.

6. **Lawyer:** "We will establish that the defendant is clearly guilty of embezzling the money and should be punished. After all, consider the enormity of his crime. He has violated a sacred trust and is the person to whom we have entrusted our pension funds. Yet he has betrayed us. We can only conclude that such behavior is deserving of the harshest punishment."

7. **Doctor:** "Here's why you should exercise. It's good for your heart, it will help firm your muscles, and it will make you look better."
Patient: "That sounds good Doc, but spending all that time exercising just to make me look better makes no sense to me."

8. **School Board Member:** "We should support the tax-levy because it will provide for more teachers for our children, help purchase new textbooks and provide for more extra-curricular activities.
   Parent: "But can we really afford more taxes just so we can have basketball and football?"

9. **Salesperson:** "It's easy to see that you need a new car. Just think of all the things you can do with a new car. You can go on trips without fear of breaking down, your maintenance costs will be lower, and you can go on that vacation you have been wanting to take. There's no doubt, therefore, that you ought to buy this new Ford car."

10. We really must pass this bill to lower the crime rate in our fair city. Here's why. Just think of the terrible suffering that must be endured by victims of murders and of the economic loss resulting from such crimes. It is clear, therefore, that murder is a crime that is tearing our city apart.

CHAPTER TWENTY-THREE

FALLACIES OF RELEVANCE

In this chapter we are concerned with fallacies of relevance. Fallacies of relevance involve arguments whose premises are largely, if not completely, irrelevant to the truth of their conclusions. These arguments often have the appearance of being good arguments. At first glance, the premises may even appear not only to be relevant to the truth of the conclusion but even to strongly support the conclusion. This appearance of cogency, you may recall, is one of the characteristics of fallacies. Despite such appearances, when we examine the arguments more closely, it turns out that the premises of such arguments fail to support their conclusions because they are logically irrelevant to their truth.

ARGUMENT TO THE PERSON (Argumentum ad Hominem)

Literally, *argumentum ad hominem* means "argument to the man." As the name suggests, this fallacy involves attacking the person, rather than the person's views. In the process, one generally ignores the reasons given in support of those views, but claims that because of some characteristic pertaining to the person, that person's views must be false. There are three specific types of the ad hominem fallacy. Each will be discussed in turn.

Ad Hominem (Abusive)

The *abusive* version of ad hominem occurs when one attacks a person's *character*, instead of attacking the person's views or arguments. One then claims that because of this allegedly undesirable personal characteristic, what the person is asserting must be false. A bit of reflection will show that the character of a person, generally, is not really relevant to the truth or falsity of what the person is saying. This can be seen clearly in the following example:

> Jones says that the city council must raise taxes, since its income is falling and its expenses are not. But Jones was once convicted of tax evasion, so how can you believe anything he says? Obviously, his position is absurd.

This argument commits the fallacy of *abusive ad hominem*. Although it may be true that Jones was convicted of tax evasion, that is logically irrelevant to the truth or falsity of what he is saying. It might be true that city council will be forced to raise taxes. In any case, it is difficult to see how the fact that Jones was once convicted of tax evasion has any bearing on whether city council must raise its taxes. Thus, the premise of the argument, that Jones has been convicted of tax evasion, is irrelevant to the argument's conclusion that Jones' position is false. Since the argument is based on an attack on Jones' character, this is an example of the fallacy of *Abusive Ad Hominem*.

In the example we have been discussing, Jones' character is attacked on the basis of a past criminal conviction. Other aspects of a person's character can be attacked as well. It has been argued that we shouldn't accept someone's position because he or she is a political radical, a homosexual, of a certain religious persuasion, a conservative, a Marxist, a radical feminist, an atheist, a liberal, and so on.

In all such cases it is the person who is being attacked, not the person's position or argument. Obviously, it is often easier to attack a person's character than it is to show that the person's position is unsound, and, undoubtedly, such arguments often have a powerful psychological effect. However, despite their persuasiveness, abusive ad hominem arguments do nothing to establish the truth of their conclusions.

Now it must be pointed out that not all attacks on a person's character or personality are cases of the fallacy of abusive ad hominem. One must keep in mind that the fallacy is committed when one argues that because of certain aspects of a person's character or personality, that person's position is false. Thus, for the abusive ad hominem fallacy to occur there must be an argument that has this basic character. Merely attacking someone's character or personality is not enough to commit the fallacy. Also, there is at least one case in which attacking someone's character is relevant to the conclusion you want to draw. Consider the following example.

> Ralph cheats on his wife, abuses his children, doesn't pay his bills and mistreats animals. Therefore, Ralph is a scoundrel.

This is a perfectly good argument (assuming the premises are true) that does not commit the abusive ad hominem fallacy. Although it is true that one is arguing ad hominem, or "to the person," in this case, however, the premises are relevant to the conclusion, since the conclusion is about

Ralph's character. However, this is quite different from arguing that because Ralph cheats on his wife, abuses his children, etc., that his views about politics or some other matter must be false.

It should also be pointed out that there are times when an attack on a person's character is relevant to the truth of what the person is claiming. For instance, in a court of law the testimony of a witness is often called into doubt by pointing out that the witness is a known perjurer. In this instance, the argument is that because of some *relevant* characteristic about the person, we should not trust the person's testimony. Although, again, this is arguing ad hominem, that is, "to the person," it does not commit a fallacy.

Ad Hominem (Circumstantial)

The *circumstantial* variety of ad hominem also involves an argument directed to the person rather than to the person's arguments or views. But in this case the claim is that because of the *circumstances* surrounding the person advocating a position, that position must be false. Here is an example.

> Victor Kiam, owner of the company that markets Remington electric shavers, argues that they give the closest, most comfortable shaves of any electric shavers. But who could expect him to say anything else? After all, he owns the company. Therefore, his claims ought to be rejected.

In the above example, it is being argued that what Victor Kiam says about Remington electric shavers is false, because of his special circumstances, that is, he is the owner of the company. In this case the suggestion is that since he has something to gain from what he is advocating, what he is advocating must be false. But even if he does have something to gain from what he is advocating, his claims about Remington shavers could still be true. Thus, the premises that take note of the fact that he is the owner of the company, are largely irrelevant to the truth of the conclusion. That is, they are irrelevant to the conclusion that Victor Kiam's claims regarding his electric shavers are to be rejected. Since the argument is directed to the person's special circumstances, rather than demonstrating that the person's views are false, this is an example of the fallacy of *Circumstantial Ad Hominem*.

Tu Quoque (You're Another)

The third type of ad hominem fallacy, like the other two, involves attacking the person rather than the person's argument or position. However, in this case, the attack takes the form of arguing that the person criticizing someone for a particular shortcoming, is guilty of the *same* or *similar shortcomings*. Here is an example:

Mother to Son:	You simply must be more diligent about your school work. You have missed several days of school and according to your teacher, your assignments are always messy and turned in late.
Son to Mother:	You're a good one to criticize me. You're always missing work because you claim to be "under the weather," and you are often quite late in completing your jobs at work. Thus, your criticism of me is invalid.

In this example, the son appears to be arguing that because his mother is guilty of the same sort of shortcomings she is accusing him of, it follows that her criticism of him must be false. But the premises of the son's argument are *irrelevant* to his conclusion. The fact that his mother has shortcomings similar to those for which he is being criticized, does nothing to show that the criticisms being made of him are false. Therefore, the son is guilty of the *You're Another* variety of the ad hominem fallacy.

If the mother is guilty of the same sorts of shortcomings for which her son is being criticized, this may raise a question about whether the mother is being fair in making the criticisms. This may be why one is tempted to respond to the criticisms in the way the son does. However, it fails to show that the criticisms themselves are not justified. That is, even if the mother has similar shortcomings to those she identifies in her son, it doesn't follow that the son does not have those shortcomings. Since that is what the son is claiming, he is guilty of the *You're Another* version of the ad hominem fallacy.

All three versions of the ad hominem fallacy commit essentially the same error. They attempt to refute someone's argument or position by attacking the person, rather than the person's argument or position. Whether the argument attacks the person's character, or the person's special circumstances, or accuses the other person of failings similar to the ones he is being accused of, in all cases it is being argued that because the person has those characteristics, the person's position is false.

Of course, it is often much easier to attack the person than it is to show why the person's position is faulty. But the fact remains that in the case of ad hominem arguments, the premises are irrelevant to the conclusion. Thus, they do nothing toward establishing the truth of their conclusions.

ARGUMENT FROM IGNORANCE (Argumentum ad Ignorantiam)

There are many beliefs for which we do not have conclusive evidence or even very good evidence. When our evidence about a matter is not very good, the most prudent behavior is to suspend judgment about it. Sometimes what we do, instead, is to attempt to turn our lack of information about a matter into an argument. This gives rise to the fallacy known as the *Argument From Ignorance*.

There are two basic versions of this fallacy. The first version argues that a given belief must be true, because it has never been proven false. Here are two examples of the first version.

> Ghosts must exist, since it has never been proven that they don't.

> It has never been established that eating a lot of sweets doesn't cause diabetes; therefore, it is obvious that eating sweets must be the cause.

Both of these examples have the form: **(1) X is *true*, because x has not been proven *false*.** In the first example, the argument is that because it hasn't been proven that ghosts do not exist, it must follow that they do exist. In the second example, it is being argued that eating sweets must cause diabetes because it has never been proven that they don't cause it.

The second version is the opposite of the first. Here are two examples:

> It should be obvious to any rational person that there are no ghosts. After all, despite their best efforts for hundreds of years, no one has succeeded in proving that they exist.

> No one has been able to prove that eating a lot of sweets causes diabetes; therefore, it's obvious that eating too many sweets isn't the cause.

The second version of the Argument From Ignorance has the form: **(2) X is *false*, because x has not been proven *true*.** Thus, there can be no ghosts, because no one has managed to prove that they exist. Or, in the second example, it is claimed that eating too many sweets isn't the cause of diabetes because no one has been able to prove that it does.

Both versions result in arguments whose premises do little if anything toward proving their conclusions. This should be obvious from the above examples, since we have used the Argument From Ignorance to support both the views that ghosts exist and that they do not exist. Obviously, something must be wrong with that sort of reasoning. The mistake being made here is that a belief is *not* shown to be false because it hasn't been proven true. Conversely, a belief is *not* proven true because it hasn't been proven false. To argue in either of these two ways is to argue from *ignorance*. The correct inference to draw from our ignorance about a subject is that we don't know, not that a belief is either true or false. To claim otherwise is to be guilty of the fallacy known as the *Argument from Ignorance*.

There are *two qualifications* to be made about the second version of the Argument From Ignorance. The necessity of the first qualification can be understood by considering the following example:

> There is no evidence that shows I have won the lottery. Therefore, the belief that I have won it is probably false.

Here we have a case in which if the belief were true, there would be evidence for it. Since there is no evidence for it, it is reasonable to believe that it is false.

The other qualification occurs in courts of law. Under our system of criminal justice, a person is presumed innocent until proven guilty. If the defendant is not proven guilty, then the verdict is "not guilty." Thus, one can argue:

> The prosecution was unable to prove that my client was guilty, therefore, we must find the defendant "not guilty."

This looks very much like the second version of the Argument From Ignorance. That is, it appears that one is arguing that it is false that the defendant is guilty because we were unable to establish that the defendant is guilty. However, it must be kept in mind that the conclusion is only that the defendant is not "legally guilty." It does not follow that the defendant did not commit the crime.

It should be kept in mind that these are *exceptions* to the rule that the Argument From Ignorance is a fallacious way to argue. However, in almost every case, to argue that a belief must be false because it hasn't been proven true, is to reason improperly.

APPEAL TO AUTHORITY (Argumentum ad Verecundiam)

The fallacy of *Appeal to Authority* is committed when one claims that a certain belief or position is true because someone (who is not a legitimate authority) says it is true.

Arguments that involve appeals to authority have the following form:

> A *asserts* that p is the case.
> Therefore, p *is* the case.

In general there is nothing wrong with appealing to authority to support the truth of a belief or position. This is because, given the complexity of our world, it is impossible for any one person to know more than a small fraction of what there is to know. Thus, in many cases, depending on authorities is inescapable. But there are *legitimate* and *illegitimate* appeals to authority. An appeal to authority is *legitimate* and, therefore, does not commit a fallacy, provided that the following conditions obtain:

1. The person being appealed to is an authority (expert) in the subject being discussed.

2. There is general agreement among the experts concerning the matter being discussed.

The *fallacious* Appeal to Authority occurs when either one or both of the above conditions fail to obtain. Unfortunately, all too often these conditions are not satisfied. Consider the following examples:

> Singer Ray Charles says that Diet Pepsi tastes better than Diet Coke. Therefore you should drink Diet Pepsi and not Diet Coke.

> Our family doctor says that our school system is outmoded. Since she is such a fine physician, we should accept her judgment regarding our schools.

Notice how these appeals to authority follow the form outlined above. A (where A is some person) says that p is true (where p is some belief). But why should we believe p simply because A says it is true? The answer is that the testimony of A provides us with a reason for believing p, if A is an expert regarding p and there is general agreement about the matter among experts. However, the problem with the first example given above is that we have no reason to believe that Ray Charles is an expert when it comes to the question of which diet cola tastes best. Neither is it clear that even if there were taste experts, there would be general agreement among them. Therefore, this is a fallacious and improper appeal to authority. The premise, that Ray Charles says that Diet Pepsi tastes best, is irrelevant to the truth of the argument's conclusion.

The same is true in the second example. The family doctor may be an expert in diagnosing illnesses, but we have no reason to think that she is an expert in education. Thus, her claim that our school system is outmoded, gives us little reason for believing that it is true. The fact that she is a doctor, gives us no reason for attaching special weight to her testimony. Both arguments, then, commit the fallacy of *Appeal to Authority*.

Sometimes even if the authority being appealed to is an expert in the area under discussion, appealing to that expert to settle the issue commits the fallacy of Appeal to Authority.

> Wotten, the famous theologian, says unequivocally that abortion is wrong. That proves the immorality of abortion.

The problem here is not that Wotten is not an expert on morality. Let's suppose he is. The difficulty here is that this argument violates the second of our conditions, given above, for a legitimate appeal to authority: there must be general agreement among the experts about the matter being discussed. However, moral experts are not in agreement regarding the morality of abortion. Thus, for every moral expert who says abortion is wrong, there is another expert who says, at least under some conditions, that abortion is morally permissible. Attempting to settle such an issue by appealing to experts, therefore, commits the fallacy of *Appeal to Authority*.

IRRELEVANT CONCLUSION (Ignoratio Elenchi)

This fallacy occurs when one draws the "wrong conclusion" from a set of premises that actually support a different but related conclusion. The premises, then, are irrelevant to the truth of the conclusion that is actually stated. When this fallacy is committed there is often, in the argument, some hint of what the correct conclusion should be, but a different conclusion from the one hinted at is drawn. Here is an example:

> If one tries hard, although there may be setbacks, one will succeed. This can be seen in countless instances. The evidence, then, is that trying hard is something within everyone's control.

The difficulty with this argument is that the premises are irrelevant to the truth of its conclusion. The premises do nothing to show that trying hard is something within everyone's control. Instead, it looks as if the premises are designed to show that trying hard is the key to success.

You may have noticed that the fallacies of *Misdirected Argument* and *Irrelevant Conclusion* are quite similar. Both involve attempting to establish a "wrong conclusion." But the difference between them is clear. In the case of Misdirected Argument, one announces that one is going to prove a conclusion, but then presents an argument directed to proving a different conclusion. The premises may support the conclusion actually drawn, but not the conclusion the person claimed to be proving. Hence, the irrelevance is not between the premises and the conclusion actually drawn, but between the premises and the conclusion the person claimed to be proving. Consider the following example:

> Salty potato chips are made with only the finest ingredients. It is the case, after all, that Salty sells more chips than anyone else. We must conclude, then, that they are America's favorite chips.

In this example, one announces that they are going to prove that "Salty potato chips are made with only the finest ingredients." But then an argument is offered that attempts to establish that "Salty potato chips are America's favorite chips." The premise provided to establish that conclusion is not irrelevant. Instead the problem here is that this is not the conclusion the person set out to prove. Hence, the argument is "misdirected," since it attempts to prove a conclusion different from the one it set out to prove. The premise provided is irrelevant to the original conclusion announced at the outset of the argument.

In the case of Irrelevant Conclusion, the irrelevance occurs because the premises provided are irrelevant to the conclusion actually drawn. Thus, there is no "misdirection" resulting from a confusion about what the argument's conclusion is. The problem is simply that the premises provided are irrelevant to the conclusion.

Now, of course, this description fits most of the fallacies of relevance we have talked about. Therefore, you may ask, how do we know when to call a fallacy Irrelevant Conclusion, since fallacies of relevance are all cases of irrelevant conclusion? The answer is that we can regard the fallacy of Irrelevant Conclusion as a sort of "catch all" or generic fallacy. If we encounter an argument whose premises are irrelevant to the conclusion, but it doesn't fit any of the other specific fallacies of relevance, then it commits the fallacy of Irrelevant Conclusion. But if it falls under one of the specific fallacies of relevance, then use that as the name of the fallacy.

Exercises

Identify the fallacy contained in the following examples.

1. General Quale argues that the army needs more and bigger tanks. He claims that even though they are expensive, they are vital to the nation's security. But that is exactly what one would expect a member of the military-industrial complex to say. We don't need them and cannot afford them.

2. General Quale claims that wearing a copper bracelet greatly reduces the symptoms of arthritis. He should certainly know, after all he is a famous general.

3. General Quale argues that we can know that copper bracelets reduce the effects of arthritis, because it has never been proven that they don't do so.

4. One can't accept Professor Bayle's analysis of the causes of alcoholism. Although Bayle is considered an authority in such matters, he cheats on his taxes and is a known felon.

5. Your claim that I drive too fast can't be taken seriously. After all, according to the newspapers, you have, yourself, been arrested for speeding several times.

6. This legislation on crime control is certainly worthy of your support. Why, William Hurt, the famous movie star supports it as well as Sparky Anderson, the great former Tiger manager. Obviously the legislation has great merit.

7. How can you doubt that capitalism is the best economic system? Where have you been? All of the Communist countries of Eastern Europe have turned toward democracy. Thus it is clear that capitalism is best.

8. Adolph Hitler maintained that the growth of communism presented great dangers to the rest of the world. That can't be true. Hitler was a racist who was responsible for murdering millions of innocent people.

9. It must be false that copper bracelets relieve the symptoms of arthritis, since this has not been scientifically established.

10. The good doctor has provided us with many arguments against the Medicare bills before us. But we shouldn't even bother to listen to her. After all, historically, physicians have always opposed Medicare. Her position is just what we should expect.

11. Clinton says he has done nothing wrong regarding the Whitewater affair. But who can believe him? He has been untruthful in the past. It's obvious that he is guilty of serious wrongdoing.

12. We can't accept Clinton's claim that he is innocent in the Whitewater affair. It's obvious that he is just trying to save his own skin.

13. No one has established a direct causal link between cigarette smoking and lung cancer. Therefore, it should be clear that cigarette smoking is not the cause of lung cancer.

14. Tommy Jones, the great golf pro, says we should support health care reform. Who can doubt the advice of this great golfer?

15. Just look at all the traffic jams that have occurred recently. That we need a new highway located between Routes 2 and 4 is obvious.

16. It's ridiculous for the United States to complain that Japan has unfair import restrictions. The U. S., after all, has its own import restrictions.

17. The mayor's decision on the crime bill was a good one. Why, there has never been such a wise individual, such a dedicated public servant.

18. Although the present administration has complained about the Fed's recent increase in interest rates, no one has been able to demonstrate that they will result in a recession. We can safely conclude, then, that we have nothing to worry about.

19. I know that your doctor has advised extensive surgery for your condition. However, you should keep in the mind that your doctor stands to make a lot of money from that operation. It should be obvious from this that the surgery is really quite unnecessary.

20. You shouldn't believe what John says about repairing your car. Didn't you know that he is a Professor of English Literature. What could such a person possibly know about anything practical?

CHAPTER TWENTY-FOUR

ADDITIONAL IRRELEVANT APPEALS
AND FALLACIES OF FALSE ASSUMPTION

In this chapter we will continue to look at irrelevant appeal fallacies. We begin by looking at a group of irrelevant appeal fallacies known as emotional appeals. Finally, we will conclude this chapter with a discussion of some fallacies of false assumption.

APPEAL TO PITY (Argumentum ad Misericordiam)

The fallacy of Appeal to Pity occurs when, instead of using reason to support a conclusion, one attempts to use the emotion of *pity* to get a conclusion accepted. Here is an example:

> **Defense Attorney to Jury**: "You simply must agree that my client is not guilty. I know that the evidence presented by the prosecution is overwhelming. But keep in mind that my client has four beautiful little children and a wife who is an invalid. Without their father, they will surely suffer grievously. Please, please, draw the only humane conclusion. Vote 'not guilty.'"

Although it is most likely true that the defendant has four children and an invalid wife, it does not follow from this that the defendant is not guilty. The premises are, in fact, totally irrelevant to the conclusion. Rather than providing reasons for accepting the conclusion that the defendant is not guilty, the defense attorney attempts to play on the *emotions* of the jury. The appeal is to the emotions, specifically the emotion of pity, rather than to reason. This is the essence of the fallacy of Appeal to Pity.

Another example of Appeal to Pity occurs with students, particularly with college students.

> "Surely, Professor, you must agree that I deserve at least a C in Physics 101. My poor mother has scrubbed floors for years to pay for my college education. Anything less than a C would simply break her poor old heart."

Note again that this argument does nothing to support the truth of its conclusion that the student *deserves* a C in the course. There is, for instance, no appeal to grades earned on an examination, or to projects completed or papers written. Rather, the student attempts to appeal to the emotions of the instructor. It may be true that receiving a D or F in the course will cause pain for the student's mother. The instructor may even take that fact into account in giving the student a grade. However, the argument's premises are clearly irrelevant to showing that this is the grade the student deserves. The student appeals to the emotion of pity, instead of providing reasons, to support the contention that a higher grade is deserved.

APPEAL TO POPULARITY (Argumentum ad Populum)

The Appeal to Popularity, like the appeal to pity, is an emotional appeal. In this case, however, the appeal is to *popular sentiments* such as patriotism, prejudices, snobbery, and the like, to get one's conclusion accepted. In the Appeal to Popularity fallacy, rather than providing reasons in support of a conclusion, one appeals, instead, to popular sentiments. As a result, the premises employed in such arguments are irrelevant to the truth of their conclusions.

> Our troops fought for your freedom. You can support them by buying U. S. Savings bonds. Therefore, buy U. S. Savings Bonds, an investment in your future.

In this example we are told that we ought to buy savings bonds because it is the patriotic thing to do. There is also the suggestion that it is a good investment. But it's not clear that we ought to do something *simply* because it is patriotic. One could, for instance, volunteer to pay more taxes than one owes. While this would probably be patriotic, it's not clear that one ought to do it. Hence, it appears that being patriotic, by itself, is not a very good reason to believe that one should behave in a certain way. Perhaps this is why, in the above example, there is also the suggestion that buying bonds is a good investment. The appeal here is largely to one's emotions, in this case the emotion of patriotism, rather than to reasons that would be relevant to showing that one ought to buy savings bonds. Consequently, the argument fails to provide reasons in support of its conclusion.

Another version of the Appeal to Popularity, or "the mob," is a more direct appeal to the popularity of a certain product or way of behaving. Here are some examples:

> More people use *Choke* hair spray than any other brand. It must be the best. Shouldn't you use it too?

> Come on, Sam, we think you ought to kick in a couple of bucks too. After all, everyone else in the office has given.

This version of the Appeal to Popularity, exemplified in these examples, is sometimes known as the "bandwagon argument." It basically claims that you ought to do something because it is a popular thing to do or that everyone else is doing it. Perhaps *Choke* hair spray is the largest selling brand of hair spray. It doesn't follow that it is the best or that it is the brand you ought to use. In the second example, Sam is told that he ought to contribute money because everyone else has. But just because everyone else at the office has given doesn't imply that he ought to give. It may be that Sam's financial condition is such that he can't afford to give or, perhaps, enough money has already been collected so that Sam's contribution is not really needed. The form of the argument is "Everyone's doing it, therefore, you ought to do it too." Small children and teenagers are especially vulnerable to this sort of emotional appeal because of the strong peer pressure to conform in order to be one of the group. The sale of jeans, athletic shoes, illegal drugs and many other items all benefit from this sort of reasoning.

Despite the success of such arguments, all of them are fallacious. They all appeal to popular sentiments instead of providing good reasons for accepting their conclusions. Therefore, they fail to provide premises that are relevant to the truth of their conclusions.

APPEAL TO FORCE (Argumentum ad Baculum)

The Appeal to Force is an argument that relies on a threatened use of *force* or bad consequences to gain acceptance of a conclusion. Thus, the emotion of *fear*, produced by either psychological or physical means, is employed, instead of providing reasons for the truth of a conclusion. Children often resort to this sort of reasoning as the following baseball example illustrates.

"I was safe! I got to first base before the throw. You know it! I am telling you right now that if you don't agree, I'll take my equipment and just go home."

To get agreement that she is safe, the child resorts to threats, in this case the threat that she will take her ball and bat and go home. The hope is that the other players will prefer to accept the conclusion that she is safe, to the prospect that the game will have to end. Nevertheless, the fact that the child has the power to end the game is irrelevant to the question of whether she was safe or out. Thus, the argument relies on the threat of force to gain acceptance of its conclusion and commits the fallacy of Appeal to Force.

Adults, even academics, are not immune to the use of such fallacies. Consider the following example:

> **Tenured professor to untenured professor:** "I'm sure you'll agree that Dr. Howe is the best candidate for the position and ought to be hired. You do recall that a decision on whether to grant *you* tenure comes up next month."

The suggestion here is clear. If the untenured professor doesn't agree with the tenured professor and vote for hiring Dr. Howe, then his own tenure vote may be adversely affected. But just because one professor has that power over another does nothing to show that Dr. Howe is the best candidate for the position. Hence, the implicit premise, that the untenured professor may not be granted tenure, is irrelevant to the truth of the conclusion, that Dr. Howe is the best candidate for the position.

ACCIDENT

This fallacy occurs when one applies a rule that is generally true, to cases whose *peculiar* or *accidental* characteristics make the application of the rule inappropriate. Here is an example:

> One should tell the truth. Therefore, a physician should always tell her patient the truth about his condition, even if doing so will complicate his medical problems.

The above example commits the fallacy of Accident, since it applies a general rule to a case whose special features render the rule inapplicable. It may be true, in general, that one ought tell the truth. However, should a physician do so even if it will cause harm to the patient? Actually this situation is even more complicated because the physician takes an oath that, in effect, promises not to knowingly do anything to harm the patient. Thus, a second example of the fallacy of Accident is generated.

> One should keep one's promises. Therefore, a physician should keep her promise not to knowingly do anything to harm her patient, even if that requires lying to the patient.

Obviously, the conclusions of these two arguments cannot both be true since they are logically incompatible with each other. It can't be the case that the physician is both obligated to tell the truth *and* to lie to the patient. But in fact both are instances of the fallacy of Accident. Each makes the mistake of applying a general principle to a particular case when there is something about that case that makes it clear that applying the rule is inappropriate.

One way of thinking about the fallacy of Accident is to consider it a false assumption fallacy. Lying behind the application of general rules to particular cases is the assumption that there is nothing special about the particular case that renders the rule inapplicable. In cases in which the fallacy of Accident occurs, that assumption turns out to be false.

CONVERSE ACCIDENT

The fallacy of Converse Accident, as the name suggests, is just the *opposite* of the fallacy of Accident. It involves generalizing from an *atypical* case to a general rule based on that case.

> Seventy-five persons attending the Baptist Convention were asked about the importance of religion in American life. The results of the survey are convincing that religion is of central importance.

The example clearly commits the fallacy of Converse Accident. The persons attending the religious convention are not likely to be typical of the American public as a whole. One would certainly expect that they would give more importance to religious values than the ordinary person on the street. Thus, generalizing from this atypical case to a conclusion about all Americans commits the fallacy of Converse Accident.

Like the fallacy of Accident, we can think of Converse Accident as a false assumption fallacy. Here the false assumption is that the case we are generalizing from is typical rather than atypical. In the above example, that is not the case. We are generalizing from an atypical case to a conclusion that is probably not justified. Thus, we commit the fallacy of Converse Accident.

FALSE CAUSE

There are two basic versions of this fallacy. The first is known as *post hoc, ergo propter hoc,* "after this, therefore, because of this." The *post hoc* version claims that A, where A is some event, is the cause of B, another event, because A occurred before B. The basic form of the argument is:

> <u>A occurred before B.</u>
> ∴ A is the cause of B.

The following are all examples of the *post hoc* version of the False Cause fallacy:

> I developed a terrible cold.
> I took lots of vitamin C.
> <u>In a few days my cold was gone.</u>
> ∴ That vitamin C really works.

> <u>Every time I wash my car, it soon begins to rain.</u>
> Thus, if you want it to rain, just wash your car.

In each of these examples, the only evidence presented for the causal claim is that the second event occurred *after* the first event. The inference is drawn that, therefore, the first event *caused* the second event. Now, of course, we generally do think of causes as occurring before their effects. Nevertheless, many events occur before other events without being their causes. Thus it is fallacious to argue that simply because A occurs *before* B, A is the *cause* of B.

The question concerning the first example is whether the argument gives us any reason to think that taking large amounts of vitamin C is causally relevant to getting over the cold. Certainly the fact that we got over the cold *after* taking the vitamin C does not establish the causal connection. One usually gets over a cold in a few days, even if one takes no medication. Thus, we might have gotten over the cold just as quickly if we had taken no medication at all. Since the only evidence presented in this argument for the conclusion is that vitamin C was taken before the cold went away, the argument commits the *post hoc* version of the False Cause fallacy.

The tendency to commit this fallacy is responsible for the sale of millions of dollars of medications whose efficacy is either non-existent or questionable. As long as we are willing to assume that because we got better *after* taking a certain medication, that taking the medication *caused* us to get better, this will continue to be the case.

Television commercials encourage this sort of reasoning. Think of commercials for pain relievers, for example. A typical commercial goes like this. "I had a terrible headache. I took two *Excedrin*. Now I feel great. That *Excedrin* really works." What are we to make of the reasoning reflected in this commercial? First, let us make it clear that we am not arguing that *Excedrin* doesn't work. Presumably, there is scientific evidence to show that it does. Our point is, however, that the type of reasoning in the commercial is a blatant example of the *post-hoc* version of the False Cause fallacy. The argument is clearly a case of reasoning "after this, therefore, because of this."

The car washing example is probably an instance of someone making a joke. Do we really believe that washing our car *causes* it to rain? Nevertheless, the example does exhibit the *post-hoc* form of reasoning. The argument is that because it rains *after* I wash my car, it follows that washing my car *caused* it to rain.

It should also be pointed out that such reasoning is the basis for many superstitions. One breaks a mirror, and expects seven years of bad luck, or walks under a ladder and one or more bad things happen to him. These superstitions undoubtedly arise from the tendency to reason in the *post-hoc* fashion. Because the bad things happened *after* walking under the ladder or breaking the mirror, we infer that they happened *because* we walked under the ladder or broke the mirror.

The second version of the False Cause fallacy may be described as follows. For any two related events, one is either the cause or the effect of the other. A television commercial from a few years back perfectly illustrates this fallacy:

Successful business people read the *Wall Street Journal*. So, get the edge, read the *Wall Street Journal*.

This ad appears to imply that reading the *Wall Street Journal* causes business people to be successful. However, no evidence is presented to show this. At best the argument shows that there is a correlation between reading the *Wall Street Journal* and being successful in business. But it certainly does not show that reading the *Wall Street Journal* causes them to be successful. Many successful business people also live in large houses, but do we want to claim that this is the cause of their success?

It is also quite possible that, in the above example, the *cause* has been confused with the *effect*. One is a successful business person and as a result one needs to keep abreast of what is going on in the world of business. Thus, one reads the *Wall Street Journal* because one is a successful business person. Now this is not to deny that reading the *Wall Street Journal* might contribute to that success. But it would be a mistake to think that if one simply reads the *Wall Street Journal* this will *cause* one to be successful.

Exercises

Identify the fallacy contained in the examples below.

1. Please, officer, you must believe that I had nothing to do with the scheme. You must consider that my family would suffer terribly if the community believed that I was involved. You must conclude that I am innocent.

2. Soon after I began taking the vitamin supplement, I began to feel much better. Why, that stuff really works. I would recommend it to anyone.

3. More people drive the Ford Taurus than any other car. That proves that it is the best car.

4. I say that I didn't foul you on your attempt to make a basket. If you don't agree, I'll take my basketball and go home. How are you gonna like that?

5. Since everyone has the right to free speech, it follows that professors have the right to promote their personal political and religious views in their classes.

6. Law enforcement personnel are allowed to carry guns in this town. It seems clear that gun control is not popular here.

7. Everyone is wearing 501 jeans these days. It's clearly the thing to do. Don't wait another day to buy a pair for yourself.

8. Our team had lost every game this season. Then, I started wearing my Dad's old sweatshirt and we started winning. I'll tell you, I'm never taking this shirt off.

9. I'm sure you will agree that my plan is the right one for cutting costs in our department, Bob. It seems to me that you mentioned something to me about wanting a raise.

10. Those who commit criminal acts should be punished. Since Sue did the act, she should be punished, despite the evidence that she is insane.

11. If you buy our new model Mustang, you'll impress your neighbors and be the envy of everyone who sees you. Clearly, then, buying the new Mustang is the right thing to do.

12. Vanilla ice cream is the best. If you don't agree, I simply will not help you buy any ice cream and you will have to do without.

13. You should never steal anything. Therefore even if you are starving and no one will help you, it would be wrong to steal a slice of bread.

14. There are more bars in Bowling Green than ever before. There is also more crime. The solution to our problem is simple. If we reduce the number of bars, we will reduce the amount of crime.

15. We must make the Chinese government see that the denial of human rights is wrong. If we threaten to deny them most favored nation trade status, that will help them see the light.

16. Allowing unlimited immigration of the poor of the world to the United States will, in the long run, be good for the nation's economy. After all, how can we turn our backs on the poor, pitiful, starving children of the world?

17. You really must read the latest novel by John Grisham. Can you believe that it is number one on the *New York Times* best-seller list?

18. It seems that the United States is not really committed to the freedom of all, because we lock up dangerous criminals and those who are dangerously insane.

19. Well, you can believe what you want to. But I broke a mirror yesterday and then I flunked my math test. I just know that breaking a mirror is bad luck.

20. You say that you believe in freedom of speech. How, then, can you ask me to be quiet in your class when an exam is going on?

CHAPTER TWENTY-FIVE

MORE FALSE ASSUMPTION FALLACIES

In this chapter we will continue our discussion of false assumption fallacies. One of the most commonly committed false assumption fallacies is known as the *Gambler's Fallacy*.

GAMBLER'S FALLACY

The Gambler's Fallacy is sometimes called the *Monte Carlo Fallacy*. It occurs when one treats statistically *independent* events as if they were *dependent* upon each other. Here are two examples of arguments that commit the Gambler's Fallacy:

> You have rolled a seven four times in a row. Therefore, there's no way you can roll a seven this time.

> **Baseball Announcer:** "Wade Boggs has no hits in four official times at bat today. He is a .350 hitter. He's due."

Many people find arguments like these not only plausible but even self-evident. Somehow we think Boggs is much more likely to get a hit now, if he has gone hitless the first four times at bat, or that since a seven has been rolled four times in succession, it is highly unlikely that a seven will be rolled the next time. Despite the appeal of such thinking, these examples commit the Gambler's Fallacy.

Such arguments gain their plausibility by blurring the distinction between *dependent* and *independent* events. The distinction can be explained as follows:

1. For any two events, x and y, they are *independent* if the outcome of x does not affect the outcome of y.

For instance, consider the odds of drawing a spade from a standard deck of cards. A standard deck of playing cards has four suits of thirteen cards each of hearts, diamonds, spades and clubs. Therefore, the odds of drawing a spade are obviously one in four. Now suppose I draw a spade on the first draw, then replace it and draw again. The odds again for the second draw are one in four. The odds remain one in four even if I have drawn ten spades in a row, provided that after each draw I replace the card drawn and reshuffle the deck. In fact, it doesn't matter how many spades in a row I have drawn. The odds each time of drawing a spade will be one in four. Since each draw is an *independent* event, the outcome of prior draws does not affect the probability of the next draw.

On the other hand:

> 2. For any two events, x and y, they are *dependent* if the outcome of x affects the outcome of y.

Let's imagine again that we are attempting to draw a spade from a standard deck of cards. Once again we want to know the odds of drawing a spade. The odds for the first draw are one in four. We draw a spade on the first draw. But this time suppose that we do *not* replace the spade. We lay the spade aside and proceed to draw again. What are the odds of drawing another spade? Well, since there is one fewer spade in the deck relative to the other suits, the odds are slightly less than one in four. Suppose we have now drawn three spades in our first three draws and that none of the three have been returned to the deck. What are the odds that we will draw a spade on the fourth draw? Since there are now forty-nine cards in the deck, and ten of them are spades, the odds of drawing another spade are roughly one in five.

The reason the probability changes in the second example is that each draw after the initial draw is now a *dependent* event. Drawing a spade in each of the prior cases affects the probability of drawing a spade on the next draw. In contrast, in the first example the probability of drawing a spade was not affected by the outcome of prior draws because each draw was an *independent* event.

Now let's look again at the examples presented earlier. In the dice example, notice that each roll of the dice is an *independent* event. Thus, what happened in the prior instances does not affect the probability of the present toss of the dice. The probability of throwing a seven on any single roll of the dice is one in six. This is true on the first roll and it still holds even if I have thrown a seven four times in succession. On the next roll, the odds against rolling a seven do not become greater, but remain one in six. To conclude that the odds are affected because of the outcome of previous throws commits the Gambler's Fallacy.

In the baseball example, it is being suggested that since Boggs has no hits in four official times at bat, he is now much more likely to get a hit this time at bat. So, in one way this example is just the opposite of the dice example. In the dice example it is being argued that because an event has occurred several times in a row, it is *less* likely to occur again. In this case the argument is that because an event has *not* occurred several times in succession, it is *more* likely to occur now. Nevertheless, the mistake in the two cases is identical. In both cases, independent events are treated as if they are dependent events.

If you listen very often to baseball commentators on radio or television, you have no doubt heard an example similar to the Boggs example. However, the point is that if Boggs is a .350 hitter, his chances of getting a hit on any one official time at bat are slightly better than one in three. This is true whether he has gone four times without a hit or has managed five hits in a row. Each time at bat is an independent event. Thus, what the batter did the last time at bat does not affect his chances of getting a hit this time at bat. To reason that Boggs is more likely to get a hit now because he has just gone hitless four times in succession is to commit the Gambler's Fallacy.

Let's close this discussion of the Gambler's Fallacy with one more example. In a game between the Detroit Tigers and the Kansas City Royals, George Brett, earlier in the game, had already hit two home runs. Brett came up late in the game with its outcome on the line. The Tiger manager reasoned that the odds against Brett (or any other player) hitting three home runs in a single game were phenomenal. He decided to pitch to Brett rather than walk him. Brett hit a home run.

The reasoning in this case was faulty. What Brett had done before was *irrelevant* to the probability of what he would do this time. The question was not, "What are the odds against someone hitting three home runs in a single game?" Rather, the question was, "What are the odds that this batter will hit a home run in a single time at bat?" Had the manager reasoned this way, he probably would not have pitched to Brett. But because he apparently believed that the probability of what Brett would do this time at bat was somehow *dependent* on what he did earlier in the game, he decided to pitch to Brett. He reasoned that because Brett had already hit two home runs, he was less likely to hit a home run this time. In other words, Brett's last time at bat, on which he hit his third home run, was treated as a *dependent* event when, in fact, it was an *independent* event. The manager was guilty of committing the Gambler's Fallacy.

The Gambler's Fallacy, then, occurs when one treats independent events as though they were dependent events, and argues that because of what has occurred previously, a certain outcome is either more or less probable than it actually is.

BEGGING THE QUESTION (PETITIO PRINCIPII)

The fallacy of Begging the Question occurs when one *assumes*, as a premise in an argument, what one ought to be proving. The fallacy can occur in at least two ways. Sometimes one of the premises is simply a *restatement* of the conclusion. Consider the following examples.

> Of course I'm the owner of the coat. That follows because I'm its rightful possessor.

> The only acts for which one ought to be held responsible are those that are voluntary. Therefore, one should not be held responsible for involuntary acts.

In these examples, the fallacy of Begging the Question is committed because the premise in each argument is simply a *restatement* of the conclusion. "I'm the rightful possessor of the coat" means the same as "I'm the owner of the coat." In the second example it is also clear that the premise and the conclusion say the same thing. In both examples, then, the premise is merely a restatement of the conclusion.

The fallacy of Begging the Question also occurs when one of the premises of an argument *depends* for its truth on the truth of the conclusion. Here are two examples:

> I must be my logic students' favorite professor. After all, they all tell me that I am, and not even logic students would lie to their favorite professor.

> The Bible asserts that there is a God. What the Bible says must be true, since it is God's divinely inspired Word. Therefore, God exists.

In the first of the two examples, notice that neither premise is a restatement of the conclusion. The conclusion asserts that "I am my logic students' favorite professor." The first premise says that "my students all tell me that I am their favorite professor" and the second premise that "not even logic students would lie to their favorite professor." Although neither premise is a restatement of the conclusion, the second premise *depends* for its truth on the truth of the conclusion. The second premise says that I can trust what my students tell me because they would not lie to their favorite professor. However, that is to *assume* the very thing the argument seeks to prove, namely, that I am their favorite professor. Hence, the argument begs the question.

Again, in the second example, neither premise is a restatement of the conclusion. But the truth of one of the premises *depends* for its truth on the truth of the conclusion. That is, the premises could not be true unless the conclusion is also true. The premise asserts that what the Bible says must be true because "the Bible is God's divinely inspired Word." However, suppose someone doubts the truth of the conclusion, "God exists." Then that person could not accept the premise's claim that "the Bible is God's inspired Word." Thus, the truth of the premise *depends* for its truth upon the conclusion being true. Since we are assuming, in the premises, the truth of the conclusion, this argument is guilty of committing the fallacy of Begging the Question.

Now that we know what the fallacy of Begging the Question is, we must raise the question of what is wrong with such arguments? Are such arguments invalid? The answer is clearly, no. If we look carefully at the first two examples, in which the premise is merely a restatement of the conclusion, it is easy to see that both of the arguments are valid. Since the premise in each case is saying the same thing as the conclusion, it would be impossible for the premise to be true and the conclusion to be false. Hence, the arguments are clearly valid. Remember that our definition of a valid argument is one in which it is impossible for the premises to be true and the conclusion false.

The second set of examples are also valid arguments. In the first example, the premise is that I can know that my student's won't lie to me because I am their favorite professor. From that premise it follows that I am their favorite professor. In the second example, I know that what the Bible says is true because it is God's Word. If that premise is true, then it must be true that there is a God. How could God have a Word if there is no God? Thus, given the connection between the premises and conclusions of arguments that beg the question, all such arguments are always valid.

If arguments that beg the question are never invalid, then that cannot be the reason they are fallacies. Are such arguments unsound? Here the answer must be that such arguments are not necessarily unsound. That is, there is no reason why arguments that beg the question must have false premises. If we look, for instance, at the argument that attempts to prove that God exists, it is clear that the first premise is true and it is quite possible that the second premise is also true. Therefore, arguments that beg the question are not fallacies because they are necessarily unsound.

If arguments that beg the question are neither invalid nor necessarily unsound, why are they fallacies? Arguments that commit the fallacy of Begging the Question are fallacies because they violate the point of presenting an argument. In an argument, premises are supposed to provide *independent* support for the truth of their conclusion. That is, one is supposed to provide premises that one could accept as true, while at the same time having doubts about the truth of the conclusion. In all the examples given above, if one has a reason for doubting the conclusion, one will have at least as much reason for doubting one of the premises. That is, if one doubts the conclusion, one could not accept the truth of the premises. Thus, ultimately, the premises provide no real support for the conclusion and the argument does nothing toward establishing the truth of its conclusion.

COMPLEX QUESTION

To understand the fallacy of Complex Question, we must first understand what a complex question is. A complex question is a question that assumes the answer to another unasked question. Perhaps the most famous complex question is, "Have you stopped beating your wife?"

This question is complex in the sense that there are two questions here, not one. "Have you beaten your wife in the past?" and "Do you still beat your wife?" The question presupposes that you did at one time beat your wife. Thus, if you answer "yes," you are in effect admitting that you did, at one time, beat your wife. If you answer "no," you suggest that you are still beating you wife.

Complex questions are, of course, a favorite tactic of lawyers. "Where did you hide the weapon?" or "Why did you steal the money?" are questions that *presuppose* that you did hide the weapon or steal the money. In the heat of questioning in a court of law, sometimes such questions are effective in getting the defendant to betray his or her guilt.

The *fallacy* of Complex Question involves drawing an incorrect conclusion as a result of being misled by a complex question.

Father: "How much more time are you going to waste writing that music of yours, Son? It's time that you go out and find a job."

Son: "Maybe you're right that I have been wasting my time. I'll start looking tomorrow."

The father, in this example, asks a complex question. He assumes that his son's music writing is a waste of time. This leads him to conclude that his son should quit trying to write music and find a job instead. (Actually, the son may be a talented writer who will someday be successful.) But the conclusion may be the result of the father's failure to see that he has *assumed* an affirmative answer to another question, "Is your writing music a waste of time?"

The son commits the fallacy of Complex Question by also assuming an affirmative answer to the prior question, "Is your writing music a waste of time?" He draws the conclusion that he should stop trying to write and begin to look for a job. However, this conclusion would follow only if it is true that the son is wasting his time. Thus, both the father and the son are guilty of the fallacy of Complex Question. Both draw an incorrect conclusion as a result of being misled by a complex question.

COMPOSITION

The fallacy of composition occurs when one *assumes* that what is true of each part of something must also be true of the whole. The following are examples:

It's clear that State is going to have a great basketball team next year. This is obvious since every player on the team is an outstanding player.

What do you mean I'm asking too much for this car? Each payment is only $129.99 per month.

The first example assumes that what is true of each player on State's basketball team must be true of the team as well. Since each member of the team is a great player, the team will also be great. But upon reflection it is clear that the conclusion doesn't really follow from the premises. The argument fails to take into account the importance of team work, and the balance between speed, rebounding, ball handling and quickness, for example, in order for a team to be outstanding. Although each player on the team may individually be outstanding, it doesn't follow that the players together provide the proper balance and team work necessary for an outstanding team. Thus, the assumption that what is true of *each part* must also be true of the *whole* results in an argument that commits the fallacy of Composition.

The second example is guilty of the fallacy of Composition as well. In this case, we are confronted with a common ploy in automobile merchandising. The salesperson attempts to get the customer to consider only the monthly payment, not the cost of the car as a whole. The assumption is that what's true of *each part*, must be true of the *whole*. Since each payment is reasonable and affordable, the salesperson argues, it follows that the car is reasonable and affordable. But, of course, a monthly payment may be reasonable, while the cost of the car is not. One, of course, must look at the price of the car as a whole, and at the number of monthly payments, not simply at the amount of each payment, to determine whether the price of the car is reasonable. The argument by the salesperson overlooks the fact that although each payment is in itself reasonable, the price of the car as a whole may not be. It assumes, in other words, that what is true of each part must be true of the whole. The argument, therefore, commits the fallacy of Composition.

It is generally true that assuming that what is true of each part must be true of the whole will lead to fallacious reasoning. However, there is a qualification that should be mentioned. Not every argument that reasons from parts to wholes is necessarily a fallacy. Consider the following example.

> Every piece of candy in that box is a piece of chocolate candy.
> Therefore, that is a box of chocolate candy.

This argument is clearly valid and therefore does not commit the fallacy of Composition. Nevertheless, it is often true that what is true of the part is *not* true of the whole. The fallacy of Composition occurs when one assumes that what is true of the part must *always* be true of the whole. As we have seen, that is not necessarily the case.

DIVISION

The fallacy of Division is just the opposite of the fallacy of Composition. In this case one assumes that what is true of the whole, must be true of each of its parts. The following example is adapted from a television commercial.

> Midas has installed mufflers on more than 5 million cars.
> <u>That's more than any other muffler shop.</u>
> At Midas you'll have your muffler installed by a real professional.

This ad may be comforting to one who needs a new muffler and may even be effective in getting one to take one's car to Midas. But does the commercial give us a good reason for supposing that our car's muffler will be installed by an experienced professional? Well, the argument is that since Midas has installed so many mufflers, the person installing the muffler on your car will be an experienced professional. Notice, however, that your muffler is not going to be installed by the Midas chain as a whole, but by one or two individuals working at a local shop. Now from the fact that Midas as a whole has installed 5 million mufflers, we can infer nothing about the experience of the individuals who will be installing the muffler on your car. In short, the argument commits the fallacy of Division. It assumes that what is true of the whole, must be true of each of its parts. Since the Midas chain as a whole is experienced, the commercial suggests, then each part of the Midas chain is experienced. Clearly the conclusion doesn't follow from the premises.

Another example comes from a sports commentator on CBS-TV. In the pre-game show the announcers were trying to whip up excitement for an up-coming basketball game. They argued that it was likely to be a great game because:

> <u>In their last 42 meetings, Philly has won 22 games and Boston 20.</u>
> Therefore, it's going to be a really close game.

Upon examination, however, this argument does nothing to show that the game about to be televised is likely to be close. Just because the *series* between the two teams over the last few years has been close, that doesn't mean that this game is likely to be close. For example, it could be the case that most of the 42 games have been one-sided. Moreover, even if most of the past games had been close, that is consistent with one team being very strong this year and the other being very weak. In that case, one would not expect the game to be close.

The sports commentator has committed the fallacy of Division. He has assumed that what is true of the series (the whole), must be true of the upcoming game (the part). Actually his argument is a bit more complex than that. He has assumed that since the *series* as a whole between the two teams has been close, 22 games to 20, that *each* of the games in the series must have been close games. As we have seen that is not necessarily true. Then, because he has assumed that each of the games was close, he argues that today's game is likely to be close as well. But such reasoning is obviously based on the assumption that what is true of the *whole* must be true of each of its *parts*. In other words, the argument commits the fallacy of Division.

It should be pointed out that not every argument that moves from the whole to its parts commits a fallacy. For example:

> Every human is mortal and John is a human. Therefore, John is mortal.

This argument represents correct reasoning from whole to parts. However, as we have seen, many arguments that move from wholes to parts are fallacious. Lying behind the fallacy of Division appears to be the assumption that whatever is true of the whole *must* be true of its parts. As we have seen, that is not true.

Since both the fallacies of Composition and Division are arguments dealing with the relationship of parts and wholes, it is easy to confuse them. However, there is a way of keeping them straight. First, distinguish the premises of the argument from its conclusion. Second, remember that in the case of the fallacy of Composition, the argument moves from parts to whole. Thus, the premises will talk about what is true of a part or each part and the conclusion about the whole. (One is "composing." The argument begins with the parts and moves to a conclusion about the whole.) On the other hand, arguments committing the fallacy of Division move from the whole to some claim about its parts. Thus, the premises will talk about what is true of the whole and the conclusion about each part or a part. (One is "dividing." The argument begins with the whole and moves to a conclusion about the parts.) Keeping this in mind should allow you to easily distinguish the fallacies of Composition and Division.

Exercises

Identify the fallacy contained in each of the following examples.

1. I don't care if he did steal only a candy bar. Shoplifting is a serious offense that amounts to millions of dollars of losses for businesses each year. I think we should lock him up and throw away the key for committing such a serious offense.

2. Are you still cheating on all of your exams? No, you say. So you admit to having cheated in the past.

3. I've been losing at cards all night long. So, I'm bound to win this hand.

4. Every member of city council is under 45 years of age. It follows that city council is less than 45 years old.

5. John always tells the truth. You can be certain of that. If you don't believe me, ask John. He will be glad to tell you so.

6. Don't worry about being able to afford this set of tools. Each tool, you agree, costs very little. So, the set of tools costs very little.

7. Bengal tigers are an endangered species. Since your team mascot is a Bengal tiger, it must be endangered as well.

8. Rice has just hit five baskets in a row. He has the hot hand. Therefore, make sure you get the ball to him.

9. Why are *Tummies* best for your tummy? Because they use a formula developed by a physician. Therefore, get *Tummies*.

10. Classical music must be superior to rock music. I know that this is true because it is preferred by people with refined tastes. Obviously, it is easy to distinguish those with refined tastes from those lacking it. Why, the ones who prefer classical music, naturally, are the ones having refined tastes.

11. All professors are smart. This is obvious from the fact that they are all so bright.

12. Statistically, we know that two out of three throws will be successful in hitting their targets. Since she missed her first throw, she is bound to hit it this time.

13. Are you still drinking beer to excess? By answering "no" you have admitted that you once drank to excess.

14. Since these supports are holding up the bridge, it follows that each support is quite capable of supporting the bridge.

15. So, you like the looks of our latest model, too. Shall I sign you up for our new lease, or do you prefer to buy? In any case, I'm grateful for your business.

16. At our last basketball game I understand that my team scored over 100 points. So, Bill, the starting guard for the team, must have scored a lot of points.

17. I can assure you that this new stereo is something you can easily afford to buy right now. Since each component is clearly affordable, it follows that the stereo as a whole must be affordable.

18. I've been putting money in these slot machines for years and have never won a dime. The odds are now in my favor. Hence, I'm sure to win tonight.

19. The United States is by far the richest nation in the history of the world. It's ludicrous to think, therefore, that there are people starving here.

20. Since each and every living thing on earth will someday die, it must follow that the day will come when no living thing will exist.

CHAPTER TWENTY-SIX

VERBAL FALLACIES

Verbal fallacies occur because of some lack of clarity in what is being asserted. They may result from a word or phrase used in an argument that is either vague or ambiguous. Verbal fallacies can also occur because the grammatical structure of statements contained in an argument is incorrect or misleading. Sometimes verbal fallacies result from an undue emphasis on a particular word or phrase. In all cases, verbal fallacies are the result of a lack of clarity that causes one to draw a mistaken inference.

FALLACY OF EQUIVOCATION

An equivocation occurs when one uses a word in more than one sense in a single context. The fallacy of Equivocation occurs when, as a result of a word or phrase being used equivocally, one draws a mistaken inference. One form of the fallacy of Equivocation results from the fact that certain words in our language are *ambiguous*. A word is ambiguous if it has more than one distinct meaning. There are many such words in the English language. Here are a few examples:

> The word "plant" is ambiguous--it can refer to a house plant, or a factory, or to the act of planting something or even to someone placed in a position to do a certain task, for example, laugh at the jokes of a comedian.

> The word "ring" is ambiguous--it can refer to something one wears on one's finger, or what a bell or telephone does, or a group of people.

> The word "pen" is ambiguous--it can refer to something one writes with or to something used to constrain an animal.

> The word "free" is ambiguous--it can refer to something that costs nothing or to the state of not being constrained.

The word "duck" is ambiguous--it can refer to an animal or to the act of avoiding a collision with an object.

Here are a few more examples for which you may supply the meanings: "bank," "bark," "sign," "bass," and "mad."

Most of the time ambiguous words and phrases cause little difficulty. This is because the *context* in which a word is used usually makes clear which of its meanings is intended. Thus, if we see a sign saying "free coffee" we know the word "free" means that one is not going to be charged for the coffee. No one would suppose that it is being implied that the coffee has somehow been liberated or has free will.

However, sometimes the necessary context is either missing or is insufficient to make one's meaning clear. Suppose someone says, "Would you please get the ring?" meaning that I should answer the phone. If I happen not to hear the phone, I might suppose I am being asked to pick up the person's ring that is lying on the dresser.

When one uses a word or phrase in more that one of its senses in a single context, one is said to "*equivocate*." If the shift between meanings is subtle, it might not be noticed. When the equivocation occurs in an argument, it can often give the appearance of validity to an argument, when in fact the argument is invalid. If, as a result of the equivocation, one draws an incorrect inference, then the *fallacy* of Equivocation has occurred. Here is an example:

Only man is rational
No woman is a man
∴ No woman is rational.

This argument may appear to have a superficial plausibility. The argument on the surface appears to be valid. But once we notice that in the first premise the word "man" is used in the sense of "human being" and in the second premise as "male human being," the argument loses its initial plausibility. This can be seen clearly if we restate the argument substituting the two different meanings for the term, "man."

Only human beings are rational.
No woman is a male human being.
∴ No woman is rational.

Now the argument no longer has even the appearance of validity. One could make the argument valid by substituting for "man" in the first premise what the term actually means in that premise.

> Only male human beings are rational.
> <u>No woman is a male human being.</u>
> ∴ No woman is rational.

This change makes the argument valid. But notice that the first premise in the revised argument is obviously false. The argument only appeared to be valid, and to have true premises, because of the equivocation on the term, "man." Once the equivocation is revealed, the argument is either obviously invalid or obviously has a false premise.

The other form of the fallacy of Equivocation occurs because certain words are *vague*. A term is vague if its extension is not definite. The extension of a term is the collection of objects to which the term refers. For example, the extension of the term "computer" is all the computers that exist. A term is vague, then, when it is not clear whether the term applies to a given object or not. Such cases of unclear application are often called "borderline cases."

An example will make this clear. The word "old" is vague. This is because there are many cases in which it is not clear whether the term correctly applies or not. How many years must have elapsed since the birth of a person before the term "old" correctly applies to that person? Is a person "old" when he is 40? Or must he be 50? Or perhaps 65 years is the point at which one becomes "old?" In a particular case, therefore, it may not be clear whether the term "old" is correctly applied. Since the term "old" has an indefinite extension, it is vague.

Words such as "old," "hot," and "big" are vague because they are what we call *relative terms*. The meanings of such terms vary with the context in which they are employed. Sometimes a term's shift in meaning can cause an argument to have the appearance of validity, when in fact it is invalid. If this causes one to draw an incorrect inference, one has committed the fallacy of Equivocation. Here is a rather obvious example of an incorrect inference in which a relative term is involved.

> All mice are animals.
> <u>All gray mice are gray animals.</u>
> ∴ All big mice are big animals.

This argument overlooks the fact that "big" is a relative term. What is big for a mouse is actually quite small for, say, an elephant. As animals go, a big mouse is still a small animal. The conclusion, therefore, that a big mouse is a big animal doesn't follow. The argument commits the fallacy of Equivocation.

AMPHIBOLY

Expressions that are ambiguous because of their *grammatical construction* are called *amphibolies*. The grammatical structure of the statement allows for two or more interpretations of the statement. Sometimes the instances are humorous. For example, here is an ad from an auto dealer:

> We stand behind every car we sell.

One is tempted to add: "Therefore, don't put the car into reverse." Another example is:

> She was taken to the emergency room and seriously injured. She should have gone someplace else instead.

The first statement in this example probably means that the woman was taken to the emergency room *because* she was seriously injured. However, given the way it is stated it could be interpreted to mean that the she was injured at the emergency room. Thus, the suggestion that she should have gone someplace else instead.

Usually, amphibolies occur because of poor or careless writing. But sometimes they are used intentionally. In an article appearing in the *Toledo Blade*, this was brought home in a dramatic way. The article points out that in a litigious country, such as ours, people who write letters of recommendation are often reluctant to make negative comments about an applicant because they fear being sued. They are also, understandably, reluctant to simply lie about the applicant's qualifications. Consequently, the amphiboly is employed. To describe a lazy employee one might write:

> In my opinion you will be very fortunate to get this person to work for you.

This is likely to be taken as a positive comment about the applicant. Nevertheless, it actually says that the person is lazy.

To describe a totally inept candidate one might say:

> I most enthusiastically recommend the candidate with no qualifications whatsoever.

To describe a candidate who is so awful that the position would be better left unfilled, one might write:

> I can assure you that no person would be better for the job.

Finally, to describe a candidate who is not worthy of further consideration, one could say:

> I would urge you to waste no time in making this candidate an offer of employment.

Each of these examples embodies an ambiguous statement, that is, a statement capable of more than one interpretation, because of faulty syntactical construction. Now the *fallacy* of Amphiboly occurs when, as a result of such a statement, one draws an erroneous conclusion. Suppose one argues as follows:

> She must really like the book I gave her. After all, she said "Thanks for the book. I'll waste no time reading it."

But the question is what did she mean when she said "I'll waste no time reading it?" Did she mean "I'll read it as soon as possible," or "I'm not going to waste my time reading it"? If she meant the latter, then the inference drawn in the above example commits the fallacy of Amphiboly.

ACCENT

The meaning of a statement can sometimes be altered by stressing or emphasizing a particular word or words in the statement. The word or words are then said to be *accented*. Sometimes the word being stressed conveys a meaning different from that intended by the author. If one, as a result, infers from the statement a conclusion not following from the original statement, the *fallacy* of Accent has occurred.

Consider, for instance, the old maxim: "We should not speak ill of our friends." On the surface the maxim seems quite clear. However, depending upon which word in the sentence is stressed, we can alter the meaning of the statement. If we emphasize the word "friends," the statement could be taken to imply that it's fine to speak ill of those who are not our friends. Since that is probably not what the speaker intended, if we draw that conclusion we have committed the fallacy of Accent.

Remember that fallacies are *arguments*. Merely misunderstanding a statement because of an "accented" word is not to commit the fallacy of Accent. Rather, it is when, as a result of misunderstanding the statement, one draws an unwarranted inference that the *fallacy* of Accent takes place. Using the above example, one is, in effect, creating the following argument:

> We should not speak ill of our *friends*. Therefore, it's fine to speak ill of those who are not our friends.

There are other words in the maxim that, if stressed, give the maxim other meanings. For example, if we emphasize the word "ill," it might be inferred that the speaker is saying that it's fine to tell everything about a friend's private life provided that we don't speak "ill" of him or her. Again, that inference is based on emphasizing a word in the statement probably not intended by its author. By drawing that incorrect inference, I have committed the *fallacy* of Accent.

Sometimes words in a statement are emphasized by placing them in italics or underlining them. This, of course, can affect the meaning of the statement. If we are quoting an author and we underline words not underlined in the original, we run the risk of distorting the author's meaning. That is the reason that, in scholarly writing, if one wants to call attention to certain words in a quote through underlining or italics, the author will indicate that the emphasis is that of the current author, not the original author being quoted. This alerts the reader to the possibility that the meaning intended by the original author may have been altered.

In advertising words are often emphasized by using bold or large print for part of the ad, but very small print for another part. Here are two examples:

Store wide Sale: Everything 10% to **50% off.**

Biggie drinks and biggie fries, only **99 cents** each.

In the first ad, because the "50%" is in huge print, while the "10%" is in very small print, one may draw the wrong conclusion from the ad. It seems likely that we are supposed to ignore the "10%" and conclude that everything in the store is 50% off.

In the second case the word "each" is so small that one is likely to ignore it. So, one may go into the restaurant assuming that one can get both the drink and the fries for 99 cents. In fact the two will cost one nearly two dollars. By drawing the wrong inference because of this sort of stressing of words, one commits the fallacy of Accent.

Exercises

Part I: Identify the linguistic fallacies contained in the following examples.

1.   They said that he wanted to be a writer in the worst way and he succeeded. I conclude that he isn't a very good writer.

2.   She said, "I don't ever want you lying to me." I guess that means she doesn't care if I lie to somebody else.

3.   Laws are made by persons. Because laws are made by persons they can, therefore, be repealed. The law of gravitation is obviously a law. Therefore, it can be repealed.

4.   For sale: "One small puppy by owner with white and brown spots and a long tail." Just getting a look at the owner might be worth the price of the puppy.

5.   All diamonds are stones. It follows that a large diamond is a large stone.

6.   The review said: "Except for the script, the acting, the casting and the photography, this is a great movie." Since the reviewer said it was a "great movie," she must have liked it.

7. A lost paper clip is difficult to find. Difficult to find items are usually expensive. It follows that lost paper clips are usually expensive.

8. Some triangles are obtuse. To be obtuse is to be stupid. Thus, some triangles are stupid.

9. It says here that the Amish farmer threw the cow over the fence some hay. It seems that it would have been easier to throw the hay to the cow. I conclude that the farmer could have saved himself a lot of effort.

10. She said that I shouldn't preach at her. So, I infer that it's acceptable to preach to others.

Part II: This exercise is meant to test your knowledge of all of the fallacies we have covered. Identify each fallacy by name.

1. This bridge across the ocean is bound to last a long time. I say this because each part of the bridge is designed to last a long time.

2. We have a duty to do what is right. We have a right to say what we think. Therefore, we have a duty to say what we think.

3. Our movies and television shows have more violence than ever before. The amount of violence in society has also increased. It's obvious that to control violence in our society, we must clean up our movies and television.

4. You have spent most of your life on an Iowa farm and have just recently graduated from college. Now you want us to accept your proposals for reforming the welfare system? Your proposals could not possibly be sound.

5. The distinguished professor of music has said several times that the current administration's economic policies are misguided. How can we doubt that this is true?

6. Everyone who habitually lies is not to be trusted. But everyone lies in bed every night. So, no one is to be trusted.

7. Since I have a right to life, it follows that every cell of my body has a right to life.

8. You really should sign this protection agreement. If you don't, then I can't be held responsible for what might happen to your family. You may recall that several others have declined to sign with us and their families have been mysteriously injured.

9. Our University is bound to have a strong future because its new programs will succeed. And why, you may ask, am I so confident? Well, we know that they will succeed because of the strong future of the University.

10. You can't prove that she was to blame for the incident, so it must have been someone else who was responsible.

11. Wilson is clearly the best person for president of our club. She suffered terribly from poverty as a child and she is the sole supporter of three young children. So vote for the best, vote for Wilson.

12. Capital punishment must be a better deterrent to murder than life in prison. This is, after all, what most people believe.

13. I know that you claim that smoking harmful and that I shouldn't do it. But how can that be true? Haven't I seen you smoking?

14. You say that you want to buy the house because it is in a good neighborhood, it is convenient for school and shopping and you like the way the lawn is landscaped. Well, I like the landscaping too, but that is hardly enough to justify buying the house.

15. This must be my lucky night. I have been getting great poker hands all night long. It's obvious that this last pot is going to be mine.

16. You can't believe what Jones says about the safety of our cars. He is nothing but a trouble maker and malcontent.

17. There is no question that our car is the best value on the market. Just compare our sticker price to that of any other car and you will see that our car is priced lower than any other model. So, clearly, our car costs less.

18. The professor must have really liked my paper. She said, "It is impossible to praise it too highly."

19. I agree that we should not ask for more funds for this project. But I suppose, then, that you would approve of having someone else request the funds for us.

20. It obvious that we no longer value work and self-reliance in this country. Otherwise, we would not have a welfare system.

21. So you say your coffee is too hot. I guess I can infer that you want it ice cold.

22. Will that be cash or do you want to charge it? Well, even if you can't decide on the method of payment, I'm glad you are buying the item.

23. According to the Constitution, we have the right to bear arms. Although Brown is a convicted felon, it follows that he should be allowed to purchase a gun.

24. It's obvious that everyone must have a guardian angel. You should believe this because it has never been demonstrated to be untrue.

25. It's not surprising that environmentalists say that the new highway project through the national park will cause all sorts of damage to the environment. They have been saying the same thing for years. But you should just ignore what they have to say. This is just what you should expect from them.

26. Susan says this novel is really great. So, it must really be worth reading.

27. Professional baseball players now average over one million dollars a year. Thus, if I can become a professional baseball player, I will earn over one million dollars a year.

28. Since putting tariffs on imported Japanese cars is good for the domestic automobile industry, it follows that it must be good for the country.

29. **Sports reporter:** "Well, Coach, the Browns have lost fourteen straight games here in Three Rivers Stadium. How do you feel about today's game?" **Coach:** "There are several ways to view the problem. One would be that the odds are now in our favor."

30. Electing Clinton as President has been good for our economy. Shortly after he was elected the economy started to recover.

31. Aristotle, the great Greek philosopher, claimed that watching violence provides a release for our violent emotions, and thus reduces acts of violence in society. Hence, there can be nothing wrong in violent programming.

32. Studies show that during the same period that violent acts increased on T.V. shows, acts of violence have increased in our society. It's obvious that violence on T.V. increases the amount of violence in our society.

33. It has not been established that watching violent T.V. shows and movies causes violent behavior. Thus, there can be no connection between the two.

34. Whenever I wear my Falcons cap to our baseball games, our team always wins. That sure is a lucky cap.

35. Century 21 sells more houses than any other realty company. Thus, you ought to see your local Century 21 agent if you want to sell yours.

36. Everyone is listening to country music these days. Shouldn't you be listening to it too?

37. The death penalty should be opposed. This is because it is opposed by the best informed and most sensitive of our citizens. You can identify those who are the best informed and most sensitive by their opposition to the death penalty.

38. Joe, the shortstop for the baseball team, had two home runs and three runs batted in during yesterday's game. Clearly, it was a high scoring game.

39. Immediately after watching a movie in which one teenager killed another, John killed another teenager. It's clear that violence in our movies contributes to violent acts in our society.

40. Brown, Harvard and Yale all use Macintosh computers on campus. It's obvious that they must be the computer to buy.

ANSWERS TO SELECTED EXERCISES

Chapter One, p. 2

1. Logic is a discipline that studies <u>reasoning</u>.

3. To say that logic is a discipline implies that logicians study the <u>principles</u> that distinguish good from bad reasoning.

Chapter One, p. 3

1. statement   3. not a statement.

5. statement   7. not a statement

9. statement

Chapter One, pp. 6-7

1. argument. <u>Premise</u>: No great oratorio has been written in English since Mendelssohn completed his *Elijah*. <u>Conclusion</u>: It seems safe to hold that the tradition of great English oratorio writing is dead.

3. not an argument

5. argument. <u>Premise</u>: Compared to the many markets that are opening, available capital is scarce. <u>Conclusion</u>: The demand for capital will probably increase the price people are willing to pay for it.

7. not an argument

9. argument. <u>Premises</u>: All scholarly books are dull. Kant's Critque of Pure Reason is not a scholarly book. <u>Conclusion</u>: It is not dull.

Chapter Two, pp. 11-12

1. <u>Premise</u>: I am simply looking for certain words. <u>Conclusion</u>: I shouldn't have much trouble picking out premises and the conclusion. <u>Conclusion indicator</u>: "so"

4. <u>Conclusion</u>: In fact, I must have been wrong to say that I was looking for certain words. <u>Premise</u>: I am really checking whether the author is using a statement either as support or as supported. <u>Premise indicator</u>: "because"

7. <u>Premises</u>: The sidewalk is wet. Only rain would make the sidewalk wet. <u>Conclusion</u>: It must have rained. <u>Premise indicators</u>: "given that," "since." <u>Conclusion indicator</u>: "it follows that"

10. <u>Premises</u>: Every plant is a living thing. All living things require oxygen. it must be the case that <u>Conclusion</u>: all plants require oxygen. Premise Indicator: "because" <u>Conclusion indicator</u>: "it must be the case that"

Chapter Two, pp. 14-15

1. not an argument

4. <u>Premises</u>: Many students take logic. Only a minority of them take the LSAT. <u>Conclusion</u>: The others would probably lack such a direct confirmation of whether taking logic improves reasoning skills. Conclusion indicator: "then"

7. <u>Premises</u>: All crows are black. This bird is white. <u>Conclusion</u>: It is not a crow. <u>Conclusion indicator</u>: "consequently"

10. <u>Premises</u>: My life will be complete only if the Yankees win the World Series. They are not doing well this year. <u>Conclusion</u>: I should seek fulfillment elsewhere. <u>Premise indicator</u>: "since"

Chapter Two, pp. 18-19

1. argument

4. not an argument. Conditional statement: If I am asked politely, I will comply.

7. argument

10. not an argument. Conditional statement: I will go to the game only if I have a ticket.

Chapter Three, pp. 22-23

1. Whales suckle their young.

4. Books costing less than $100 dollars for a semester are cheap.

7. Persons who read a lot are smart.

10. Tonight I'm going on a date that involves dinner and a movie.

Chapter Three, pp. 31-32

1.

①
↓
②

3.

② ③
↓↓
①

5. This argument rests on two assumptions.
<u>Hint #1:</u> What does the speaker assume about where "you" are and what you are doing?
<u>Hint #2:</u> What does the speaker assume about you relating what you would want to what you should do?

7.

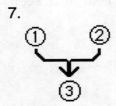

Chapter Four, p. 36

1. "it follows that"   4. "bound to"

7. "it has to be the case that"   10. "it's clear that"

Chapter Four, p. 40

1. false   4. true

7. true   10. false

Chapter Five, pp. 44-45

Part I

1. inductive   4. inductive

7. deductive   10. inductive

Part II

1. inductive   4. deductive

7. inductive   10. inductive

Chapter Five, pp. 48-49

1. true   4. true

7. true   10. true

Chapter Six, pp. 51-52

1. A class is a <u>set</u> or <u>collection</u> of objects.

4. A categorical statement asserts that one of the classes to which it refers is either <u>included</u> in or <u>excluded</u> from the other class.

Chapter Six, pp. 53-55

Part I

1. The quality of a statement is either <u>affirmative</u> or <u>negative</u>.

4. If a categorical statement is negative in quality, it is called an <u>exclusion</u> statement.

7. If a categorical statement refers only to part of its subject class, it is called a <u>particular</u> statement.

10. The words "all" and "no" tell us that a statement is <u>universal</u> with respect to its <u>quantity.</u>

Part II

<u>UA</u> 1. All computers are useful tools.

<u>UN</u> 4. No bugs are cute things.

<u>UN</u> 7. No dogs are felines.

<u>UA</u> 10. All doctors are persons opposed to socialized medicine.

Chapter Six, pp. 57-58

Part I

1. A categorical statement contains two terms, a <u>subject</u> term and a <u>predicate</u> term.

4. The letters <u>**A**</u> and <u>**E**</u> are used to represent universal statements.

Part II

1. All S is P   4. No S is P   7. Some S is P   10. All S is P

Chapter Seven, pp. 61-62

Part I

1. The diagrams that we are using to represent categorical statements are called: <u>Venn Diagrams</u>.

4. When diagramming an **I** statement an x is placed in the S͟P͟ region to show that there is at least one thing that is both an S͟ and a P͟.

Part II

1.   3.

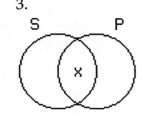

Chapter Seven, pp. 67-68

Part I

1. A statement having existential import asserts that there is at͟ least͟ one͟ member of the subject class.

4. When diagramming an **E** statement employing the Boolean interpretation, the S͟P͟ region is shaded to illustrate that it is empty͟.

Part II

1. type of statement: **E**

    symbolic notation: SP= 0

4. type of statement: **I**

    symbolic notation: SP ≠ O

6. type of statement: **O**

    symbolic notation: SP̄ ≠ O

10. type of statement: **A**

    symbolic notation: SP̄ = 0

Part III

1.

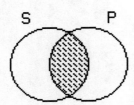

4.

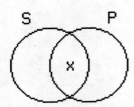

6.

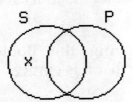

10.

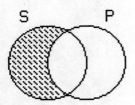

Chapter Seven, pp. 71-73

Part I

1. When an **A** or **E** statement is interpreted as asserting or implying that its subject class has at least one member, the statement has <u>existential import.</u>

3. Then, in order to reflect the Aristotelian interpretation of an **A** statement, an "x" is placed in the <u>SP</u> area of the diagram.

5. Then, in order to reflect the Aristotelian interpretation of an **E** statement, an "x" is placed in the $\overline{S}\overline{P}$ area of the diagram.

Part II

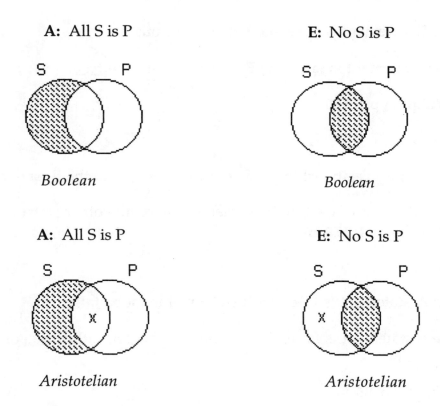

A: All S is P

Boolean

E: No S is P

Boolean

A: All S is P

Aristotelian

E: No S is P

Aristotelian

Chapter Eight, pp. 77-78

Part I

1. An **A** statement is the contradictory of an <u>O</u> statement.

3. When two statements contradict each other, they will always have <u>opposite</u> truth values.

5. When the first statement of a contradictory pair is false, the other statement will be <u>true</u>.

Part II

1. If the **A** statement is true, the **O** statement must be <u>false</u>.

4. If the **O** statement is false, the **A** statement must be <u>true</u>.

7. If the **E** statement is false, the **I** statement must be <u>true</u>.

8. If the **I** statement is false, the **E** statement must be <u>true</u>.

Chapter Eight, pp. 79-80

Part I

1. The contrary relationship holds between the <u>A</u> and the <u>E</u> statements.

4. If one of a pair of contrary statements is false, the other statement's truth value is <u>unknown</u>.

Part II

1. If the **A** statement is true, the **E** statement must be <u>false</u>.

4. If the **E** statement is false, the **A** statement may be either <u>true</u> or <u>false</u>.

Chapter Eight, p. 85

Part I

1. The subaltern relationship holds between the <u>A</u> and <u>I</u> statements and between the <u>E</u> and <u>O</u> statements.

3. The falsity of the particular statement implies the <u>falsity</u> of the corresponding universal statement.

5. If a universal statement is false, then its subaltern's truth value may be either <u>true</u> or <u>false</u>.

Part II

1. If **A** is true, then **I** is <u>true</u>.

3. If **A** is false, then **I** is <u>unknown</u>.

5. If **E** is true, then **O** is <u>true</u>.

7. If **E** is false, then **O** is <u>unknown</u>.

Chapter Eight, pp. 91-92 (Note: "T" = true, "F" = false and "U" = unknown. I, II, III, IV refer to assumptions you are to make for each exercise. e.g., under 1:I you are assuming that "All soldiers are brave persons" is true and you are using the Aristotelian interpretation.)

1. All soldiers are brave persons.

	I	II	III	IV
a. Some soldiers are brave persons.	T	U	U	U
b. No soldiers are brave persons.	F	U	U	U
c. Some soldiers are not brave persons.	F	T	F	T

3. No soldiers are brave persons.

	I	II	III	IV
a. Some soldiers are brave persons.	F	T	F	T
b. All soldiers are brave persons.	F	U	U	U
c. Some soldiers are not brave persons.	T	U	U	U

6. Some moral judgments are matters of taste.

	I	II	III	IV
a. All moral judgments are matters of taste.	U	F	U	U
b. No moral judgments are matters of taste.	F	T	F	T
c. Some moral judgments are not matters of taste.	U	T	U	U

8. Some moral judgments are not matters of taste.

	I	II	III	IV
a. No moral judgments are matters of taste.	U	F	U	U
b. Some moral judgments are matters of taste	U	T	U	U
c. All moral judgments are matters of taste.	F	T	F	T

Chapter Nine, pp. 94-95

Part I

1. An immediate inference is an inference from <u>one</u> premise immediately to a <u>conclusion</u>.

3. Two statements are said to be logically equivalent whenever they always have the same <u>truth</u> value.

5. When the subject and predicate terms of a categorical statement are interchanged, the resulting statement is called the <u>converse</u> of the original statement.

Part II

1. Some green reptiles are frogs.   4.   No radios are televisions.

Chapter Nine, pp. 98-100

Part I

1. Conversion by limitation can be validly performed only on an <u>**A**</u> statement.

4. The second step in the operation of conversion by limitation is to change the quantity of the statement from <u>universal</u> to <u>particular</u>.

7. Because the **A** statement and its converse make claims about different regions, the statements are not <u>logically</u> <u>equivalent</u>.

10. When the subject and predicate terms of an **O** statement are interchanged, the resulting statement is not <u>logically</u> <u>equivalent</u> to the original, and the original statement does not <u>guarantee</u> the truth of the resulting statement.

Part II

1. Some mortals are humans.

4. No drivers are children

7. No reptiles are fish.

8. cannot be converted

Chapter Nine, pp. 102-103

Part I

1. Obversion can be validly performed on the A, E, I, and O form categorical statements.

4. The complement of a class includes <u>everything</u> which is not part of the original class.

Part II

1. All bill collectors are non-sensitive individuals.

4. Some wrestlers are non-sensitive persons.

7. All meter-readers are non-interesting conversationalists.

10. Some dog lovers are non-cat lovers.

Part III

Items 1, 3, 5, and 7 can be converted.

Items 2, 6 and 9 can be converted by limitation.

Items 4, 8 and 10 cannot be converted.

Part IV (since all categorical statements can be obverted, all statements converted in Part III can be obverted. Here are a few samples.)

1. All sensitive individuals are non-bill collectors.

5. Some buses are not non-vehicles.

7. All interesting conversationalists are non-meter readers.

Chapter Ten, pp. 105-107

Part I

1. A categorical syllogism is an <u>argument</u> which consists of two <u>premises</u> and a <u>conclusion</u> all of which are <u>categorical</u> statements.

4. The three class terms of a categorical syllogism are known as the <u>major</u>, <u>minor</u>, and <u>middle</u> terms.

7. The predicate term of the conclusion is always the <u>major</u> term of the argument.

10. Determining the major, minor and middle terms and labeling them will allow us to represent the argument's <u>form</u>.

Part II

1. major term: "unique plants;"   minor term: "trees;"   middle term: Redwoods.

4. major term: "persons who love candy;" minor term: "dieters;" middle term: "underweight persons"

Chapter Ten, pp. 110-111

Part I

1. Some P is M, No S is M, ∴ No S is P

3. All P is M, Some S is not M, ∴ Some S is not P

5. All S is M, Some M is P, ∴ Some S is P

Part II

1. The validity or invalidity of a deductive argument is determined by its <u>form</u>.

4. Refutation by logical analogy is a technique used to demonstrate the <u>invalidity</u> of an argument.

7. Refutation by logical analogy cannot be used to show that an argument is <u>valid</u>.

Part III

Yes. The form for each is Some S is M, All M is P, ∴ Some S is P.

Chapter Eleven, p. 114

Part I

1. Since categorical syllogisms refer to three classes, diagramming them requires <u>three</u> circles instead of two.

4. The lower circle in the lower middle represents the <u>M</u> class.

Part II

See p. 113 of text for labeled regions.

Chapter Eleven, p. 119

1. All S is M $S\overline{M} = 0$
    <u>All M is P</u> $M\overline{P} = 0$ <u>valid</u>
    All S is P $S\overline{P} = 0$

(The Venn Diagram is at the top of the next page)

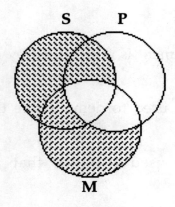

4. All M is S $M\overline{S} = 0$
    No M is P $MP = 0$ invalid
    No S is P $SP = 0$

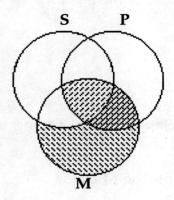

Chapter Eleven, pp. 123-125

Part I

1. When a categorical syllogism has one premise which is a universal
    statement and one premise which is a particular statement, then the
    <u>universal</u> <u>statement</u> must be diagrammed first.

3. Diagramming an argument's premises represents what it would be like
    for the premises to be <u>true</u>.

5. After diagramming the premises of an argument if the diagram fails to
    show that its conclusion must be true, the argument is <u>invalid</u>.

Part II

1. Some S is M, All M is P, ∴ Some S is P (valid)

5. All P is M, Some M is S, ∴ Some S is P (invalid)

9. All P is M, All S is M, ∴ All S is P (invalid)

Chapter Eleven, pp. 132-134

Part I

1. The conditions under which a Venn Diagram should be modified to reflect the Aristotelian assumption are:

    a. We must have good reason to assume that the classes we are talking about have <u>members</u>.

    b. The argument must have both of the following characteristics:

        i. Both premises are <u>universal</u> statements.

        ii. The conclusion is a <u>particular</u> statement.

4. If the assumption that a class has at least one member forces us to put an "x" in a region that diagrams what the conclusion says, then the argument is <u>valid</u>.

Part II

1. valid

4. invalid

Part III

1. valid

4. invalid

7. invalid

10. valid

Part IV

4. This argument is invalid on the Boolean interpretation but valid on the Aristotelian interpretation.

Chapter Twelve, p. 136

1. A categorical statement that is in standard form will consist of four components. The four components are a <u>quantifier</u>, a <u>subject term</u>, a <u>copula</u> and a <u>predicate term</u>.

Chapter Twelve, pp. 137- 138

1. Some cats are mistreated animals.

3. All accomplished artists are talented persons.

5. No facts are things easily denied.

Chapter Twelve, p. 138

1. All cows are animals that grass.

3. No poor people are people who have money

5. All faculty are persons who may use the lounge.

Chapter Twelve, p. 140

1. Some cats are not cuddly animals.

3. Some humans are not mortal.

5. No witnesses are persons telling the truth.

Chapter Twelve, pp. 142-143

Part I

1. Some wines are red things.

3. Some spider bites are not fatal events.

5. Some snake bites are fatal events.

Part II

1. All persons who know her are persons who love her.

4. All records selling more than one million copies are platinum records.

7. Some spider bites are not fatal events.

10. Some horses are intelligent animals.

13. Some cats are smart animals.

16. Some plans are things that go astray.

19. No bartenders are bashful persons.

Chapter Thirteen, pp. 145 - 146.

Part I

1. When translating an "only" statement, there are two steps to be followed:
    a. <u>reverse the order of the subject and predicate terms</u>.

    b. <u>replace "only" with "all."</u>

Part II

1. All persons who are pro-labor are persons who are pro-union.

3. All persons who will be prosecuted are persons who are apprehended.

5. All persons who can get free services are persons with medical insurance.

Chapter Thirteen, p. 147

1. All bears are carnivores.

3. Some trees are plants that lose their leaves in the fall.

5. Some computers are programmable machines.

Chapter Thirteen, pp. 148-149

Part I

1. Syllogistic statements referring to individuals instead of classes are called <u>singular</u> statements.

3. Singular statements are assumed to have <u>existential</u> <u>import</u>.

5. An affirmative singular statement is diagrammed as an <u>A</u> form statement.

Part II

1. All persons identical to Jerry are married persons.

4. No animals identical to Spot are cats.

Chapter Thirteen, pp. 151-152

Part I

1. Exceptive statements actually make <u>two</u> assertions.

3. When a categorical syllogism contains an exceptive statement as a premise, both of the <u>statements</u> implicit within it must be represented in the diagram.

Part II

1. "Some runners are persons who have finished the course." *and* "Some runners are not persons who have finished the course."

4. "Some administrators are persons who favored the union." *and* "Some administrators are not persons who favored the union."

Part III

1. No auctioneers are quiet people.
   Some quiet persons are well mannered persons.
   <u>Some quiet persons are not well mannered persons.</u>
   ∴ Some auctioneers are not well mannered persons.

Chapter Thirteen, pp. 153-155

Part I

1.   All persons who die young are good persons.

4.   No computers are user friendly machines.

7.   No persons identical to Susan are happy persons.

10. All snails are slow movers.

13. Some of our actions are insignificant events.

16. All things that one sows are things that one will reap.

19. All barbers are extroverts.

Part II

1.   All savings and loan companies are organizations in financial trouble.
     All organizations in financial trouble are organizations needing to be
     very cautious.
     ∴ All savings and loans are organizations needing to be very cautious.

     valid

3.   Some unintentional acts are not criminal offenses.
     All criminal offenses are acts that should be punished.
     ∴ All acts that should be punished are unintentional acts.

     Note: the conclusion is derived by first converting the original
     conclusion, then obverting the resulting converse and finally replacing
     "non-intentional" with "unintentional." The argument is invalid.

Chapter Fourteen, pp. 158-159

1. simple statement 3. compound statement 5. compound statement

7. compound statement 9. simple statement

Chapter Fourteen, pp. 161-162

1. temporal compound 3. truth-functional compound

5. truth-functional compound 7. causal compound

9. causal compound

Chapter Fourteen, pp. 164-165

1. false 3. false 5. true

Chapter Fourteen, p. 168

1. true 3. false 5. false

Chapter Fourteen, pp. 169-170

Part I

1. true 3. true 5. false

Part II
1. p • q 4. p v q 7. p • q

11. ~p v ~q 13. p • ~q 15. p

Part III

1. false 4. true 7. false

11. true 13. true 15. true

Chapter Fifteen, p. 174

Part I

1. The first simple statement in a conditional is known as its <u>antecedent</u>.

3. A conditional statement is false only when its antecedent is <u>true</u> and its consequent is <u>false</u>.

5. Conditional statements do not assert that either their antecedents or their consequents are <u>true</u>.

Part II

1. false   3. true   5. false

Chapter Fifteen, pp. 176-177

Part I

1. Biconditionals are really two <u>conditionals</u> rolled into one.

3. When the components of a biconditional have a different truth value, the biconditional is a <u>false</u> statement.

5. Biconditionals assert that their components have the same <u>truth</u> <u>value</u>.

Part II

1. false   3. true   5. false

Chapter Fifteen, p. 180

1. false   4. true   7. true   10. true

13. true   16. true   19. true

Chapter Sixteen, pp. 187-188

Part I

1. p v q   4. p • q   7. (p • q) v r

10. p • q   13. ~p • ~q   16. p v q

19. p • q   22. ~(p v q) • ~r   25. ~p

Part II

1. true   4. false   7. true

10. false   13. false   16. true

19. false   22. false   25. false

Chapter Seventeen, p. 193

1. p ⊃ q   4. p ⊃ q   7. q ⊃ p

10. q ⊃ p   13. p ⊃ q   15. q ⊃ p

Chapter Seventeen, pp. 197-198

1. p ⊃ q   4. p ⊃ q   7. ~p ⊃ ~q

10. ~p ⊃ (q v r) 13. p ⊃ (q • r)

Chapter Seventeen, pp. 199-200

1. p ≡ q   3. p ⊃ q   7. p ⊃ (q v r)

10. (p ⊃ q) ≡ ~r   13. (p • q) ≡ (r v s) 15. (~p ⊃ ~q) ⊃ ~r

Chapter Eighteen, pp. 206-208

Part I

1. The number of rows in a truth table is determined by the number of
    <u>variables</u> in the statement.

4. A statement with three variables requires a truth table with <u>eight</u> rows.

7. When there is more that one logical operator in a statement, one
    should begin determining the truth values for the part of the
    expression contained in the <u>innermost</u> parentheses.

10. Consequently, truth tables provide a complete picture of the conditions
    under which an expression is either <u>true</u> or <u>false</u>.

Part II

1.

p	q	p ⊃ q
T	T	T
T	F	F
F	T	T
F	F	T

4.

p	q	p ∨ q
T	T	T
T	F	T
F	T	T
F	F	F

7.

p	q	r	p	∨	(~r	•	q)
T	T	T	T	F	F	F	T
T	T	F	T	T	T	T	T
T	F	T	T	T	F	F	F
T	F	F	T	T	T	F	F
F	T	T	F	F	F	F	T
F	T	F	F	T	T	T	T
F	F	T	F	F	F	F	F
F	F	F	F	F	T	F	F

10.

q	r	s	(r v s) ⊃ ~q		
T	T	T	T	F	F
T	T	F	T	F	F
T	F	T	T	F	F
T	F	F	F	T	F
F	T	T	T	T	T
F	T	F	T	T	T
F	F	T	T	T	T
F	F	F	F	T	T

Chapter Eighteen, pp. 211-212

Part I

1. A tautology is a statement that is always <u>true</u>, regardless of the truth values of its component statements.

4. A truth table for a contradiction will have all <u>F's</u> in its final value column.

7. Tautologies are sometimes called <u>necessarily true</u> statements.

Part II

1.

p	p ⊃ p	
T	**T**	tautology
F	**T**	

5.

p	q	p ⊃ (p • q)			
T	T	T	**T**	T	
T	F	T	**F**	F	contingent
F	T	F	**T**	F	
F	F	F	**T**	F	

10.

p	q	~(p v q)		
T	T	**F**	T	
T	F	**F**	T	contingent
F	T	**F**	T	
F	F	**T**	F	

15.

p	q	r	(p • (q • r)) ⊃ r		
T	T	T	T	T	T T
T	T	F	F	F	T F
T	F	T	F	F	T T
T	F	F	F	F	T F
F	T	T	F	T	T T
F	T	F	F	F	T F
F	F	T	F	F	T T
F	F	F	F	F	T F

tautology

20.

p	q	r	(p v r) ≡ (q v p)		
T	T	T	T	T	T
T	T	F	T	T	T
T	F	T	T	T	T
T	F	F	T	T	T
F	T	T	T	T	T
F	T	F	F	F	T
F	F	T	T	F	F
F	F	F	F	T	F

contingent

Chapter Nineteen, pp. 215-216

Part I

1. The first step in determining whether two expressions are logically equivalent is to do a <u>truth</u> <u>table</u> for the two statements.

3. The third step in determining whether two expressions are logically equivalent is to do a truth table for the <u>resulting</u> statement.

5. When two statements are logically equivalent, the statement of their equivalence is a <u>tautology</u>.

Part II

1.

p	q	(~q	⊃	~p)	≡	(~p	v	q)
T	T	F	T	F	**T**	F	T	T
T	F	T	F	F	**T**	F	F	F
F	T	F	T	T	**T**	T	T	T
F	F	T	T	T	**T**	T	T	F

logically equivalent

5.

p	(p)	≡	(~~p)
T	T	**T**	T
F	F	**T**	F

logically equivalent

9.

p	q	r	((p	⊃	q) v	r)	≡	((p	v	q)	⊃	r)
T	T	T		T	T **T**	T	**T**		T	T	T
T	T	F		T	T F **F**	F	**T**		T	F	F
T	F	T		F	T T **T**	T	**T**		T	T	T
T	F	F		F	F F **T**	F	**T**		T	F	F
F	T	T		T	T T **T**	T	**T**		T	T	T
F	T	F		T	T F **F**	F	**T**		T	F	F
F	F	T		T	T T **T**	T	**T**		F	T	T
F	F	F		T	T F **T**	F	**F**		F	T	F

not logically equivalent

Chapter Nineteen, pp. 220-223

Part I

1. When an argument is valid, it is impossible for there to be true premises and a <u>false</u> conclusion.

3. A truth table shows an argument to be invalid if there is even one case of all true premises and a <u>false</u> conclusion.

5. An argument form containing four statement variables requires a truth table having <u>sixteen</u> rows.

Part II

1.

		1	**2**	**C**	
p	q	p ∨ q	~q	p	
T	T	T	F	T	valid
T	F	T	T	T	
F	T	T	F	F	
F	F	F	T	F	

4.

		1	**2**	**C**	
p	q	~p ∨ q	q	p	
T	T	F T	T	T	invalid
T	F	F F	F	T	
F	T	T T	T	F	
F	F	T T	F	F	

7.

			1	**2**	**C**	
p	q	r	(p ≡ q) ∨ r	~r	p ≡ q	
T	T	T	T T T	F	T	valid
T	T	F	T T F	T	T	
T	F	T	F T T	F	F	
T	F	F	F F F	T	F	
F	T	T	F T T	F	F	
F	T	F	F F F	T	F	
F	F	T	T T T	F	T	
F	F	F	T T F	T	T	

Part III

1.

		1	**C**			
p	q	p ≡ q	~q ⊃ ~p			
T	T	T	F T F	valid
T	F	F	T F F	
F	T	F	F T T	
F	F	T	T T T	

6.

		1	**2**	**C**	
p	q	~(p • q)	~q	p	
T	T	F T	F	T	invalid
T	F	T F	T	T	
F	T	T F	F	F	
F	F	T F	T	F	

10.

p	q	r	1 p ∨ q	2 ~r ⊃ ~q	C p ∨ r	
T	T	T	T	F T F	T	valid
T	T	F	T	T F F	T	
T	F	T	T	F T T	T	
T	F	F	T	T T T	T	
F	T	T	T	F T F	T	
F	T	F	T	T F F	F	
F	F	T	F	F T T	T	
F	F	F	F	T T T	F	

13.

p	q	r	1 (q ⊃ p) ∨ r	C q ⊃ p	
T	T	T	T T T	T	invalid
T	T	F	T T F	T	
T	F	T	T T T	T	
T	F	F	T T F	T	
F	T	T	F T T	F	
F	T	F	F F F	F	
F	F	T	T T T	T	
F	F	F	T T F	T	

Chapter Twenty, pp. 227-228

Part I

1. A statement that attributes a specific property to an individual or thing, is called a <u>singular</u> <u>affirmative</u> <u>statement</u>.

3. A singular statement attributes a specific <u>property</u> to a single individual or object.

5. In a singular statement the uppercase letters A - Z are used to stand for <u>properties</u>.

Part II

1. Td

3. Hk

4. ~Lc

Chapter Twenty, pp. 232-233

Part I

1. Because they are not statements, propositional functions are neither <u>true</u> nor <u>false</u>.

3. Instantiation involves replacing a <u>variable</u> with a <u>constant</u> .

5. An important difference between propositional functions and statements is that while statements are either <u>true</u> or <u>false</u> propositional functions are not.

Part II

1. (x) Bx

4. (∃x) ~Rx

7. ~Hs

10. (∃x) Gx

Chapter Twenty, pp. 235-237

Part I

1. (x) (Sx ⊃ Bx)

4. (∃x) (Bx • Sx)

7. (x) (Px ⊃ Ex)

10. (∃x) (Lx • Ux)

Part II

1. (∃x) (Bx • Gx)   4.   (∃x) Wx

7. Ls   10. (∃x) (Cx • ~Sx)

13. (x) ~Lx   16. (x) (Ex ⊃ Fx)

19. (∃x) ~Sx

Chapter Twenty-One, pp. 248-251

Part I

1. inductive generalization. Weak, because it fails to indicate the total number of dentists surveyed.

4. inductive analogy. Argument provides some reason to think conclusion is true.

7.   inductive generalization. Relatively, weak because it fails to say how many peanuts have been tasted.

10. inductive analogy. Relatively strong inductive argument.

Part II

1. a.   stronger; number of instances. b. weaker; strength of the conclusion. c. stronger; number of similarities among instances mentioned in premises and instance mentioned in conclusion. d. stronger; weaker conclusion. e. stronger; dissimilarities among instances in premises.

4. a. stronger; number of instances. b. stronger; dissimilarities among instances mentioned in the premises. c. no effect; irrelevant. d. weaker; strength of the conclusion. e. stronger; number of similarities between instances mentioned in premises and instance mentioned in conclusion.

Chapter Twenty-Two, pp. 257-259

Part I

1. true   3. false   5. true

Part II

1. Straw Person   3. Misdirected Argument

5. Misdirected Argument   7. Straw Person Fallacy

10. Misdirected Argument

Chapter Twenty -Three, pp. 269-271

1. Ad Hominem (circumstantial)   5. Ad Hominem (you're another)

9. Argument from Ignorance   14. Appeal to Authority

17. Irrelevant Conclusion   20. Ad Hominem (abusive)

Chapter Twenty-Four, pp. 279-281

1. Appeal to Pity   5. Accident

9. Appeal to Force   14. False Cause

17. Appeal to Popularity   18. Converse Accident

Chapter Twenty-Five, pp. 292-293

1. Division   5. Begging the Question

9. Complex Question   12. Gambler's Fallacy

16. Division   20. Composition

Chapter Twenty-Six, pp. 300-305

Part I

1. Amphiboly   5. Equivocation (on "large")

10. accent ("at her")

Part II

1. Composition   5. Appeal to Authority
9. Begging the Question   12. Appeal to Popularity

16. Ad Hominem (abusive)   20. Converse Accident

23. Accident   27. Division

30. False Cause   33. Argument from Ignorance

36. Appeal to Popularity   40. Appeal to Authority